A Messenger of Love

A Messenger of Love

The Biography of Dada J. P. Vaswani

**KRISHNA KUMARI AND
PRABHA SAMPATH**

MACMILLAN

This edition first published in India 2019 by Macmillan
an imprint of Pan Macmillan Publishing India Private Limited
707, Kailash Building
26 K. G. Marg, New Delhi – 110 001
www.panmacmillan.co.in

Pan Macmillan, 20 New Wharf Road, London N1 9RR
Basingstoke and Oxford
Associated companies throughout the world
www.panmacmillan.com

ISBN 978-93-89109-09-2

Typeset in Adobe Jenson Pro by Manmohan Kumar
Printed and bound in India by Gopsons Papers Ltd., Noida

This book
is an offering
at the Lotus Feet
of our Guru
Tera Tujhko Arpan
whatever we are
whatever we have
is due to Your Grace.

Our every breath is beholden to You,
our every step is guided by You,
our hearts are set ablaze by You,
our souls are nourished by You,
the very light of our life is You, just You!

Contents

Preface   ix

1. A Carefree Childhood   1
2. The Years of Loss and Learnings   12
3. The Making of a Disciple   44
4. New Beginnings: Pune, the Chosen City   96
5. In the Footsteps of the Master   138
6. Everyone's Beloved Dada   158
7. Dada: The Man for All Seasons and Climes   176
8. His Life is His Message   219
9. What Dada Means to Us   268
10. How to Embrace Pain   290
11. Khuda Hafiz   317
12. Dada Enters the Eternal   342

Appendix   352
Select Bibliography   381

Preface

We wish to state, at the very outset, that this book is not the outcome of an act of writing; it is born out of an act of devotion, it is an expression of our *guru bhakti*. It is also a fulfilment of our responsibility and commitment to present an authorized biography of Dada J. P. Vaswani for his thousands of devotees as well as readers across the globe, who can derive inspiration from his illustrious life.

Above all, it is an offering of love ...

'Love is never blind,' Dada would say to us again and again. 'Love is never blind – for love sees not only with the eyes, but the mind, the heart and the spirit ... Love goes about with eyes wide open, looking for opportunities to be of service to those in need. Love blesses the one who offers it and the one who receives it.'

Yes, this book is an offering of love; an expression of our love and devotion for one of the greatest spiritual luminaries of our times – the very personification of love – Dada J. P. Vaswani.

'What is the meaning of life?' asked the greatest scientist of our age, Albert Einstein. 'To know an answer to this question, is to be religious,' he asserted. We rephrase his question, 'What is it to live?' and the answer comes to us from the living precept of our dearly beloved Dada, 'TO LIVE IS TO LOVE!'

Truly, Dada was a great believer in the strength and sustaining power of love. His emphasis was on what he called 'love-in-action', which manifests itself in sympathy, service and sacrifice. 'In love,' he stated, 'is the solution to all the problems of life.'

Dada's life is his message; for he is, indeed, love-in-action.

'Love is not an attribute of God,' Dada would say. 'Love is God.'

A question was asked to him, 'What is love?' And he answered, 'You will know when you become love!' We might venture to add, 'To know Dada, is to know the meaning of love.' To know Dada even from afar, to read about his life, to let our lives be touched by his influence – even remotely – is to feel the magic of his love! This is the magic we have tried to capture for you in the pages of this book.

When we say an 'act of devotion', let us make it clear that we are not into idolatry or adulatory writing. Our intention is to present the facts of Dada's life, authentically recorded events from his life to which other people may not have access to, and collate from the systematically stored archives of the Sadhu Vaswani Mission, his major books and addresses, his extensive travels, his essential message, his interactions with the masses and his devotees as well as with great personages who happened to cross his path, and an attempt to give a few glimpses into his life and teachings.

Yes, it is a book written by his devotees. But we see ourselves also, as record keepers, entrusted with the responsibility of maintaining, communicating and disseminating the life and works of a great spiritual leader who has been the life and soul of the humanitarian organization to which we belong, namely the Sadhu Vaswani Mission. In all humility, we see ourselves as chroniclers entrusted with documenting a great life of our great master.

There is poetry in Dada's life, the lyrical poetry of compassion and empathy; there is magic in his life, the magic of an understanding heart; there is music in his life, the music of selfless service and sacrifice. This magic, music and poetry have flowed into our pages.

We dedicate this book to the love which is never blind – the love which sees not only with the eyes but more so with the mind, the heart and the spirit.

ONE

A Carefree Childhood

'For in every adult there dwells the child that was, and in every child there lies the adult that will be.'

– John Connolly, *The Book of Lost Things*

2 August 1918, Hyderabad–Sind: As the hands of the clock met at 2, indicating 2:10 p.m., the sun shone resplendent in all its glory, greeting the eldest grandson of the Vaswani family with a warm welcome, for on this auspicious day was he born to Pahlajrai Vaswani and his wife, Krishnadevi. A fascinating smile played upon the lips of the infant, while his eyes seemed to gleam with an unearthly light.

The father with pride held the newborn in his hands. The mother whispered softly, 'Welcome, Jashan! You are indeed a reason for us to rejoice.' The parents offered gratitude to the Almighty for blessing them with a son.

They were ecstatic at the birth of their first son. Before him, Pahlajrai and Krishnadevi had given birth to two daughters, Shakuntala and Hari. It was, therefore, apt that the boy who brought joy to all the family, was named Jashan, as his birth marked celebration.

Just as a single ray of the sun can dispel darkness, Jashan's arrival in the world was an affirmation of a miraculous light. He had been blessed abundantly with the sunshine of God's love. However, little did humanity know that he was born with a golden touch – he could bring light where there was darkness, usher hope where there was despair.

Jashan was raised in an environment defined by piety, dedication and character. His father was an erudite scholar and more importantly, a remarkable human being. He had a distinctive penchant for selfless service, complemented by an open, friendly and warm disposition, the fine qualities Jashan inherited. At the time of his son's birth, Pahlajrai was posted at the Hyderabad Training College for Teachers. Well-versed in both the Persian and Sindhi languages, he was a voracious reader, and loved reading the poetry of Shah Abdul Latif and other Sindhi poets. He was also awed by the Persian masters, Rumi and Hafiz. In addition to being learned, Pahlajrai was also an eloquent speaker. He was often asked to address community meetings that tackled serious social issues. With his flair for public speaking, he appealed to the people to engage in acts of service and commit themselves to social causes. Given his good nature, warmth and dedication, his pleas were met with resounding success.

Widely known and respected in society, the Vaswani family won many hearts with their utter simplicity and devotion to God. They came from a scholarly background and had a marked inclination towards social responsibilities, selfless service and social reform. While Jashan's grandfather, Diwan Lilaram belonged to a wealthy, noble family of landowners and was known to be a man of learning and faith, his uncle, Thanwar Lilaram Vaswani, had made a name for himself as a professor and principal of some of the prestigious colleges in North India. This celebrated Son of Sind had won great acclaim, representing India at the World Congress of Religions held in Berlin in 1910. Later revered as Sadhu Vaswani – carrying the message of India's rishis and its deathless culture to the world, as Swami Vivekanand had done earlier – he was a patriot, a visionary, a poet, and an educationist, sought out by distinguished luminaries of the likes of Rabindranath Tagore and Pratap Chandra Mazumdar.

Jashan's mother, Krishnadevi, was among the few women during those times who benefited from an education in the English language. A woman of courage, unparalleled will-power and progressive disposition, she broke age-old conventions by not conforming to the orthodox way of life – confining herself to the kitchen, a fate countless Sindhi women were subject to. At the time when the Sindhi cultural norm dictated that women should wear long skirts, cover their person and veil their faces, she was among the first few women to move about in a saree, her serene face fully visible to the onlookers. A devout woman with a sharp intellect, Jashan's mother steered the destiny of her family in the right direction after her husband died an early death.

A LOVING FAMILY AND A HAPPY HOME

At home, Jashan was raised in a happy and loving environment, always bustling with energy. Pahlajrai, being a warm and welcoming host, always kept his doors and heart open to those who sought his advice. As teachers, social workers and neighbours came calling, Krishnadevi lent all the support she could by extending her hospitality. Pahlajrai took up several activities for community welfare, among which was the founding of one of the major institutions of social work in the city in those days, the Social Service League in Karachi, which ran a night school for the underprivileged sections of the society, particularly male domestic workers looking to better their prospects.

Life in the Vaswani household epitomized simplicity, bordering on austerity. The family adopted a minimalistic approach, following the ideal of simple living and high thinking. The children grew up watching their parents juggle their time, effort and resources between various activities, which had a strong bearing on their futures.

When asked what he would like to become when he grew up, Jashan, an imaginative, intelligent child, had amazing answers to give. A tram driver who would give free rides every day, or a street lamp-lighter, who would enter the dark streets and magically leave a trail of light behind him. Indeed, he would grow up to be a giver of hope and joy, illuminating every life he touched!

In addition to their parents, all the children of the Vaswani family held utmost regard and affection for their uncle, Sadhu Vaswani, who in turn adored them.

When the news about Jashan's birth first reached his uncle's ears, he was overjoyed. He made a beeline to his brother's house, and oh, how delighted was he to see his nephew! There was a look of wonder on his face, as though struck by a premonition about the karmic link with the child, and the incredibly spiritual future that awaited the little boy. While Jashan was an adored child, the driving force that moulded his life was Thanwar, Sadhu Vaswani, who was his guiding star that led Jashan on the path of enlightenment and righteousness.

Just as the Hindu scriptures emphasize how *sanskaras* or values imbibed during childhood years shape an individual's character, Jashan's soul being nurtured by a living saint from a tender age was the supreme assurance of his brilliant future.

One evening, while they were playing their favourite game, Word Making, Jashan put together the word M-A-N. It was Sadhu Vaswani's turn to make the next move. He drew the letter E out of the collection of letters but did not make use of it.

Jashan won the round by rearranging the letters to make the word N-A-M-E. While celebrating his triumph in his usual childlike manner, he asked his uncle with curiosity, 'You could have easily made the word N-A-M-E with the letter E you picked up!'

Sadhu Vaswani smiled warmly at the boy and answered, 'Not only could I have made the word N-A-M-E, but also the word M-A-N-E. But I like to give rather than take! I did not want to take victory away from you; I wanted to give you the joy of winning.'

This little exchange with Sadhu Vaswani left an indelible impression on the little boy's mind. He followed his uncle's precept in letter and spirit, and his life became an unending saga of selfless service. Truly, he lived for others; he became happy seeing others happy.

The children of the Vaswani household were also acquainted with the value of self-reliance at an early age. It was a quality that was ingrained in them. Although there was a full-time and a part-time domestic helper at the beck and call of the family members, Pahlajrai, a man of principles, expected his children to do their own chores. They were required to fold their own clothes, make their own beds, and fetch and carry for themselves too.

Once, the father overheard Jashan asking the helper to bring him a glass of water. He discouraged the habit forthwith. He asked his son, 'Have you hurt your hands or feet?' 'No, Papa,' replied his son sheepishly. 'If you are in perfect health, then please get yourself a glass of water,' he admonished his son. 'Yes, Papa,' said the boy, complying immediately.

One wonders if little Jashan realized that the father's insistence on self-reliance and self-help would always stand him in good stead.

What set the Vaswani household apart was that the prophets and saviours from all traditions and religions of the world were venerated equally. Pahlajrai, who was also a theosophist, had faith in all religions and considered them a pathway leading to the same great goal of humanity – liberation.

The walls of their home were adorned with pictures of Krishna, Rama, Buddha, Zoroaster, Guru Nanak and Jesus Christ. Jashan would marvel at the heroism of the Sikh gurus and admire the infinite tenderness and love given selflessly by St Francis of Assisi; the spirit of renunciation of the Buddha and the supreme sacrifice made by Jesus for humanity never ceased to inspire him. He was, however, most drawn to Rishi Dayaram, a noble social reformer of Sind and a devout man of God.

When left alone, delighting in the quiet, the child would talk to the rishi from the deep recesses of his heart. In particular, he learnt three things from the rishi: simplicity of dress and demeanour, silence, and humility.

A lively and playful boy, Jashan often got into trouble for making mischief. One such episode from his primary school days deserves mention.

The bell rang, signalling the end of the dull Math class. All the boys leaped out of their seats and started dancing and frolicking. Jashan climbed onto a bench and began to dance happily. Creak! came the sound from the bench he was dancing on. Fear gripped the little boy. Jashan was in panic, a soft whisper echoed into his ears, 'Son, you are not alone. Always remember, you are not alone.' The words sounded familiar, for it was a song his dear mother would often sing to him as a lullaby.

When the teacher saw the broken bench, he was livid. 'You will pay a fine of five rupees as a cost of mending the broken bench. And if the fine is not paid by tomorrow, you will not be allowed to enter the class!' he thundered at the boy who was scared out of his wits.

Lost in these thoughts, a miserable Jashan went home. In the evening, when his mother stepped out, he rummaged through her money box and picked out five rupees. As he felt relieved that he had solved the problem, the same old refrain rang in his ears, 'Son, you are not alone. Always remember, you are not alone.'

'Someone is always with me!' thought Jashan to himself. 'He is watching over me, constantly keeping a check on my deeds. How could I do such a thing as stealing money from my own mother?'

Jashan put the money back in the box, but continued to feel miserable. Upon her return from the stroll, his mother found Jashan in a downcast, and asked him why he looked so terrible. Between sobs and tears, he narrated the story truthfully to his mother: 'O Ma, what shall I do?' he begged her.

'Here, Jashan,' she said, wiping the child's tears away. 'Let me give you some money. Pay the fine and apologize for your mistake.'

For Jashan, life itself was a school; every experience, his teacher.

At primary school, he took lessons in knitting. One day, while he was knitting a sweater, the wool got tangled into several knots. Jashan turned to his mother and pleaded for her intervention. His mother gave him a reassuring smile and said, 'Leave it with me. I will sort it out in a few minutes.'

Jashan went out to play. When he returned, the ball of wool was neatly rolled up so he could start afresh.

'If there is something you cannot handle, go to God as you would go to your mother,' Dada tells us. 'Place your problems before your Divine Mother and trust her to sort it out for you in all her love and wisdom!'

In his childhood, Jashan made the discovery that changed his life forever, from the most minuscule to the mightiest of problems, prayer has the strength to overcome any eventuality.

Jashan was extraordinarily gifted. At the tender age of three, when most boys were busy playing in the sun, he began his formal education. At seven, he earned double promotions, completing primary education from T. C. Primary School, Karachi, in three instead of the usual five years. A special tutor in the English language was arranged for the little boy, as his father left no stone unturned to help him blossom in every way.

Soon enough, Jashan was admitted to the Rosary School, Karachi. Not contrary to expectations, the little boy excelled at academics once again, with a triple promotion, and joined high school earlier than most children.

Apart from his sharp intellect, Jashan showed early signs of spiritual maturity. Whenever he could find the time, he would choose a quiet corner and reflect upon life in absolute silence. Sometimes, he would interrogate himself with perplexing questions, 'Why am I here? What is the purpose of my visit on this planet, which is like a traveller's inn? People arrive and depart from the world without leaving a trace. What is the meaning of the mystery of this endless adventure of existence?'

Having been a lover of silence throughout his school years, Dada would later urge children to keep aside some time every day to practice silence: 'If only everyone in the world would spend just five minutes in silence every day, our world would indeed become new!'

Solitude, silence and kinship with nature were Jashan's preferences. He was compassionate and more inclined to looking inwards than most other children. The sight of someone's suffering never failed to touch his heart. Once, on his way to school, Jashan was drawn towards a toy train at a shop. Every morning and evening, he would stare longingly at it from a distance. One day, his curiosity got the better of him, and he went up to the shopkeeper. 'How much does that toy train cost?' he asked timidly, as he fixed his gaze on the toy. 'Fourteen *annas*,' came the reply from the other side of the counter. Alas! It was too expensive for Jashan. But day after day, he looked earnestly and lovingly at the train and continued to enquire its price, hoping it would become cheaper.

On his birthday, Jashan's mother gave him a one rupee coin. He was thrilled. He clutched it tightly in his hand and dashed out of the door. He would now be able to buy his favourite train. Outside the shop, a beggar caught his eye. She had tears in her eyes and a child in her arms. She cried out, 'Won't you give me a rupee? My little one has typhoid and the doctor demands a rupee for the medicine.' While the sound of the moving train was music to Jashan's ears, he could not shut out the piteous cries of the woman. Leaving behind the train, he put the rupee coin into the poor woman's outstretched palm. The joy and gratitude that lit up the eyes of the mother awed the young boy. It was the most precious gift – much more adorable than the toy train – that Jashan had received on his birthday.

Jashan's sensitivity was limited not just towards human beings; his sympathy went out to animals and birds too. One day, he went to visit his neighbour Diwan Gopaldas, who was the proud owner of a beautiful parrot. He told Jashan affectionately, 'Come, I will show you my most prized possession!' and led the inquisitive boy to his parrot.

Jashan gazed at the bird, admiring its beauty, when suddenly his heart grew heavy with grief. He imagined how lonely it must be, separated from others of its kind; he began to feel sorry for the bird. He felt as though the piercing gaze of the parrot was trying to communicate the story of its empty and lonely existence.

In a small voice, Jashan said, 'Uncle! Why have you confined this lovely parrot in a cage?'

'Cage?' the uncle said incredulously, not expecting to be asked such a question. 'This is its cozy home, Jashan! I give it the food it loves to eat: chillies, guavas and seeds. It is very happy and content in its cage. I talk to the parrot every day and everyone who comes to the house admires it.' he explained.

'Papa says that the greatest treasure of a living being is freedom,' Jashan continued in a sad voice. 'You have deprived the parrot of its freedom. I cannot believe that he is truly happy.'

Gopaldas was taken aback by what Jashan had just told him. Eager to humour the boy, Gopaldas said, 'Alright, Jashan, if it makes you happy, I permit you to set it free. But make sure that it is able to fly and that it does not get harmed by any other bird or creature.'

With bated breath, Jashan opened the door of the cage, his hands trembling with excitement. He had thought the parrot would rush out with joy. Instead, it seemed to cower in one corner, reluctant to come close to the door that had just been thrown open for him. Jashan put his hand inside the cage and brought out the bird gently.

He lifted it lovingly and placed it outside of the cage, thinking it would finally flap its wings and fly. The little boy was disappointed again. The bird could not fly. Jashan began stroking its wings, hoping to infuse energy into them. The poor creature hopped around but was unable to fly. The parrot tried to spread its wings but after making a few attempts got tired and gave up.

Jashan was discouraged to see the bird in such a state. He stared at it disappointedly. After a while, when he had least expected it, the parrot summoned all its strength to hop onto the parapet. Just then, a flock of parrots flew by. The sight and sweet sound of these parrots gave the bird new hope. With one upward surge, away it flew into the blue skies that had been beckoning it all along. Jashan smiled and ran towards the neighbour to give him the good news.

All of us can be likened to the parrot except that his cage was made of steel, while ours has been built block by block with desires and attachment. Dada would later ask, 'Aren't we all like the caged parrot in the story? Why have we imprisoned ourselves when we are meant to soar higher and higher?'

Even as a child, Jashan subjected himself to acts of self-discipline and service. He vowed to perform at least one good deed every day which helped strengthen his character. Once, after a very hectic day at school, he returned home rather late. Completely exhausted, he slipped into his cosy bed, his mind recounting the happenings of the day. To his utter shock, he realized that he had not done a single, selfless, good act the whole day.

Up sprang young Jashan and ventured out of the house in search of an opportunity to serve someone or the other. Weary and tired, he could not find anyone to serve. But he had to show loyalty to the vow he had taken. So, he picked up an ant very carefully, put it into a puddle of water. What happened next is rather amusing. Very benevolently, the young boy placed his finger under the struggling ant and rescued it. It was just a mock situation, but he managed to keep his word. Jashan went back home happy and relieved.

Jashan's carefree childhood came to an abrupt end when he was just ten years old. On 17 April 1929, on the auspicious day of Ram Navami, his beloved father, Pahlajrai, passed away. His mother was bereft, inconsolable, with seven young children: sons Jashan, Ram, Hiro, and Harkrishin, and daughters Shakuntala, Hari, and Sundri. The youngest child, Harkrishin, was only six months old.

The children kept asking their mother why she had told them that their father would never return. To console them, Krishnadevi would say, 'If you stay awake the whole night and repeat the Holy Name "Rama! Rama! Rama!" then your father will come.' Innocently believing what she said, the children would resolve to do that. But sleep would invariably overtake them, try as they did to resist it.

It was not without reason that Krishnadevi had chosen the name of Sri Rama. Shortly before his sudden death, Pahlajrai had started writing the Ramayana in Sindhi especially for the youth. It was a project very dear to his heart. Therefore, Sri Rama had figured constantly in his conversations at home. For that reason, Krishnadevi could think of no better way of keeping her children connected with their father.

Thus, at a very early age, little Jashan came to understand the transience of human life. Only an year before his father's death, a very dear friend, Prem, had died unexpectedly. Now, his beloved father was no more. All that he had taken for granted – his father's loving presence, a sense of security and well-being and a happy family atmosphere – were snatched away in one moment. Several questions began to recur in the little boy's mind. He would often awaken at night, pondering over these questions endlessly: What was life all about? Was it only pain and suffering? What was man expected to achieve in the short lifespan given to him?

TWO

The Years of Loss and Learnings

'We cannot always build the future for our youth, but we can build
our youth for the future.'

– Franklin D. Roosevelt, *Great Speeches*

In the years that followed the death of his father, every
disappointment turned into a heartache for Jashan. The father's
sudden departure from the world put a strain on the family's
finances. Pahlajrai's altruistic life meant that he left behind very
little for the family. Silently, but with deep concern, Jashan observed
how his mother put up a brave front at the time of such a severe
financial crisis, struggling to make ends meet. He realized how
every penny counted.

Jashan also discovered that others outside the family held
his beloved father's memory in great reverence and appreciation
because Pahlajrai had touched many lives with his generosity and
selfless service. Ram Prasad, who was a peon, was one of his father's
most sincere students. He diligently attended the night school
and eventually became a teacher himself. Jashan was imbued with
pride. His father deserved every ounce of respect and admiration
that people continued to keep alive in them even after his demise.

Pahlajrai's friends in the education department went all out to offer help to the family. They created a post for Krishnadevi in one of the best primary schools in Karachi. She had no specific qualification, making her ineligible for any teaching post. To counter the inadequacy, a new subject of cookery was introduced, in which she had an expertise. Gradually and painfully, the family began to limp back to normalcy. Jashan soon began to practise austerities that were nothing short of incredible for someone so young. He was consumed by an intense yearning for God and his desire to realize him, speak to him, feel his ever-living presence prevailed over all other desires, although there weren't many.

Once, in school, he experienced a deep longing to envision God. He went up to his teacher and asked her innocently, 'What should I do in order to see the radiant form of God?'

The teacher, a sensitive and understanding lady, was quite touched by Jashan's sincerity. 'If you want a vision of God so earnestly, I will tell you a *sadhana*,' she told him. 'It is difficult, Jashan, but I want you to try it sincerely. You have to keep a vigil. You must keep awake for three nights and recite the mantra, *Om Namo Bhagavate Vasudevaya*.'

With sheer devotion, Jashan chanted the hymn for about 108 times when he fell into a sound sleep. But there were two more nights to make up for the first one. The next night, he managed to repeat the mantra for a much longer period of time. But much to his chagrin, he fell asleep soon after. 'Jashan, this is not as simple as you thought it was.' the little boy told himself.

Jashan attempted to still his wandering mind by way of *tapasya*. Not just that, he practised the *panch agni tapasya* by lighting fire on all four sides and seating himself in the middle, under the scorching heat of the sun. At times he wrapped a blanket around himself. He did everything he could to walk the path of spirituality.

At school, Jashan avoided looking at girls – a favourite pastime of most young boys. He handled money with caution, as he feared it would ensnare him. Whenever an undesirable thought crept into his mind, he would immediately slap himself and drive away the evil thought. 'It was a mosquito!' he would tell his friends who were confounded by this act of his. Every impure thought is indeed a mosquito, which must be driven away at once, he would say.

As he grew in years, Jashan got a nail fixed in his shoes. The nail served the purpose of punishing him by piercing the sole of his foot when an undesirable thought would enter his mind.

Krishnadevi began to see her son questioning everything in life and well understood the struggle that her son was going through as part of adolescence. In all fairness, Jashan had never brought anxiety to his mother. But now, she had to be mindful of the fact that her son was fatherless, at a time when he most needed a father. She could see him develop a strong determination and the ability to hold steadfast to his convictions.

Jashan's mind was flooded with questions on life and its purpose. He had received a modern education and was not really familiar with the traditional rites and rituals. When time came for the youngster to undergo the sacred-thread ceremony (*janeu*), Jashan demanded to be told the reason behind it. When he was provided the explanation of the three threads symbolizing the threefold ideals of compassion, truthfulness and purity, he announced that he would not take the janeu until he was sure of his ability to live up to the high ideals. The distraught mother did her best to persuade him to comply with the family tradition that had been followed through several generations. She remonstrated and pleaded, but Jashan refused to wear the thread. Krishnadevi gave up. Consequently, the ceremony was organized only for the younger brothers.

Jashan enjoyed solitude and was always pining for it. The unwavering desire would often send him in a frantic search of peaceful and quiet communion with nature, which was his constant companion. The Clifton Beach in Karachi was his favourite haunt, where he spent long hours by the waves, watching the sun rise and set in all its glory. The waves that rushed to touch his feet vigorously would withdraw noiselessly. Their boundless, ceaseless ebb and flow enchanted him. For hours, he would stare at the huge steamers and ships sail past him in the Karachi harbour.

On weekends, he would go out to the Manora Islands (a group of small islands to the south of Karachi, forming a protective barrier between the Karachi harbour and the Arabian Sea), where he would watch the rolling waves of the deep blue sea crash against the shore tumultuously. At times, the waves seemed to be as turbulent and stormy in nature as the thoughts that occupied his mind – 'What do I want? Where would I like to go?' How he wished to find the answer to these questions! But as he gazed at the waves, he also realized that the tumult and turbulence was only on the surface; the deeper you delve, the more silent, clear and calm the waters grow. He saw a reflection of himself in the sea. Deep within him too, there was a reservoir of stillness and silence. The million-dollar question was: How could he touch that point of stillness?

He would never grow tired of gazing at the sea and wondering about its depth. 'Life is like the sea. Its treasures lie deep within, not solely on the tempestuous surface,' he felt.

Jashan was lucky to have a couple of like-minded friends, not attracted by frivolous pleasures. The three friends would often set out on long walks to Clifton Beach, whenever they had the time and opportunity to do so.

As they walked, they would discuss various interpretations of passages from the *Sukhmani Sahib* and other holy scriptures. The friends developed an analytical attitude to life and learnt to question everything. They came from Hindu families, but instinctively questioned the rituals and practices of organized religion.

One day, Jashan visited a gurdwara. The old man who stood at the entrance would not allow him in.

'Where is your cap?' he demanded. 'Don't you know that you cannot come in here with your head uncovered?'

Jashan had to return that day without being admitted to the gurdwara. The old man had won that round, but it was not the end of the episode.

Few days later, Jashan returned to the same gurdwara, head still uncovered. The same old man was at the entrance and cast a sour glance at the recalcitrant youth.

'Where is your cap?' he demanded, as usual.

'I'm wearing my cap,' answered Jashan coolly.

The old man blinked. 'I don't see any cap on your head,' he said suspiciously.

'*Kakaji* (uncle), I am wearing a cap. How could I be here without my cap?' Jashan persisted.

'Do you take me for a blind man? Do I need some special spectacles to see your cap? You are not wearing it and you cannot enter! And that's final,' snapped the old man.

'Kakaji, you may not see it, but I am wearing the cap of faith. I would not come here without it, and you must let me in without any hindrance,' Jashan explained to him patiently.

The old man was nonplussed. Wordlessly, he let the young lad pass through, muttering under his breath, 'Cap of faith! What cap of faith?'

The strong pull of mysticism and yearning for the Divine was conspicuous in Jashan's life. It is no coincidence, therefore, that several holy men crossed his path.

Men of god and seekers often pass through a period of intense quest. During this evolutionary phase of their spiritual growth, perhaps, they do not even know for certain what it is that they seek, but remain undeterred and steadfast in their pursuit. Jashan was no stranger to this phase either.

One year, during his vacations, Jashan left home quietly to wander into the villages in and around Karachi. As his feet walked one step after the other, a million thoughts travelling at the speed of light raced in his mind.

He slept in the open, had just one simple meal a day, served at a *langar* in a temple or a gurdwara. He sought solitude and communed with the Eternal. What questions he asked, what answers he found, no one knows. But he returned home a different person – more mature, more evolved and more certain now about what he wanted from life. He would resume his studies and continue to be the brilliant scholar that he always was. Yet a gradual but certain transformation had already begun within his heart. He had seen the light, and it beckoned him in a new direction.

Jashan's zealous search for God could win over any saint. There was one such man of God, who showered his grace generously on the young man. He would often say to him, '*Pyare* (dear one), if you wish to walk the path of an aspirant, follow the way of utter and complete obedience.'

However, with Jashan's temperament of questioning everything he saw and heard, his arguments were fervent. But the holy man's words set him thinking. He had made up his mind that the path of the seeker was to be his chosen path. Now, it was incumbent upon him to practise the virtue of obedience, no matter how difficult it was.

After a few days of struggle, Jashan made up his mind to follow the saint's advice in letter and spirit. He went to the saint straightaway, sat at his feet and told him in all eagerness, 'I am ready to walk the path of obedience.'

The holy man smiled and said, 'May I put your obedience to test?'

'I am waiting to carry out your every behest,' Jashan replied in all honesty.

The saint told his disciple, 'Pyare, go to this young man (a fellow disciple) and tell him a few harsh truths. Reveal his misdoings to him. Tell him to mend his ways.' The gentleman in question was a good friend and much older than Jashan. How could he, still a teenager, go to him and utter such a warning?

Instinctively, Jashan shrank from the task. His courage and resolution failed him utterly. He despaired: Was it so tough to walk the path of obedience? Nonetheless, he had promised the saint to walk the path of obedience and he was determined to keep his word. His mind still in turmoil, but his determination indomitable, the seeker made his way to the friend's house.

It was the longest, hardest walk that Jashan had ever taken. For every step he took forward, he took back two steps in his mind. As he drew close to his destination, his reluctance grew manifold. Soon enough, he was knocking at the friend's door, his hands trembling.

The door opened and Jashan was face to face with his friend's mother. She greeted him graciously and invited him in.

Jashan inquired about her son nervously. 'He left for Shikarpur last evening. But at least I got to see you.' The mother responded warmly.

Ah! Jashan was relieved upon hearing these words. It seemed as though a huge burden had been lifted off his shoulders. He offered gratitude to the Lord, 'God! You have saved me!'

After making some polite conversation with the mother and her family members, Jashan returned to the holy man and said to him, 'I went to meet the friend as you had suggested. But he was away at Shikarpur.' Jashan paused, swallowed his reluctance and continued in a small voice, 'Tomorrow, when he gets back, I shall call upon him again and convey your message.'

'There is no need for that now,' said the saint nonchalantly. 'There is something else I want you to do.' And Jashan was assigned a simple, routine task, which he carried out meticulously.

It was indeed a lucky escape for the young aspirant.

This incident more or less set the tone for the trying duties which the holy man assigned for Jashan to perform. The tender stage of life that he was in made each of them seem insurmountable. At the same time, while being administered another challenging test at the hands of the saint, Jashan perceived life through the prism of reason and common sense.

Once, the holy man sent for Jashan and told him, 'I want you to go to the press which is printing this series on the lives of saints. I am currently reading it. Their next edition is to be printed shortly. I want you to meet the printer, who is also the publisher of the series and request him to use a better quality of paper. And here is something more important; they should also use larger fonts.'

Jashan felt daunted by the task before him: how could an unknown young student go to a well-known press and tell the printers how to do their job?

Firm as he was to keep his vow of obedience, he set out for the press, where he was requested to wait for the manager in his office.

Jashan's heart was pounding against his chest, his hands trembling at the thought of what he was about to do. He conjured up an image of what was to come: the manager giving him a piece of his mind using the choicest of words to reprimand him and then showing him the door.

Maybe, Jashan thought miserably, the entire test of obedience was to teach him to bear praise and abuse with equanimity.

Shortly afterward, the manager entered the cabin and took his seat. 'What can we do for you, young man?' he enquired affably.

Jashan cleared his throat and began on a diffident note, 'Actually sir, it is about the next edition of your series the *Lives of Saints*,' he dropped a clue.

'Ah yes, our new edition,' the manager beamed. 'Here is a brand new copy of the book, fresh out from the press. Would you like to take a look?' And he offered a hardbound copy of the book lying on his table.

'Do … do you mean to say the book has already been printed?' Jashan stammered.

'Yes, indeed!' the manager said happily, flashing a wide grin. 'We are ahead of schedule, for a change. Oh, please do keep a copy with our best compliments. It is nice to know that youngsters like you are taking an interest in our series.'

Much to his relief, the latest edition had already been published. Politely, he thanked the manager for the book and left the press in haste.

He felt indebted to God, 'God, you have saved me yet again! I could not have gone a step further on the path of obedience, without your grace.'

He returned to the holy man's abode and recounted the entire episode.

'Should I have passed on your suggestions to him despite the fact that the edition had already been printed?' Jashan asked, very humbly.

The saint radiated warmth. He sat Jashan down by his side and patted his head with affection, 'My son, you worry too much; you take things easily to heart. You have done all that was required. You obeyed me implicitly. This was meant to help you destroy your ego, your personal pride. You have, indeed, passed the test. You readily agreed to do things you did not like, carried out instructions you found difficult or unpleasant. This is all I expected of you.'

Once, Jashan was visiting a nearby town. The train was busy chugging along and Jashan was, as always, lost in contemplation. The train pulled over at a small station. The boy looked dreamily out of the window when a *sadhu* caught his eye. Several devotees and disciples had come to see the holy man off. Baskets and cartons of food, fruits and *mithai* were loaded onto the compartment. Jashan was astonished! How in the world could a man eat so much food, all by himself, he wondered.

Shortly thereafter, the train halted at another station that was brimming with people. As always, a host of beggars gathered at the windows of the compartment. They knocked on the window panes, with hopeful eyes, for food or money. The saint opened his heavy basket laden with fruits and distributed it all to the beggars. Jashan was astounded. The big basket was emptied in a jiffy. Jashan looked at the beggars. They were relishing the bananas and apples happily and bowing in gratitude to the holy man. The man had not kept any fruits for himself and had generously given it all away.

'Maybe he doesn't like fruits,' Jashan thought to himself, in his childlike innocence.

The train stopped at another station once again. It was a passenger train and moved slowly, stopping at every station. The beggars swarmed around the windows once again. This time too, the sadhu did not turn them away empty-handed. He opened a box of sweets and gave them out to the poor folk. The train kept halting every few minutes and each time the sadhu had something to give out to the hungry and poor ones. The ascetic did not treat himself to a single morsel of food; he gave it all away to the starving, poor and needy before they had crossed half a dozen stations!

Now, the holy man sat cross-legged near the window, with his eyes closed in meditation. Jashan was amazed by the sight. He swiftly moved to sit right opposite the sadhu. He had heard that when men of God went into meditation, a great power akin to electricity came into their being. When they opened their eyes after meditation, they emanated electric power, which was transmitted to those who gazed into them. So, Jashan sat there patiently, waiting to receive the great flow of current that would change his life. At last, the sadhu opened his eyes. He smiled at the expectant boy.

The hours flew by in the blink of an eye and soon, it was time for the saint to alight from the train. How Jashan longed to accompany him! But the best he could do was get off the train and bid adieu to the wise man and touch his feet one last time. In a flash, the saint touched Jashan's feet too. Jashan reluctantly boarded the train, still watching him, transfixed. A porter approached the saint and offered to carry his bag. He gave the porter some money but carried the bag himself.

Suddenly, Jashan remembered a piece of advice given to him by his revered father, 'Whenever you meet a man of God, you must never, ever forget to take a teaching from him.'

'Sadhuji,' Jashan called out to him hastily. Without a trace of hesitation, the holy man came near the compartment and stood before the young boy, 'Tell me, my child, what can I do for you?'

'Sadhuji, I would like to take a teaching from you, which I can treasure in my heart and bear witness to in daily life,' Jashan said, folding his hands in veneration.

'But I am not a sadhu!' laughed the holy man. 'I am but a simple soul. However, I am touched by your sincerity and reverence, and so, I shall share with you a simple teaching that my guru gave me.'

'Your guru!' Jashan exclaimed. 'You are so wonderful yourself. Your guru must be a truly great soul!'. 'Far from it,' the saint said. 'My guru was a humble peasant and this is the teaching he gave me: "Seek only to please God." I try to live by this teaching, and if you do likewise, you will be richly blessed.'

Jashan's keenness to learn from holy men was growing by the day. There were periods when his mother would go out of town and Jashan would make the most of these opportunities to visit the villages that formed the rural hinterland of Karachi. He would venture out in search of *fakir*s and *yogi*s. He would carry no luggage, trusting himself wholly to the loving care of God. He would sleep under a tree and eat a meal at the home of the village headman. It was the custom that any visitor to the village would be treated as a guest by the village *mukhiya*.

Once, while walking down a country lane, Jashan saw a man seated by the side of the road. The man observed him carefully as Jashan approached him. Jashan was eager to learn from him too. 'Please give me some teaching,' he said to the fakir.

'Be a lion and not a dog,' the man replied promptly.

Jashan was quite taken aback. What could such a statement mean? Jashan ventured, 'I am a lion already. My zodiac sign is Leo.'

The man smiled patiently and explained, 'The difference between a dog and a lion is that if you throw a ball or a stone at the dog it will run after the ball or the stone. But, if you throw something at the lion, the lion will come and pounce on you. He will not pay attention to what you have thrown.'

'I'm not sure that I understand what you mean, Baba,' said Jashan.

'It means that you don't have to think of all the balls and stones that come your way. In other words, you don't have to flinch at the worries and difficulties that come to you and weigh you down. You have to ask yourself, "Where are they coming from?" You will realize that everything comes from the holy hands of the Lord. If you become a lion, you will go and catch hold of the holy feet of the lord. You will not look anywhere else.'

Once, Jashan was convalescing from typhoid. He was yearning to retreat to a quiet place, for a change of climate always did him good. But he had his reservations since he felt reluctant to seek others' hospitality.

One fine day, out of nowhere, he received a letter from a strange baba: 'My son, if you would care to come to me, I shall gladly share my roof and simple meals with you. I will serve you and be blessed!' He was confused yet pleased to read the words written in the letter.

True, Jashan was flabbergasted to have received a letter from a stranger, who wanted to invite him over to his abode without knowing him. But the still, small voice whispered to him that the writer of the letter was a long-lost friend, perhaps an older brother from his previous birth. He could not resist the simple invitation and decided to accept it.

The train steamed into the platform of a small town. Jashan had arrived at his destination. He looked around for the friend whom he had never met before. There he was, unfamiliar yet familiar. Jashan instinctively knew it was him. One look at the baba kindled a flame within him. Within no time, one kindred spirit had recognized another.

The two met not as strangers, but as long-lost friends, who had chanced upon one another one fine afternoon. When he first saw him, Jashan spontaneously addressed him as 'Baba'. During his brief stay, Jashan practised many spiritual disciplines and was enriched with many spiritual experiences.

On one occasion, the two kindred souls sat together in a meditative mood, when Baba said to Jashan, 'Remember that you are a pilgrim here, a wayfarer in quest of your lost homeland. Your home is in eternity. Be patient in the midst of the difficulties and dangers of life. Remind yourself again and again, "This too shall pass!"' After a momentary pause, Baba added, 'Meditate each day on death, as death approaches with each passing moment; give your service of love to all, and seek fellowship with saints and holy men so that the tiny drop that you are, may become a mighty ocean, vast enough to hold within it a thousand oceans.' Baba's voice trailed off as he closed his eyes to ponder over life.

By no means was Baba a wealthy man, but many counted on him when in need of material help as the kind-hearted man was always willing to part with whatever little he had. He kept nothing to himself. The more he received, the more he gave. He emptied himself over and over again. Only God filled him. He ate but once in twenty-four hours. Often some hungry people would drop in at his doorstep during mealtime and he would joyfully share his food with them. On the days that no one showed up, the street dogs claimed their share and baba had no qualms about it.

'You eat only once a day,' Jashan said to him on one occasion, 'and if you do not eat your fill, you must be feeling hungry!'

Baba's answer was enigmatic. 'What I share with others,' he said, 'comes back to me tenfold and I feel full!'

Baba kept awake for the greater part of the night, at times, reading aloud from the *sant-bani* (the words of the saints); at other times, communing, in silence, with the Beloved. Jashan tried to keep up with him, but his weak state after the illness would not permit him. Ultimately, sleep would always overpower him. But the small, still voice was always up to serve as a reminder, 'Wake up! O ye, who are lost in the slumber of the senses!' It wouldn't die down, 'The night hath come to an end. Do you not realize that with each passing moment, someone or the other, is passing out of the body and starting upon the inevitable journey? Whose turn will come next, who knows? Wake up! Beware of the temptations of this transient life, and direct your mind and heart to God!'

'It is so difficult to keep awake,' Jashan confessed to baba, who went into a fit of rage and fumed, 'If you cannot keep awake, why don't you put on black clothes as a mark of mourning? Is it befitting for you to spend your time in feasts and festivals, in foolish merriment and vain rejoicings? It will do you good to hide your face in shame. For I tell you, until you have reached the stage of union with the Beloved, you can only weep without ceasing!'

His words touched the core of Jashan's being. 'If you attain the Beloved, be asleep even when you seem to be awake! In our waking hours, we are absorbed in the affairs of the world. Be asleep to the world,' baba stormed. 'Be asleep to all that the world stands for. In this sleep, the soul is released from the snare of the body. In this sleep, memory is lost and attachments and enmities cast themselves off. In this sleep, the poor man forgets his broken cottage and the rich man, his luxurious couch. In this sleep, there is no fear of the future, no burden of the past, no thought of selfish gain or loss. Live and move in the world as if you are asleep!'

'Give me some simple, realistic guidelines,' Jashan said to him at once, 'whereby I may regulate my daily living and enrich my inner being.'

Calm descended over Baba. 'I will pass on three simple rules to you. If you will live up to them, your life will bloom as a garden in spring, blessing all who cross your pilgrim-path.' Jashan was all ears as the devout man spoke, 'Talk little or not at all. And when you open your lips, see that your talk concerns God.'

Jashan was intrigued by what the Baba had to offer him. 'Judge no one! Behold the good in all! Everyone you see or meet has something good to teach you. Learn from them in all humility. Criticize no one. Give the service of love to all. And, even in your secret thoughts, send your goodwill and good wishes to all.' Baba's voice became deeper, 'Do not depart from the truth. Even when caught in tumultuous times, do not flinch in your loyalty to truth.'

While at Baba's house, Jashan appeared engrossed in reading a book. But in reality, he was just reading the same page over and over again. The words failed to penetrate his mind, and he seemed clueless.

Sensing his discomfort, Baba finally asked Jashan, 'What are you reading?'

Jashan responded honestly, 'I do not know. I cannot remember what I have read. There are thoughts and questions welling up within me. I am wondering about situations such as floods, robberies, famine, poverty and wealth. What is their cause? Why do they occur? I ponder over why I have come here. I cannot understand what it is that I want.'

Patting him on his back, baba told him, 'Son, you already know what you want and why you have come here. You want Allah. You also know that until you don't attain God, you will keep wandering, you will be haunted by the question "What for?"' Baba paused as Jashan soaked in his words.

Baba said, 'In this world, if you get everything, but you don't attain God, then what? Nothing can give you peace. You receive this precious gem only when you attain God.'

'If I really and truly want Allah, why don't I get him?' asked Jashan, growing impatient.

Baba explained, 'You have put up a block, a barrier between you and him. My dear son, remove the veil which is obstructing you, so that you can meet the Beloved.'

Jashan probed further, 'What is the sign of one who has become one with Allah?'

Baba answered, 'He is fortunate that he is dead to the world and has killed his ego. He is free from the shackles of the ego. We are ensnared by it. The ego is a tyrant, like a hooded snake guarding a treasure it sits on us, overpowering all. It strangles and chokes everyone. Fortunate is he who can sublimate his ego. Then for him the world is dead. There is no attachment to anyone or anything.'

'Be dead to the world,' Baba emphasized. 'We have to be able to walk through the cemetery, unaffected by dualities such as likes and dislikes, joy and sorrow, praise and censure and victory and defeat. We often talk about not being attached. But the minute we are deprived of something, we become sad. When our rights are denied and we are not accorded our due, we are miserable. We are only happy when we are satisfied with the way things are around us,' he said. 'Don't let the ego dictate its terms to you! Detach from the ego!'

Jashan reflected on these words. The Bhagavad Gita too mentions that when you are not affected by the *dwanda*s (binaries of life), then you are like a calm ocean. In such an ocean, the waves lap gently. You are steadfast like a mountain, even in a storm. You are the same, in sorrow and in joy. Blessed is the one who has risen above the ego. He repeats constantly, '*Shukur*', gratitude to the Lord. The rest of us, the unfortunate ones, are still in slumber.

Jashan felt that his good fortune had led him to Baba. He valued immensely the fortnight spent with him. Baba, on the other hand, served the young guest as only a mother can serve her child. He blessed Jashan as a mother would bless her only child, giving him all the love he could draw from his pious heart. He taught Jashan how to contemplate in silence and by entering into the depths within, rise above time and space to be absorbed in the One Name of the Beloved. 'Repetition of the Name,' he emphasized, 'is perhaps the simplest and the most effective *sadhana* you can practice.' And he asked all who came to him to repeat, again and again, the Name of God, the Holy Name. He himself spent several hours of the day and night in repeating the Name of God and in reading aloud the *sant-bani* and the *gurbani*, the inspired utterances of the saints and the gurus of humanity.

When the time came for Jashan to take leave from him, he was mired in grief. He bowed and clung to Baba's feet as tears rolled out of his eyes in an unending stream. He softly whispered to him through his tears, 'My heart is sad, as the time has come when I must leave you. For fifteen days, your grace has been a shining light upon my life. And now I must go ...'

The memory of this man, whom Jashan refers to in all love and reverence as the 'Unknown Baba', continued to be a source of ceaseless blessing to him, lighting up his path.

Whenever the unknown Baba visited Karachi, he would send word to Jashan of his arrival and Jashan would, unfailingly, walk from home to the distant Soldier Bazaar to seek his blessings and gain from his words of wisdom.

Jashan offered to bring whatever Baba needed. One day, Baba said, 'You could bring a bowl of curd for me every day.' But he set a prerequisite for Jashan, 'However, you should fulfil one condition.'

'I will do anything that you command me to do,' said Jashan, eager to be of service to Baba.

'I want you to repeat the Name of God with every step that you take towards me whilst you bring me the curd. And if, perchance, you forget to do so, retrace your steps to the last point where you positively remember to have repeated the Name of God. From there, start afresh,' he added. Jashan readily agreed.

The next day, Jashan walked three miles to Soldier Bazaar in the merciless heat of the afternoon sun. He dedicatedly kept repeating the Name of God. Of course, sometimes he had to retrace his steps to the point where he felt he had forgotten to repeat the Holy Name.

So, far from imposing his rules on the young seeker, Baba invested tremendous faith in young Jashan. The simple act of carrying curd impressed the Name Divine on the young lad's mind and heart.

Another saint to have a bearing on Jashan's early life was a homeless yogi, whom Jashan met on the streets of Karachi. The young boy would meet him every now and then. The saint had no permanent residence and Jashan could never be sure where he would meet him next. But when he did see the holy man and sat at his feet, he was filled with peace.

The holy man carried a parrot with him. The bird would go on talking as the yogi went about his work.

One day, as Jashan sat at his feet, the yogi turned to him and said loudly, 'Who do you think you are? What gives you the right to criticize others?' Jashan was taken aback at this sudden outburst, but he sat there quietly. The holy man softened his voice a few moments later, 'Be cordial. Be amicable. Be friendly with everyone.' The advice of the yogi was an eye-opener for Jashan. He now consciously worked on himself and treated everyone he met with love and reverence.

The next day, when Jashan went to see the saint, he asked him out of sheer love, 'Dearest Jashan, did you feel I was angry with you yesterday?'

'Yes,' replied Jashan in a soft voice. 'You shouted at me.'

'You are mistaken. I did not shout at you. I shouted at the little devil who was inside you – a little devil who was disrespectful and critical of everyone.' The yogi enlightened Jashan with a simple sadhana.

Jashan also spent some time in the company of a wandering dervish. The dervish, for his part, would always greet the seeker with love and share insights and wisdom with him. It seemed to Jashan that the dervish had a special affection for him; if perchance Jashan was unable to meet him for a few days, the dervish would send for him and inquire about his well-being.

One day, when Jashan turned up for his usual evening meeting, the dervish greeted him rather coldly. When Jashan attempted to talk to him, he seemed to turn away; when Jashan tried to draw his attention, he brusquely commanded him to leave and come another time.

Jashan, still very young, felt both hurt and humiliated at this. Though the dervish's abrupt and rude behaviour was very difficult to accept, Jashan obeyed him implicitly. He rose from the front row where he was seated and left at once.

Jashan was deeply concerned over what had happened. He instinctively realized that the dervish was not a volatile man of moods, given to kindness and love one day, and pouring out hatred and indifference the next. 'Why did he behave with me in such an unusual manner?' Jashan wondered, 'And in public? How could someone who has treated me with such love and affection all these days suddenly turn hostile towards me?' He dwelt on the questions for a while and began looking inward for the answers, 'What have I done, knowingly or unknowingly, to deserve such treatment from my mentor?'

The moment of reflection supplied an answer. He recalled that he had been nursing strong feelings of bitterness and resentment against a friend who had behaved badly towards him. He was in the grip of wrath when he had gone to see the dervish that day, deliberately suppressing his anger, so that it did not show on his face or eyes. But the dervish had sensed the resentment and negative force that he was emanating.

As soon as he found the answer, Jashan struggled to quell the tumultuous storm in his mind. He made a valiant effort to understand himself and remove all traces of bitterness against the friend who had angered him. At last, he was able to still his raging mind, and in the reflection and introspection that ensued, he realized how to make amends. Though reconciliation was far from easy, Jashan did not shy away from it.

The following day, Jashan approached the brother who had caused him so much anguish and exchanged loving greetings with him. Perhaps the friend had realized that he had offended Jashan in some way, for he ventured an explanation for his earlier behaviour. Jashan, however, was over the incident. He had already buried the hatchet and the two parted amicably.

Having overcome the animosity that he had been nursing in his heart, Jashan went to meet the dervish, who greeted him with great warmth and affection and asked him, as usual, why he had not come to see him earlier. He gestured towards Jashan to come and sit at his feet and spoke to him as lovingly and kindly as before.

On that unforgettable day, the dervish spoke to the gathering on empathy, 'The path of the aspirant,' he told the seekers, 'is the path of detachment. When one walks this path, there should be no room for enmity or hatred in one's heart. If we are God's children, how can we entertain negative feelings against each other? If we practise hatred, envy and malice, how can we claim to love God? The genuine aspirant understands and empathizes with the pain of another. Your brother's suffering is your own; your sister's joy is your own.'

'All we need to do,' he said, radiating warmth, 'is open the door of our hearts and feel the pain and joy of others as if it were our own.'

The dervish's noble advice struck a chord with Jashan. Even today, Dada tells us: 'Hatred corrodes. It does not merely poison your relationship with the people you choose to hate; it corrodes you from within. This hatred is like an unseen virus that infects the whole environment around us. It is not merely destructive, but a severe form of self-punishment. Very often, our ill-will and resentment cannot touch the other person, but we are poisoned by our negative feelings. We lose our inner peace and this leads to anguish and misery all around.'

The words of an enlightened one never go in vain: like an archer's arrow, they hit the bullseye.

When Jashan was a college student, he would frequent the Adam Soomar confectionery shop in Sadar. The shop was famous for its delicious pastries and other desserts. He was particularly fond of the scrumptious eggless pastries sold there. Considering Jashan had the habit of walking long distances, the shop particularly came in handy as a snack stop, where he could refuel, recharge his energy and continue his pursuits.

One evening, as he headed towards Adam Soomar, in the pleasant anticipation of relishing the fancy pastries, the striking figure of a fakir wearing a fez cap arrested his attention. He wondered why the dervish stood outside the shop. At this hour, when the evening was about to give way to a starlit night, the man should have been at the mosque for his prayers.

Jashan was dumbfounded when the fakir called out to him, his eyes aglow, 'Life is not meant to eat and make merry, to consume pastries and devour sweets. Control your palate!'

Jashan stood there, mesmerized by the sharp injunction.

The young collegian was listening intently, so the sage continued, 'Listen, my child, he who wishes to serve the Lord must not seek things of the world. He must not hanker after delicacies.' In his soft voice he sang a couplet:

> Be ever awake, ever watchful, ever vigilant,
> Nor unmindful remain
> Even for a single moment.

Even before he could realize it, Jashan struck a conversation with the holy man. The exchange turned out to be both engaging and enriching. 'Are you eager to tread the spiritual path?' asked the fakir. Jashan nodded his head in eager assent. The fakir passed on a treasure trove of wisdom to the hopeful seeker, 'Never live a life of indolence and indulgence. These can be likened to thieves that rob you of your spiritual treasures. They are waiting to pounce on you and overpower you. It is, therefore, very important that you remain alert every single moment.' The sound advice of the fakir was etched on Jashan's mind. He continued with his hand on his chest, 'Build your life in constant remembrance of God.'

Jashan never met the fakir again. He disappeared as mysteriously as he had appeared. He would pass by the spot every day, hoping against hope to catch a glimpse of the strange and majestic figure, but it was not to be.

But the words had done their magic. Never again would he walk all the way from Gadikhatta to Sadar Bazaar merely to indulge in a pastry.

There was another instance which Jashan holds dear to his heart; it was the memory of a dervish, who left behind a valuable message for him, even when he could not meet him personally.

Jashan first met him when he was in college. The dervish had given him a locket and told him to wear it around his neck. The locket had a special message for Jashan, but the dervish extracted a promise out of the young man, 'Promise that you will not open the locket as long as I am alive.'

Though Jashan was sorely tempted to open the locket and take a sneak peek into what was inside, he paid loyal obeisance to the promise and chose not to open it. However, he did not wear the locket around his neck, but guarded it by keeping it safely among his books.

Years flew by and one day, the unthinkable happened. India was partitioned and the Sindhis lost their homeland to political divisions and man-made borders. Many of them were compelled to flee the land of their birth, which was now a part of Pakistan. Left with no alternative, they moved to India in hordes. Jashan too had to move out. But the holy man continued to stay in Pakistan.

One day Jashan received the sad news of his demise. He was heartbroken.

Almost instantly, his mind wandered to the locket. With mixed emotions, he opened the locket, and found inscribed in it, the following message:

> Beloved, this is also good.
> Beloved, that is also good.

Jashan was profoundly moved. The saint had indeed gifted him the most priceless lesson. To this day, this belief of Dada is asserted firmly at the Mission: that all that the Divine Providence sends to us is for our own good.

All holy men seemed to develop a fondness for Jashan. The look in his luminous eyes was a mirror of his profound spiritual aspirations.

During those days, Jashan was given to keeping a fast on Thursdays. He went to meet a holy man who, at that time, happened to be in Karachi. The fakir received him with great warmth and affection and offered him something to eat. Jashan was torn between the two choices before him: refusing the *prasad* in order to keep his fast or having it, thereby accepting blessings but breaking his fast. The holy man noticed Jashan's hesitancy in accepting his offering and enquired gently, 'What is it, dear one? Will you not accept this little offering from my humble abode?'

'No, no,' responded Jashan hastily. 'It is a blessing to receive anything from you! I only hesitated because, you see, I am fasting today, as it is a Thursday,' he mumbled.

The holy man nodded and put away the food he had offered Jashan. They spoke on other things for a while, and then the old fakir asked Jashan, 'Son, do you really know what a fast is?'

'It is to abstain from food for a certain length of time, or during the whole day. It is a discipline of the tongue and the appetite,' replied Jashan.

'Do you know which fast is the most arduous to keep?' the fakir asked a question which Jashan had not anticipated. Confused, Jashan shook his head. 'The real fast, the most arduous fast is not just abstaining from food or water, but to abstain from falsehood! Real fasting is pledging to tread the path of truth, no matter how tough it is. All of us should undertake this fast, and anchor our lives on the rock of truth.'

'Baba, why do you say that adhering to the truth is challenging and arduous?' Jashan was curious.

'All truth is not the perfect truth,' smiled the fakir. 'You have to tamper the truth with compassion and love! Of what use is truth if it hurts or wounds others? It is like a raw mango, so sour, it brings tears to the eyes and a grimace to your face. Truth should be ripened with sweetness and understanding. It is only then that it will taste like the ripe mango that everyone loves!'

'And shall I tell you what is the best truth?' he asked Jashan, with a twinkle in his eyes.

'Please tell me,' begged the young boy.

'The best truth is silence! That is why, when Jesus was asked by the Roman governor to state his case and speak in his own defence, he was silent.'

Strangely enough, from that day on, fasting never appealed to Jashan.

Despite following spiritual sadhana, Jashan's mind was plagued by constant doubts. He wished to excel at academics; he knew it all too well that his mother had pinned great hopes on the eldest son of the family. Jashan was thus conscious of all that he owed her. He was also well aware of his obligations to his family. But did that mean he could not nurture higher aspirations or attain self-realization? How would he ever have the much-longed-for vision of God if he were to entangle himself with familial responsibilities?

Once, he had the opportunity to meet a man of God whom he promptly asked, 'I want both God and the world. What must I do to balance the two?'

The holy one smiled and replied, 'Dear Jashan, go to the bazaar and buy some sugarcane. Tonight, when you have your dinner, do eat the sugarcane with your meal. You will surely get the answer to your question.'

Jashan was surprised by the suggestion. Sugarcane was in no way connected to his question even remotely. Yet being the obedient devotee that he was, Jashan implicitly followed the holy man's bidding. He bought some sugarcane on his way home. At dinner, he took alternate bites of the sugarcane along with the simple roti-sabzi that his mother had cooked. He would take one bite of the sugarcane, and follow it with a bit of the chapatti. While the sweet juice of the sugarcane went down with ease, the remainder, the unchewable fibres, stayed back in his mouth. They mingled with the roti and the result was dreadful! Neither could Jashan swallow the fibres nor the roti! The peculiar blend of textures and flavours was unpleasant to say the least. Jashan realized that sugarcane and roti do not go well together! But the lesson learnt from the experience was more profound than that.

The next day, Jashan promptly reported his experience to the holy man. The saint smiled and nodded, 'You wanted to have both God and the world. Well, dear Jashan, you have seen what it is to eat sugarcane and roti at the same time. When you take both together, you relish neither. Was it not Jesus who said, "You cannot follow two masters at the same time!" You must choose either the world or God. These are two flavours that do not go well with each other.'

One balmy evening, Jashan was out for a walk, becoming one with nature. He was soaking in the cool breeze, marveling at the trees swaying with joy, enjoying the luxury of solitude and silence.

Suddenly, the melodious music of the flute fell on his ears. He was drawn irresistibly in the direction of the heavenly music. His steps led him to a man who, oblivious of his surroundings, was lost in playing notes on a simple reed flute. Jashan stood absolutely still, careful not to disturb the flautist. He was content to drink in the Divine melody that flowed out of the flute!

All of a sudden, the flautist opened his eyes. Upon seeing Jashan standing by, he smiled warmly. Jashan sat down beside him and soon enough, the two were engaged in a conversation.

'How is it that you draw out such divine music from this simple instrument?' asked Jashan, his curiosity piqued.

'The gift of music was bestowed on me by a divine power,' said the man. 'It was something very special and peerless. And, let me tell you, I am incapable of playing the flute by my will alone. I can do so only when the spirit within me is stirred!'

He gazed at the sky as though he could see beyond the canopy of clouds into the heavens above. 'One beautiful day,' he said dreamily, 'as I sat in silence near a bubbling brook, I heard the sweet tinkle of a little bell. It filled my entire being with its resonance and a voice within me said it was bestowing a gift upon me, "Dear one, from now on, music shall flow from your flute!" Since then, all I do is place the flute to my lips and music just streams from it.'

'Do you think I could also hear the sound of that little bell?' Jashan asked innocently.

'Of course you can, my dear child,' he replied. And, taking Jashan's hand in his, he led him to his hut. As they approached his humble shack, Jashan found himself overwhelmed with a sense of peace and joy. Just then, he felt the faint sound of a chime gently twirl in his ears. It resonated through the air and into his very being!

Turning to the flute player, he asked, 'Will I be able to behold the beautiful face of your Beloved?'

'Yes, my dear child, you, too, can surely see Him. But for that you must build your life on one important teaching.'

'Please share it with me,' pleaded Jashan.

'Live in this world, enjoy it thoroughly, but do not become a slave to it. That is the secret. You don't have to renounce the world and become an ascetic. Just renounce your attachment to it while you live in it and enjoy it.'

An ordinary thought, yet so far from ordinary! The world and its many pleasures are like a whirlpool, he realized. 'Let us be in this world, but not of this world,' he concluded from the splendid message that had just been handed down to him. In another instance, Jashan happened to meet a holy man on the outskirts of Karachi. Sitting under a tree, he seemed lost in contemplation. It was his serene countenance that drew Jashan to him. Approaching him, Jashan sat down and gazed upon his face with admiration and longing. The man opened his eyes. They were as kind as they were gentle.

'Oh! Teach me to pray!' Jashan beseeched him.

'You cannot learn to pray, just go and pray,' came the simple reply.

'But what is the best way to pray?' asked Jashan, determined to find an answer.

'There is no best way, just go and pray.'

'What is the best time for prayer?' continued Jashan. 'And the best place?'

'The best time for prayer is now, and the best place for prayer is here,' came the reply.

The wise man went on to explain that no learning or education was required to be able to pray. Some of the greatest saints had been completely illiterate. Sri Ramakrishna Paramhansa, for instance, had not even known how to sign his name. Yet, he was able to pray for hours together.

The teachings he received played a significant role in making Jashan the person that he went on to become – a spiritual guide to all kinds of people. However, Jashan realized through his experience that it was important for him to put into practice all that he was taught. 'It is life that is needed,' Dada would often remark. 'Life, not words.'

Jashan was once invited to have lunch with a family-friend, a wealthy landlord. When he arrived at his place, he found the food neatly laid out in covered dishes. The host was seated before his plate, in a complicated *asana* (yoga posture), with eyes closed. His legs were crossed beneath him and his hands were held in a particular *mudra* or gesture. Aloud, he repeated, 'Sri Krishna *arpanam*!' several times, following the mantra with complicated gestures. After several such repetitions, he opened his eyes and saw his young guest. At once, he welcomed Jashan warmly and invited him to share the meal with him, adding how happy he was to have Jashan as a guest at his home.

'Uncle, you were saying a *sloka* when I came in,' Jashan began. 'It is a familiar sloka which I have heard several times. But you were also doing some asana with it, and I wondered what it was. Can you explain its significance to me?' Jashan asked him, as a bearer began to serve food.

'I was ceremonially offering to the Lord, the food that we are about to eat,' the man explained. 'I say this sloka aloud with this yogic posture and these gestures, so that the offering is whole and complete in every respect. After I have performed this ritual, the food becomes prasad, which we consume with gratitude and devotion.'

'That is beautiful,' Jashan said. 'I have also been taught never to eat food without saying a prayer.'

'Well, I repeat Sri Krishna arpanam twenty-one times before each meal,' said his host. 'Twenty-one, they say, is a sacred number.'

'Wonderful!' Jashan exclaimed, 'I am truly impressed.'

'Eat, eat well Jashan,' said his host warmly. 'I hope you like the food. Ah, what have we got here? *Baingan bharta*! It is my favourite dish. Do try it, Jashan.' And he lifted a morsel of this traditional Indian delicacy, smoked and stuffed aubergine, and put it in his mouth.

His expression changed almost instantly. His eyes narrowed and an unpleasant frown clouded his face. 'Who made this?' he shouted.

One of the cooks rushed forward. 'I made it sir,' he stammered.

The host picked up a spoon full of the aubergines and forced it through the young man's lips ferociously. 'Eat this, eat this, you rogue!' he screamed angrily. 'Is this how baingan bharta is made? Taste it for yourself and see what a mess you have made of my favourite dish. There! Swallow it and tell me what is wrong with it if you can.'

Jashan was aghast! Only a few minutes earlier, this man regarded food as prasad. And now, he was insulting the same prasad by stuffing it down someone's throat as if eating it was a cruel punishment!

Should not our thoughts, words and deeds be integrated?

Another time, at school, the headmaster had announced that a freedom fighter was to visit. His fiery speeches and his patriotic stance had been featured prominently in the press. The students were eager to see him and hear his oration.

The *neta* arrived to a tumultuous welcome and took to the stage amid resounding applause. He chose to speak on Swaraj and the Swadeshi Movement, which was then fast gathering momentum.

The fiery orator revealed that he took pride in using goods manufactured in India. He urged them all to follow his example and abstain from the use of any foreign-made goods. 'If you do possess any of these abominable British goods,' he roared, 'take my advice: whether they are caps or shirts or ties or shoes or socks, trash them now!'

It was indeed a splendid oration, rousing, sincere and extremely convincing. The children felt as though a spark of nationalism had been ignited in their hearts. The students got so carried away by this storm of emotion that one child's British-made cap was thrown in the air, another's imported pen was smashed, and cheers greeted the spontaneous outbursts. The students were ready to translate into action the fervent plea made by the eloquent speaker. They were eager to prove that they were practising what they had heard and agreed with it absolutely.

In this mood of buoyancy and emotional involvement, the freedom fighter triumphantly stepped away from the podium, waving to the cheering boys and climbed down from the stage to go to the next meeting venue. No sooner had he left the stage than he was surrounded by a bunch of admiring students, one among whom was Jashan. It was then that he noticed that the hero of the hour was actually wearing shoes that appeared imported – they were Dawson shoes.

More in shock than in disgust, he exclaimed, 'Sir, all this while you have been telling us to abstain from the use of foreign goods, but you yourself are wearing imported Dawson shoes! Is that not deceitful of you?'

The man was by no means abashed at this unexpected outburst from a youngster, who, just a few minutes ago, had applauded his speech wildly. He just laughed arrogantly and said, 'I have done my duty by telling you what the right thing to do is. Now it is your duty to put it into practice. My job is done.' And, with a wave and a smile to the cheering boys, he was out of the school in a trice.

It dawned on Jashan that however splendid an orator one was, the impact could only be felt if one practised what one preached.

Time and again Jashan stood out as different from the other boys of his age.

'Have you ever wondered what makes you unhappy, discontented, dissatisfied, and restless?' asked young Jashan one day, of some of his classmates. 'No. Tell us,' came the prompt response.

'It is a combination of various things. It can be jealousy, resentment of others' success and prosperity; or it may be a persecution complex, the unhealthy attitude that people are deliberately placing obstacles in our path to prevent us from achieving what we desire. It could be an obsessive desire for perfection, the inability to be content with what we are and what we do; and, most importantly, it is due to the needless regret over past decisions, a futile aspiration to change the unalterable past.'

'To put it simply,' continued Jashan, 'we are unhappy because we cannot accept life as it is. We are not satisfied with what we have; we live in the past or fantasize about the future; and, finally, we resist change or, in some cases, we want to change conditions around us.'

Jashan was sharing what he had heard at the Theosophical Society. He had grown up in a home where discussions and conversations had always been conducive to thought and reflection. With the passing away of his father, he acutely felt the absence of such discussions and was thus drawn to the regular discourses offered to the public by the Theosophical Society.

Here is what a classmate remembers about Jashan, in his own words:

I was rather the gregarious sort and had many friends. I sat next to Jashan because he had a calm and soothing effect on me. Before the teacher entered the class, all the other boys would create a mayhem, shouting and screaming, but Jashan would sit quietly, absorbed in his book. At the end of the day, even after school, all the other children would crowd at the door trying to rush out at the same time, but Jashan would wait patiently, with a smile on his face, for everyone to leave. Our homes were located at two different ends so we never had the opportunity to walk back home together.

One day, a friend of mine, who lived four houses away from Jashan's, invited me over for lunch. It was then that I noticed Jashan walking with his head lowered, watching the ground as he walked. Suddenly, he bent down and picked something up. My friend and I were right behind him, curious to know what he might have picked up. A man, who had been standing close by and watching him, abruptly dashed towards Jashan and demanded that he open his fist.

'Have you picked up some money?' he asked sternly. 'You young boys must learn not to pick up money that is not yours. It is equal to stealing. You seem to be a decent boy coming from a respectable home, why then did you pick up the money?'

'Huh, it is nothing,' replied Jashan, acutely embarrassed.

'No, I insist you show what you have clenched in your fists.'

Reluctantly, the small fist was opened only to reveal a sharp piece of glass.

'Glass! Why did you pick this up?' asked the man in surprise and disbelief.

Tears quickly gathered in young Jashan's eyes and in his tremulous voice he said, 'Sir, I was afraid it might pierce some poor man who walks barefoot.'

My friend and I were speechless. We never forgot this incident and to this day, whenever we recall it, our hearts choke with emotion. Years later, we wondered what had become of Jashan.

THREE

The Making of a Disciple

'The longest journey is the journey inwards. Of him who has chosen his destiny, who has started upon his quest for the source of his being.'

– Dag Hammarskjöld, *Markings*

Jashan was a child prodigy. His impeccable academic record, not only endeared him to his teachers but also enabled him to complete school much sooner than his peers. Barely was he thirteen when he was admitted into the Science stream at Diwan Dayaram Jethamal Sind Government Science College, famously known as D. J. Sind College. While students at his college dressed fashionably, Jashan's dress was simple and unpretentious. He continued to wear half-pants to college and many mistook him for a school student, thanks to his short stature.

Jashan had an insatiable appetite for reading: he read fiction and biographies, and was fascinated by timeless wisdom. He often found himself reflecting on the thoughts propounded by the great writers of the world. He devoured book after book and became well-versed with various streams of knowledge. This earned him the membership of the Students' Library Committee at college facilitating an all-time access and unlimited borrowing of books. He could visit the library whenever he pleased and could lay his hands on any book that aroused his interest. He would often say, 'A book a day, keeps ignorance away!'

With his eager young mind and his ever-energetic intellect, he was so busy absorbing everything he read that, at first, he quite neglected the limited syllabus that was being rigorously taught in his class. As a result, Jashan, a star student, nearly failed the first year's examination in the intermediate class.

However, he soon set things right when he learnt to draw a balance between his urge for reading and class work. He made a resolution: never would his grades suffer on account of his passion for reading. That said, he continued to be an ardent reader.

Back in those days, dealers would import large quantities of foreign newspapers to be made into paper-bags for use in shops. Jashan made friends with one such dealer, who took a liking to this intelligent young man. What was paper-bag raw material to the dealer, was reading material to Jashan. Without causing any hassles, the dealer was persuaded by the voracious reader to separate the magazine sections of the old newspapers and sell it to him by weight. The dealer readily consented. He would hand over piles of freshly arrived newspapers to Jashan, who would then separate the magazine sections into two: First, that he wanted to read; second that he would return to the dealer for sale. All this was efficiently budgeted. Having armed himself with a treasure trove of newspapers, he would then walk home hurriedly and impatiently to give the sections of his choice a read.

Reading for a couple of hours together gave rise to reflections and insights in his mind and his pen began to overflow with creativity. He won several writing contests held frequently by the local magazines. Five rupees was all they could offer as a prize to the winner, but Jashan cherished it, all the same. He preferred the five rupees over a gaudy trophy or cup any day. After all, five rupees could fetch him five good books, perhaps more, if he visited the second-hand bookstores.

Dada remained an avid reader till his last days. In fact, his reading hours were sacrosanct, and he was left undisturbed to pursue his passion. Dada's personal library comprises of thousands of books on a multitude of subjects. At times he would read a line or two and then spend hours reflecting on the thought conveyed by the words.

Jashan was known to be an excellent orator and a debating enthusiast among his friends. Once, D. J. Sind College was agog with excitement. The literary and debating society had announced an elocution contest. A gold medal was to be awarded to the best speaker from an endowment made by a distinguished patron of the college.

Jashan's friends were confident that he would walk away with the first prize. So, they coaxed him into entering the contest. Could Jashan, a BSc freshman, hold his own with senior students among other competitors? Surely, it was unfair to expect undergraduates to compete with MA students. But their unwavering confidence in Jashan encouraged him to go ahead.

All the participants had queued up backstage, eyeing the diminutive boy in their midst. His courage and audacity to compete with seniors stunned them.

Over a dozen participants had expressed their views before the large audience. It was finally Jashan's turn. His name was announced. He walked up the stage with his head held high and approached the podium. He offered a respectful greeting to the audience and took them by storm when he began to speak. His fiery presentation had no match. The audience sat still, admiring the young man for his speech as well as the way he spoke.

That day, Jashan took home the first prize and the coveted gold medal.

Though Jashan excelled in English and Arts, he wanted to do something different. He switched over to the Faculty of Science. Krishnadevi nurtured the ambition of making her son appear for the prestigious Indian Civil Service (ICS) examination.

'What is your plan for the future?' Sadhu Vaswani asked his nephew one day. 'How would you like to live your life?'

Jashan was hesitant. He had a sudden urge to open up, to share with his beloved uncle, the deepest aspirations of his heart. Considering the familial ambitions he was expected to fulfil, he chose not to answer the question on an impulse. He knew that his family and friends fancied a glorious future for him.

His mother dreamt of her eldest son joining the ICS. His family and teachers believed that Jashan had every chance of cracking the coveted examination. At the moment, however, he was enjoying his respite from academics since the prestigious exam could not be taken before the age of twenty-one. Jashan would finish his post-graduation by the age of nineteen and he had three years to prepare for the exam, improving the prospects of his success.

Jashan was reminded of all this and more and he answered, 'Well, Dada, I think, after my MSc perhaps I would give the ICS a chance.'

'And after that?' Sadhu Vaswani dug deeper.

'Maybe I will pass the ICS exam and make a name for myself in the service.'

'And then?'

'Well, Dada, I will work hard to have a promising career, and I hope to make a difference to the society and help my family.'

'And then what?'

'Perhaps I will continue to write ...' Jashan's voice trailed off. It all seemed so empty. Was this what he really wanted to do? He was not so sure now.

'You may make money, receive honours, but what then? What then? What then? What is the purpose of your life? What is its goal?' persisted Sadhu Vaswani.

'You tell me, Dada, what is the ultimate purpose of life?'

'Go into silence and see what answers you get,' replied Sadhu Vaswani. 'Sit in meditation regularly. It cleanses the mind and it enables you to find the answers you seek from within. Inside you, there is enormous *shakti*, a powerhouse of energy. You only have to enter into silence, go deep within to set that power into action.'

For his BSc degree Jashan opted to major in the subjects of physics, chemistry and mathematics. Not contrary to expectations, he did exceedingly well in all three subjects. In the first year BSc examinations, he scored excellent grades and secured the first rank in general English. Jashan had an aptitude for numbers. In the second year, he specialized in mathematics and passed with distinction. The days and months flew by and Jashan was now a final-year student, about to major in physics.

The results of the university examinations were announced on the radio, and later, the newspapers carrying the results were put up on the college notice board, as was the practise in those days. Students had gathered in the campus to listen to the all-important broadcast. Silence prevailed as every student strained his ears so as not to miss out on his number. Sighs of relief or gasps of disappointment rose with each number that was read out or skipped.

Strangely, Jashan's number was not announced. His friends were stunned. Jashan was a topper and there was no way he could have failed. They turned to Jashan to see his reaction. Jashan seemed rather unfazed. He sensed there was a good reason behind the happening. In fact, he got *gulab jamun*s and distributed them among his friends.

'But ... why, Jashan, why? We have passed, but we don't feel like celebrating our success. You deserve to top the list but there has been no mention of your number. Surely something is amiss! In such a case, how do you expect us to gorge on the gulab jamuns?' his friends asked him.

'It is God's will,' Jashan explained to them. 'I must accept it in the right spirit.'

One of Jashan's friends recalls his reluctance to eat the gulab jamun that Jashan had offered him on the unforgettable occasion. Instead, he took it home and offered it to his sister, who relished them.

'Delicious! This gulab jamun is so soft and spongy! Where did you get it from?' asked the sister as she savoured the fluffy, sweet delicacy.

'You can't ever get a gulab jamun like this one,' said Jashan's friend sullenly. 'People distribute gulab jamuns to celebrate a victory. My friend has given us this to accept his failure!' The sister was awed. She knew that the slightest setback, disappointment or refusal made her dissolve into tears and go into despair. And here was a friend who accepted failure just as he would accept success. What's more, he even rejoiced in it. Unbelievable!

But the shock and grief of Jashan's friends did not last long. Long before the printed lists were published, the news that Jashan had in fact stood first in the college, delighted them.

Once again, he distributed gulab jamuns among his friends, this time, to express his gratitude for the Lord's kindness bestowed on him!

To honour Jashan's brilliant achievement of securing the top rank in college, the institution awarded him a fellowship. Since he intended to pursue his master's, being appointed as a fellow enabled him to teach alongside attending his own classes.

Two girls from a wealthy, aristocratic family in Karachi wished to excel in their studies. A little extra coaching could help them achieve their goal. The sisters expressed their wish to their parents, who were very reluctant to entrust their girls to any young tutor: the family was conservative and the two sisters were famed as the local 'beauties' and were the cynosure of all the young men in Karachi.

Jashan's acclaim as a bright and intelligent student, who had been awarded a fellowship, was known to all. The parents of the girls too were aware of this and knew him to be a young man of sterling character. They wanted to request him to coach the girls, but they were hesitant as they felt he would be unable to spare time for them owing to his busy schedule.

They finally approached Jashan, discussed their problem with him and solicited his help. They were pleasantly surprised by his kindness, patience and willingness to oblige. Jashan taught the girls diligently and charged not even a single paisa for it.

A rather amusing consequence of this was that some of Jashan's classmates became jealous of him as he was now a welcome visitor at the residence of the girls. They even tried to threaten Jashan to keep away from the girls, whom they regarded as their heartthrobs. With his geniality and keen sense of humour, Jashan was able to reassure them that he had neither the time nor the inclination for romance, and that his only aim was to oblige the parents of the girls, who had reached out to him for help.

Very few people are aware that Jashan had also studied law. To facilitate prominent legal luminaries of Karachi to conduct classes, after their day-long duty in the court, law classes were held in the evening. With a view to acquire a good foundation for the tough, competitive examination, Jashan was encouraged to join evening classes for LLB, alongside his MSc Jashan attended his law classes regularly for two years. He had to follow a very busy schedule indeed. He had a lot on his plate. He was pursuing his research and study for the MSc degree, he had to teach undergraduate students as a fellow, and then, there were his two-hour long law classes in the evening.

Jashan was hardworking and never perceived multitasking as a burden. He took the LLB classes in his stride. His favourite paper was Roman law, and he loved Latin as a language. He acquired a good background of law in the two years of his studies. But when the two years drew to a close, his mind was made up. He was not going to appear for the final examination. He was already determined to spend his future at the feet of his beloved uncle and master to be. Acquiring a degree in law would have mounted pressure upon him to take up the legal profession as a career. Quietly, he chose to forego the option.

Jashan was the first student in Sind to complete his Master's through research. Whenever time permitted, Jashan was found in the company of his uncle, when he happened to be in town. He would often discuss his findings with his much-loved uncle, who always listened to him with great interest and empathy.

It was the year 1937. Jashan was hard at work in his college laboratory. The college authorities had imported a special X-ray machine worth thousands of rupees to enable him to carry on his research work. Jashan's joy knew no bounds and he wanted to share his excitement with Sadhu Vaswani who, at that time, was in Karachi. The nephew requested his uncle to come and see his X-ray machine in the college laboratory and bless his work.

One evening during his visit to the lab, Sadhu Vaswani's attention was drawn to a telescope. He was fascinated when he looked through it and beheld the brilliance of the dazzling stars. Beckoning Jashan, he asked him to take in the enthralling sight too. Jashan was equally overwhelmed by what he saw.

Sadhu Vaswani then unexpectedly blew his breath against the lens of the telescope and asked Jashan to look through it once again. This time, the young man was unable to see anything.

'A thin film of moisture can veil the firmament, and so too, can pride, ego and selfishness cloud the face of the omnipresent God. Wipe the lens of your inner eye and you too, will behold the Lord,' Sadhu Vaswani said to his beloved nephew. The master's noble reflections on the simplest everyday happenings never ever failed to arouse Jashan's admiration.

Jashan was also fascinated by the phenomenon of light because he identified it with God. The Lord is energy and radiates light that does not singe or scorch. It was his aspiration to research the phenomenon of such a light – a light without heat.

Once, Jashan's friend was working in the laboratory with him when a blaring noise diverted his attention. Setting his work aside, the friend walked to the window and was delighted to see a splendid marriage procession pass by.

After the procession had left, he turned to Jashan and exclaimed, 'Wasn't it a procession worth seeing!'

'What procession?' asked Jashan in sheer wonder.

'Why, the one that just passed by! Didn't you hear the din and the clamour?' the friend enquired, surprised.

Jashan was so deeply engrossed in his research work that he had been oblivious to all the other noises and events other than the clinking of the equipment. Such was his power of concentration and diligence!

Jashan was known to think on his feet naturally, words would effortlessly flow out of his pen. He was a gifted writer. During his college days, he would often contribute his musings to magazines and daily newspapers, who would gladly publish his articles.

In the year 1939, with a view to bring about an awakening in the youth of Sind, Jashan and two of his friends decided to publish a monthly magazine. They approached Sadhu Vaswani, who named the periodical *Excelsior*. The master also suggested, 'Give it the motto, "O onward march ye, on and on, to greet beyond the night, the dawn."'

Jashan thought of adding a spiritual dimension to the magazine. But the idea did not go down well with his other two friends, who withdrew their support to the venture. Nonetheless, he persisted, editing the magazine single-handedly. He juggled between writing articles, correcting proofs, seeing to its printing, advertisements, circulation, packing, and posting. He looked into the very last detail, so the magazine was published error-free.

The journal caught on to an extent that it even outnumbered the circulation of the then-leading daily newspaper, *The Sind Observer*.

Even as he entered college and began to mingle and interact with young men conscious of their dress and appearances, Jashan continued to tread the path of simplicity and humility. He lived a life free of pretentions, a simple life, defined by simple food and simple dressing. No wonder then, the young man decided to wear only coarse *khadi*.

He now thought of making his own spinning wheel to weave his own khadi. He had gained mastery over the craft when he was still a boy scout at school. When a friend learnt of his intention, he offered to bring him some pieces of wood from a factory, where he was working. A young man of principles, Jashan rejected the offer outright because the wood would have to be smuggled out. 'It would be better to buy a new *charkha* than make one out of stolen wood!'

His wish to spin his own khadi was inspired by Mahatma Gandhi, a votary of truth himself. How could he then resort to untruth!

'Son, won't you go to the charcoal dealer and ask him to send me a sack of charcoal?' called out Jashan's mother even as he was getting ready to leave for college.

'Yes mother, I shall do it right away,' Jashan responded, though he knew it would delay him for classes.

'But remember,' she added, 'to wait and get it weighed yourself before asking him to send it over.'

The charcoal shop was filled with black blots as far as the eye could see. Jashan tried his best to ensure his white clothes remained unstained. Nevertheless, some of the charcoal dust stained his clothing!

Taking a cue from this, Dada would later observe: 'Beware of the company you keep. No matter how careful you are, you are coloured by the company you move in. Therefore, associate with the right type of people.'

Like any other young man, Jashan too, in his teens was suffused with idealism and goals that were too far-fetched. Yet he was different from most of them: neither were his dreams empty nor was he striving to change the world. All he wanted was to achieve perfection within himself.

In order to achieve this goal, Jashan would keep a close watch on himself, so he could make steady strides towards his goals. Every day, he would unfailingly ask himself two questions. 'How have I spent my day today? Have I drawn closer to my goal of perfection?' The questions made him reflect on every thought, every deed done.

Jashan always sought to learn from every experience that life had to offer him, therefore, the question, 'Could I have learnt something more today?' was indispensable to him. Discovering the answers to such questions was a route to rediscover opportunities lost. Last, but certainly not the least, Jashan would ponder, 'Did I do something wrong today?'

The road to perfection was not easy, but surely, there was light at the end of the tunnel. And a glint of hope was already shining through, thanks to his patience and perseverance!

'First, I must know myself' – this thought was infused in Jashan's dreams by Sadhu Vaswani.

While he was young and in his first year of college, Jashan had longed to write a novel. Thinking over the plot and characters, he would stay awake at night to write as others slept.

Jashan had a simple room to himself and would write under the light of a table lamp. In this manner, with utter diligence, he wrote several chapters of the novel. He was eager to complete it soon and get it published abroad. Thus, many nights flew by, and Jashan remained deeply engrossed in his writing.

Once, when Sadhu Vaswani visited him at home, he found him busy at work. Gently, he asked his nephew, 'Dear child, what are you doing?' Jashan replied, with a sense of achievement, 'I am writing a novel.' His uncle enquired, 'What will you achieve by writing it?' Jashan explained, 'I would like to send it abroad for publishing.'

After a pause, with a look of contemplation Sadhu Vaswani said, 'Why are you taking so much trouble, my child?' Jashan responded,

'Foreign publications promise a wider readership. As more people read my book, more people will come to know about me.' 'If more people know about you,' his uncle continued, 'what will you achieve? What is the use of fame if you have not known or realized yourself?'

The words hit Jashan like a flash of lightning. They went straight to his heart. He instantly resolved that he would first get to know himself.

While Jashan stopped writing his own novel, reading fiction still fascinated him. One night, in the still silence of the darkness, Jashan was engrossed in a novel when the reading room door opened, and a shadow fell upon Jashan's book. He looked up to find Sadhu Vaswani standing before him. 'Dada, you have come back!' he said, his voice growing louder with excitement. He rushed to greet his uncle and touch his feet.

'How is it that you are still in the library at this time of the night?' enquired his uncle, solicitously. The nephew replied sheepishly, 'It is just that this book is so gripping, Dada. I cannot put it down! I just wanted to finish it before I left.'

Sadhu Vaswani took a good look at the book, skimmed through its pages and remarked gently, 'This book does not merit the time and effort you spend on it.'

'Tell me, Dada, what kind of books I should read,' Jashan asked his role model, whom he sought to emulate in every way.

'You must read books that elevate your mind and inspire you, not just ones that entertain you,' replied Sadhu Vaswani. 'Why don't you read biographies of great people and books by noble leaders? They will give you something to think about.' He made a suggestion and needless to say, Jashan heeded it then and there. He became more selective of what entered his mind by the way of reading. Consequently, novels took a back seat and biographies and the lives of great ones clearly took precedence over them.

Soon when he came more and more under the influence of Sadhu Vaswani, things changed. He realized that many worldly desires and aspirations were worthless, meaningless and therefore colourless. They no longer held any attraction for him.

During those days, the Name of God became Jashan's source of strength and support. Through periods of adversity, of trials and tribulations, the Name Divine became his refuge.

The practice of *japa*, or repetition of the Holy Name, was intensified by the influence of yet another holy man who happened to touch his life at that time. Dada fondly recalled later, 'I was young when I received the company of a devotee of God. I became close to this holy person. He had truly bound me with his love. The day I did not meet him, I felt I had lost something.

'One day he said, "Dear child, will you do something for me?"' I replied, 'Anything you say. I will even pluck the stars for you.' He said, 'Dear one, I don't need anything. But for my sake, keep repeating the Name of the Lord. Sing His Name, meditate on His Name. Lose yourself in His Name.'

'Thus, he forcefully tied me to the habit of repetition of God's Name. Since then, I learnt to do japa regularly,' Dada reminisced.

Once, when Jashan spent the night with him, the devotee of God stayed awake all night and recited the Holy Name. Through the Name, he helped so many. He would say, 'Jesus Christ comes to me; Sri Krishna comes to me; Guru Nanak comes to visit me.' Guru Nanak was his *ishta devata*. He would say, 'God has books of accounts sitting open. Some of the sorrow Ram will remove. Some of the pain Krishna will remove, and some of the difficulties Guru Nanak will destroy.'

He would say, 'The Name holds within it unusual glory and power,' he would say. 'That is why, I say to you, repeat the Holy Name more and more. Connect your heart to it. There are sages, who by encouraging people to do japa, have removed all their sorrow. There is a unique power in it. The Name Divine removes any type of sorrow and pain. Bind your heart to the *Naam*. Unfortunately, our hearts are attached to the world instead.'

It was during his days at college that Jashan experienced what true love for God is. There was a boy who would sit next to him and take notes as the professor spoke. Jashan admired his sincerity and diligence, but he wondered why the boy failed every exam in spite of taking notes down so assiduously.

One day, Jashan peeped into his notebook in the classroom and was amazed to read 'Maina, Maina' written all over it. Apparently, Maina was his girlfriend whom he loved dearly. In an instant, it struck Jashan how, in devotion, one's thoughts dwell constantly on the Beloved and the 'I' is completely effaced.

It was this 'feeling' that Dada later laid emphasis on while speaking about devotion to God.

When Jashan had entered college, one of the first things he did was to become a member of a small and select group of students, who called themselves the 'Prayer Circle'. They would meet as often as they could to study and discuss learned treatises and articles on prayers by leading luminaries. Jashan found the group activities highly edifying and intellectually rigorous. The participants in the group talked about the degrees and levels of prayer, about low, middle and high prayer. There were earnest debates and discussions on the difference between prayer, meditation, reflection and contemplation. The youngsters regarded themselves as authorities on the theory of prayer.

Jashan discovered that his theory was flourishing; however, much to his chagrin, he found that his habit of praying was impeded. Before he joined the group, he could pray spontaneously, easily and naturally, as if he were just talking to God; now, despite having dabbled extensively in theory, his prayers had become superficial and mechanical.

Jashan quit the Prayer Circle forthwith. It dawned upon him that abstract, theoretical knowledge was not necessary to draw nigh to God. He unlearnt everything he had learnt thus far and reverted to his original approach of simplicity, humility and love, which allowed him to speak to God as a child speaks to his mother!

'God does not care for the form, the shape, the grammar, the vocabulary of our prayer. It is the feeling that counts,' Dada often said to us.

What also influenced Jashan were certain encounters with a higher power during his life as a student. One night, as Jashan persevered with his experiments in the college laboratory, the room suddenly drowned in darkness due to a power failure. Accepting it as the will of God, Jashan left the laboratory. Hoping that the electricity supply would be restored soon, he went out for a stroll, allowing himself to be led wherever his feet took him.

He found himself gazing into a pair of piercing eyes that looked deep into his own. They seemed to have appeared out of nowhere. Jashan looked for more signs to trace this person, who had jolted him with his sudden appearance. He could hear a soft, flute-like voice drawing him out of the caverns of his solitude, 'My son! Why have you taken so long in coming to me? I have been waiting for you!'

The words sounded strange to his ears. 'I beg your pardon, sir,' he said respectfully. 'I don't think we've ever met before. I'm afraid you've mistaken me for someone else.'

Nonetheless, the stranger continued, 'Our acquaintance is more ancient than the earth on which we stand. But you know it not!'

Confounded by the odd behaviour of the stranger, Jashan turned his back on him and was about to leave when the stranger held him back. 'Please let me go!' pleaded Jashan helplessly.

'It is to deliver you that I have crossed miles in the darkness of this moonless night,' said the stranger in a kind voice. 'Please bear with me for a few moments, for I rarely meet the same person twice.'

Jashan could feel the stranger smiling. The warmth radiated by him overpowered the doubt and fear that had gripped him earlier. Jashan let go, allowing himself to be led to a large stone. The stranger sat beside him, and his eyes exuded tenderness and compassion, but also probed and searched for the real beneath the surface. He looked at Jashan; he looked into his eyes, and it seemed as though he could look beyond him. His lips dropped pearls of wisdom, which went straight into the young student's heart.

Hours passed. Jashan sat there in the darkness, listening to the *pir*'s words of wisdom, spellbound. His entire being seemed to reverberate with new energy and he felt like he had been transported to new heights of love and joy!

Abruptly, the stranger rose to leave, saying, 'It's time for me to leave!' It was a desperate, heartbreaking moment. Jashan clung on to the hem of his garment and implored him, 'Oh! Take me with you! Life without you will not be worth living.'

'That cannot be, my child,' said the stranger in a kind voice. 'But call me whenever you wish and I will come to you. Ask what you will, and I will answer, for your heart is now my abode!' But before he left, he shared a few more teachings with the young man. 'Remember, my child,' he said, 'God always grants us not what we want, but what we need.' After pausing momentarily, he continued, 'We are punished not for our sins, but by our sins. Lastly, heaven and hell are not some remote regions to which we travel after death, but states of consciousness in which we abide, here and now!'

What an unforgettable mystical encounter this was!

In another such instance, Jashan sent a note to his mother that he would not be home for a few days. He would often get involved in his work and spend long hours in the laboratory and therefore, his mother was not surprised at this.

On the same day, Jashan impulsively joined a group of travellers headed towards the mountain that some called Lahut, meaning the higher reality, while others referred to it as Jabrut, or the highest realm in Islamic cosmology. In Sufi philosophy, Lahut refers to the fourth or penultimate stage of the seeker's path, when the aspirant becomes totally absorbed in the Beloved. Thus, Lahut means one who is absorbed in God, a hermit. When he reached the mountain peak, Jashan was blessed with a beauteous sight. Lahut was much favoured by the holy men of Sind who dwelt in the mountain to commune with the eternal. The very silence of this sacred space spoke to Jashan's soul.

There was never much food atop the mountain. But the water was pure, sweet and crystal clear, filled with natural nutrition. Everyone would drink a lot of water and subsist on fruit.

Many people believed that whoever reached a particular peak at the mountain-top, would surely attain a vision of God. But unfortunately, it was almost impossible to get there. Many curves and slopes had to be crossed to reach there, and a single slip could prove fatal.

Jashan did not make any attempt to get there, as at that time, he still belonged to his mother, and so did not want to endanger his life.

Here he came across an unforgettable man. Jashan felt a strong pull towards this dervish. Indeed, the dervish had a magnetic appearance. His countenance shone like a jewel and his good looks were enhanced by a well-shaped beard. There was an inexplicable charisma about him. Jashan began following him like a lamb. He stayed close to the holy man for five days and five nights, unable to drag himself away.

The sage would utter 'Allah' repeatedly, and would become God intoxicated. Once, while repeating 'Allah', his consciousness rose high, and he seemed lost to the world.

During his stay at Lahut, he asked Jashan to take a lump of clay from him. He told Jashan that whatever is touched by the clay would turn to gold. Jashan declined the offer, saying, 'What will I achieve by converting things to gold. Give me the dust of your feet, instead, to apply on my forehead.'

The dervish smiled and said, 'Then say Allah! He is above all!'

The dervish also offered to give Jashan an amulet, which when worn by someone was said to mitigate sufferings. Jashan politely but firmly reaffirmed, 'Sai, only give me the dust of your feet, to apply on my eyes, and purify myself.'

Jashan had come to Lahut with just one outfit – the one he was wearing. As he had no change of clothes, he had to repeatedly wash and wear the same clothes.

The dervish said to him once, 'Taj kar (give up)!'

Jashan asked, 'What is it that I should give up?'

The dervish replied, 'This baggage that you have brought with you. Give it up!'

Jashan spontaneously responded, 'I have given it up.'

Back in Karachi, Krishnadevi was anxious to see her eldest son married and settled down in life. Like all mothers, she wanted her son to find a lucrative job and enter into a happy marriage with a 'suitable girl' and start a family. Yes, careers are important to young men, but no mother will find contented in that alone unless the son is 'settled' in matrimony.

A brave and spiritually inclined lady, Jashan's mother had struggled against all odds to bring up her children single-handedly, making several sacrifices on the way. Now, all she wanted was for her favourite son to attain financial stability and be married.

One day, she took Jashan to a well-known astrologer. He took his own time to ponder over Jashan's horoscope, going down to the minutest details, making lengthy calculations while at it. Next, it was time for Jashan's palm to undergo microscopic scrutiny. The celebrated astrologer went over the lines on Jashan's palm with a pointer and then proceeded to look at the lines under a magnifying glass. Finally, he bade Jashan to sit on a stool and show him the soles of his feet. Jashan was truly intrigued and somewhat tired at the end of it all.

The investigation was finally complete. The astrologer solemnly put away his spectacles, pointer and magnifying glass and looked at his visitors thoughtfully. 'Jashan, be prepared,' he warned. 'Be prepared!' Jashan stared at him in surprise. As a scout, 'be prepared' had been his motto in school. But what was he supposed to be prepared for now?

Krishnadevi grew pale as she imagined an illness or an accident in Jashan's fate.

'Sir, please explain,' Jashan said to him politely. 'What should I prepare for?'

The astrologer beamed. 'Good news is indicated *Bhabhiji*,' he said, turning to the mother. 'Auspicious events are in store for your boy.' And, fixing a benevolent look at Jashan, he announced, 'Even before the end of the year, our Jashan will be married.'

The mother was delighted to say the least. And she was more optimistic than ever about Jashan's marriage as the astrologer continued to speak with great confidence and authority.

Jashan knew that marriage was not for him. He courteously tried to tell the astrologer that he was mistaken but to no avail. The astrologer was adamant. 'Prove me wrong,' he thundered, heating up at Jashan's persistent denial, 'prove me wrong, and I shall shave off my beard and moustache!'

Jashan did not take up his challenge, but he knew that the astrologer's prophecy would be a non-starter!

'The stars can only indicate; they cannot compel,' Dada says on the matters of fate and astrology.

One of Jashan's good friends, known to him since childhood, got married. He was anxious that his marriage should not come in the way of old friendships that he truly cherished. From the day he set up his new home with his wife, he persistently invited Jashan to visit him. 'You must drop in, Jashan,' he told him repeatedly. 'I do not want to lose my best friends just because I chose to marry. I want to prove to the world that married men are just as loyal and committed to their other relationships as bachelors are.'

Jashan promised him that he would visit him. But as luck would have it, Jashan's own preoccupations kept him busy, and he could not visit his friend. Nearly six months after he was married, one fine Saturday evening, Jashan decided that he would drop in on his friend and convey his wishes to the couple.

Jashan took a basket of fruits and a few books to offer them as gifts, and arrived at his friend's house around 5 p.m.

The front door was ajar and he entered his friend's house, calling out his name and announcing, 'It's me, Jashan.'

To his amazement, he saw his friend with his wife engrossed in a game of cards and he did not respond to Jashan's greeting.

Jashan decided that he would wait for some time until the current game was over and then call out to him again. He took his seat in the front hall and waited patiently. He could not see them from where he was sitting, but he presumed that the game would be over in five minutes or so. At the end of five minutes, Jashan called out to him again. But yet again there was no response.

Another five minutes passed. Now Jashan decided to get up and look into the adjoining room. The couple were so engrossed in the cards they held that they were completely unaware of his presence or repeated calls.

Deciding not to disturb them, he returned quietly to the front room, wrote his name on a slip of paper and added the message: 'Dropped in to see you, but you were busy. Will call on you some other time.' He left the note with the basket of fruits and departed as unobtrusively as he had entered.

Perhaps when it grew dark, the couple arose from their game to switch on the lights. It must have been then that Jashan's friend saw his note. Around 7 p.m. the same evening, he rushed over to Jashan's place, out of breath, overcome by a sense of shame and guilt. 'I'm so sorry, Jashan,' he said, still panting. 'Please do forgive me. I really didn't notice your arrival! It's possibly because the radio was on … I saw your note and realized you had come and gone! I really can't think how I could have been so careless.'

How mortified and ashamed the fri end was when he came to know that Jashan had come to call on him, and he had missed his arrival altogether. But then, Jashan was his dear friend, his peer and his companion. He could come running to his house the moment he realized what had happened. He could apologize for his lapse and ask him to visit again.

Recalling this incident Dada reminisced, 'Just think of God arriving at the door of our hearts, perhaps waiting there hoping that we would welcome him and invite him to make our heart his abode, while we remain blind to His presence at our threshold. Can we ever make amends for such a lapse? Can we tell God, "Come back now. I am free to receive you?"'

In their own house, Jashan's father had forbidden the game of cards. But many of Jashan's friends did not think it was such a serious issue. Once, when Jashan was staying as a house guest with family friends, the head of the household, Dr Tharumal, and his sons persuaded him to join in a game of cards. Jashan protested that apart from being told not to play cards, he was also appallingly ignorant of the rules of card games.

But his friends were very persuasive. They entreated him, 'Jashan, when friends like us play cards, we do not gamble! There are no stakes to win or lose. And when one plays intelligently, cards can keep your brains sharp. It is just a harmless way of passing time pleasantly, nothing more, nothing less. And the games we play are hardly of the calculus or quantum science variety. They are simple, and they are great fun. We will teach you the rules in a minute. An intelligent person like you can catch up in no time at all.'

And so it came to pass that Jashan was taught the game called flash. Once he began playing, Jashan felt his friends were right; it

THE MAKING OF A DISCIPLE

was easy, it was fun, it was no rocket science. And how the time
flew as they played.

The game started after lunch, around 2 p.m. The day's
programme was to get ready and leave for satsang by 6 p.m. But
so engrossed were they with the game that the clock struck 6 and
no one noticed.

Finally, it was the lady of the house who came in to stop the
game, as it was time for dinner. 'That's quite enough for one day,'
she said sternly, 'It's time we have dinner now.' Someone noticed
the time and said, 'Can you believe it, it's already 8:30 p.m. now.
We have been playing continuously for over six hours!'

Jashan was aghast. He had missed going to the satsang!

If someone had told Jashan on the previous day that he would
miss satsang for some reason, he would have laughed away the
suggestion and told them confidently, 'What? Me and miss satsang?
Never! Not for any reason.'

But it had happened that day! So engrossed was Jashan in the
new game his friends had taught him, that he had lost track of time
and his own duties and obligations!

'Where were you yesterday, Jashan?' his friends, who were at
satsang, asked him in innocence. 'We looked everywhere, but we
couldn't find you!'

Worse was to follow. Somehow it came to be known that the
guests at Dr Tharumal's house had missed the satsang, playing
cards. People began to whisper, 'Can you believe it? Jashan has
started playing cards! He was so engrossed in his card game that
he actually missed satsang the other day.'

'I tell you, nobody can escape such addictions,' someone added.
'This is how it all begins. As a happy, friendly activity; and then,
before you know it.'

Jashan's kind host defended him strongly. 'That is ridiculous,' he
said to people sternly. 'Just because Jashan played cards with friends

like us for one day, it does not mean he has become an addict. Please do not make such exaggerated statements.'

As for Jashan, he was too stunned to take in everything that was being said about him in hushed voices. So preoccupied had he been playing cards that he missed going to the satsang. This thought hurt him and made him remorseful.

'Believe me, it was a long time before I overcame the sense of shame and regret that overwhelmed me at the time. But the fear did not ever leave my heart, that I could be so preoccupied doing lesser things, when the Lord came calling on me,' Dada later told his followers.

Those were stirring times in India. People had several grievances against the British government, but they made their protests peacefully. Sadhu Vaswani too, had launched a Satyagraha movement for a socio-religious cause. As the leader of the protest, he courted arrest. He was awarded a sentence of fifteen days and was taken to the Karachi District Jail. Jashan managed to sneak into the jail with his beloved uncle!

Sadhu Vaswani was not keeping well, and was severely afflicted with gout, which required some ministration. Jashan resolved to accompany him to the jail, come what may. He secretly longed to be in the company of his uncle and spend a few days with him, uninterrupted by other calls and responsibilities. What better opportunity than to be with him behind the limiting constraints of prison bars, where nobody could intrude? As Jashan saw it, it was a great opportunity for a wonderful 'break' with the master! But the problem was: How could he, an underage college student, be sent to jail?

In the melee after the protest march, as Sadhu Vaswani and his followers were being rounded up and taken to the police vans, Jashan, still a slip of a youth, slipped under the legs of a tall policeman who was supervising the operations. Before anyone could notice, Jashan had made his way into the police van. He seated himself next to his uncle. Naturally, Sadhu Vaswani raised his eyebrows in surprise. He did not have the heart to send away his eager nephew, who looked excited as though he was off on a picnic.

The days in prison were unforgettable for Jashan! Sadhu Vaswani, a well-known spiritual leader, was not meted out the treatment of a common prisoner. The jail authorities went all out to make his stay in the prison as comfortable as possible. He was given the freedom to move around and talk to the other inmates. He met the regular jailbirds, thieves, murderers, and criminals with tender love and understanding. 'They are my friends and brothers,' he insisted. 'And I would fain be in their midst to bear witness to the love and mercy of God'. Jashan hadn't looked at it like that! His uncle's words struck a chord within him. Was it not true that many commit crimes in hunger and passion, in bitter anguish and through a sense of frustration, he was compelled to ask himself.

'A prison is a precious gift,' Sadhu Vaswani said. 'To stay here and to see God around you and within you is to be in a state of grace.' Indeed, these were the circumstances in which Jashan dwelt with his uncle in the prison!

Upon learning that a man of God was their fellow resident, scores of convicts approached Sadhu Vaswani and opened wide the doors of their hearts to him. Many of them came clean with him, while Sadhu Vaswani comforted and counselled them. Deep in the recesses of his heart was the conviction that the sin and the sinner are eclipsed by the grace of God and the mercy of his redeeming love. All are his children, Sadhu Vaswani said, who are at different stages of evolution, since all of them are striving to reach the goal. 'There is,' he said, 'a treasure God giveth in darkness, and sinners are nearer to the kingdom of love than the self-righteous.'

Jashan sat at the feet of his uncle, offering him the service of love and devotion, eagerly drinking in every word he spoke, every act he performed!

Meanwhile, Sadhu Vaswani's imprisonment stirred an uproar in the town. The authorities were left with no choice but to hasten the withdrawal of the case. A public protest was in the offing and the spiritual leader, loved and respected by many, was released along with a group of followers. The release occurred in four days instead of the earmarked fifteen.

Once out of prison, Sadhu Vaswani had his hands full. The master was surrounded by the national press, who had several questions to put to him. There were press statements to be issued and somebody was needed to type those out immediately. Jashan was good at typing, and his English was impeccable. He was only too happy to help his uncle with all the work.

In those days, Jashan actually thought of quitting his college to serve his uncle in every way he could. Sadhu Vaswani was curt in dismissing this proposal when Jashan broached the matter. There was no question of opting out of post-graduation! Jashan had to get his master's degree before he considered his future plans!

As Sadhu Vaswani's visits to Karachi became more frequent, one of the devotees decided to build a place of residence and worship for the master in the city. This was where his satsangs and classes would be held. Thus, Krishta Kunj came into being. The educated and elite sections of Karachi society soon began to gather in large numbers at the spacious assembly hall to hear the master's discourses on the Gita and other scriptures.

Despite his busy schedule at college, Jashan dedicated all his spare time and effort to assist Sadhu Vaswani. The young seeker always put himself at the master's disposal. Thus, when the construction of the building slowed down due to a severe shortage of cement, Jashan stepped in to salvage the situation. He contacted the owner of a cement factory to arrange for the supply. Leaving nothing to chance, he organized the loading of the cement on a lorry from the factory and rode on the lorry to deliver the cement at the construction site.

Seeing his dear nephew arrive with the cement, his white clothes covered in dust, Sadhu Vaswani was touched.

The deepest aspiration of Jashan's heart was always to be there to assist the work of his master. For him, this appeared to be the very purpose of his life; everything else paled into insignificance. When the building was completed, Krishta Kunj became a second home for Jashan in Karachi.

The uncle–nephew bond was to turn into something very special: they would be guru–disciple very soon.

Krishta Kunj had given Sadhu Vaswani a new base in Karachi, where he had many followers. But Hyderabad–Sind continued to be the busiest centre of activities of the Brotherhood Association, Sakhi Satsang, and of course, the fledgling Mira Movement in Education, all of which Sadhu Vaswani had founded.

Jashan's vacation after the MSc examination gave him the opportunity to spend some time in Hyderabad with his uncle. Once in the city, he completely immersed himself in the service of Sadhu Vaswani.

The breadth and sweep of his activities and the tremendous wisdom and vision with which he conceived them left a lasting impression on Jashan. He also observed at close quarters the kind of youth that flocked to his uncle to join his band of followers that was rapidly growing. The master's selflessness, his whole-hearted service to humanity and his dedication to the cause of spiritual uplifting of the youth were truly inspirational.

Sadhu Vaswani had fostered an environment where idealism and high values flourished and the young men and women of Sind were drawn to him by virtue of his spiritual magnetism. Jashan also met the many seniors who had given up their lucrative careers and personal ambitions to follow the master. He found the ambience spiritually invigorating and threw himself into this new world with renewed zeal and vigour. He soon became the unofficial secretary and personal assistant to the master, handling his correspondence, appointments and attending to all administrative tasks.

Jashan was enjoying an extended summer vacation with his uncle while the MSc examination results were still awaited. Sadhu Vaswani had been invited to speak at an International and Inter-Religious Retreat and Conference in Colombo, Ceylon (now Sri Lanka) in 1939. The master was not in good health at the time, but doctors felt that the voyage to Ceylon and the air of the emerald isle would do him good. Sadhu Vaswani accepted the invitation and Jashan was permitted to travel with him since his vacation was on. The party left for Colombo on 9 May.

After delivering memorable and well-attended lectures in Colombo, Sadhu Vaswani moved to Nuwara Eliya, a beautiful hill station, where he stayed for nearly four months. The messages of the Gita travelled far and wide in the mountain city with him as he held classes towards this end in the English language, twice a week. The citizens of Nuwara Eliya gravitated towards Sadhu Vaswani.

Meanwhile, Jashan was on cloud nine. He couldn't have asked for more. He had the saint, who was his own uncle, in his constant company. In fact he had been following Sadhu Vaswani like a shadow and wished to dedicate his life to him.

Amidst it all arrived the month of June. Jashan received a letter from Professor Ganesh Gopal Paldhikar, head of the department of physics in D. J. Sind College, Karachi. The post of a lecturer was vacant and the professor wrote to inform his favourite student that it could be his for the asking. The question was, could Jashan return to Karachi at the earliest? Would he be able to make it to the city by 20 June, when the college was to reopen after the vacation?

Jashan told his beloved master of the offer and sought his guidance on the matter. At the same time, Jashan could no longer conceal the aspirations of his heart. He told the master frankly that his heart longed to be with him and that he had no wish to pursue a worldly career for money or for fame.

Sadhu Vaswani listened to his nephew patiently. He explained to his nephew, who seemed determined to follow his heart, 'My dear one, you must do as your mother wishes. She has taken great pain and effort to educate her beloved son and bring him up well. Isn't this the time for you to express your gratitude towards her?'

Jashan was in a dilemma. How could he write to his beloved mother and tell her that he had no desire to pursue a career – in fact, that he had no desire to go back home at all? How could he make her understand that he wished to devote his life to the service of his beloved uncle and guru? Jashan had to figure out an answer at the earliest.

Several decades ago, Sadhu Vaswani had himself been in Jashan's shoes. He had made known his desire to become a fakir, but the tears of his mother had held him back for a while. He had to pursue an academic career before he could tread the chosen path.

Jashan chose a well-considered way out of the dilemma. He wrote to his younger brother Ram, telling him of the offer from the college, adding that he personally wished to continue to be with Sadhu Vaswani. In the letter, he asked Ram if he could put in a word to their mother about his aspirations and gauge her feelings about it. If she refused, he would return to Karachi. If, however, she did not say anything, it meant she was not averse to the idea.

A few days later, he received Ram's reply. Their mother had consented to his wish of staying with his guru. Jashan was ecstatic and felt relieved. He enthusiastically communicated the message to his master, who heard it with a gracious smile.

However, D. J. Sind College was not yet ready to let go of its star student. The college authorities wrote to tell Jashan that the post was still open and would stay open for him until he decided to come back.

Jashan was not tempted by the flattering offer from his alma mater. He had chosen a different path for himself. The offer of a prestigious job and the prospects of a successful career had no charm on him. He had chosen to take 'the road less travelled' meant for the few whose aspirations were far from worldly.

Happy in the thought that his mother had not stood in the way of his aspirations, Jashan continued to be with his beloved master, rejoicing in every second he spent in his presence. But his newfound joy was short-lived.

A visitor from Karachi arrived to see Sadhu Vaswani in Colombo. In the course of his conversation, he mentioned meeting Bhabhi, Jashan's mother, Krishnadevi. He recalled how she had narrated with pain the story of bringing up her son with a great deal of effort. She had expressed regret that after raising her son so well, she had to face the reality: her brother-in-law had just taken her beloved son away from her.

Sadhu Vaswani grew thoughtful when he heard this. He summoned Jashan and told him, 'I want you to go back home. Your duty is to be with your beloved mother.'

A broken-hearted Jashan uttered not a word of protest, but his silence conveyed his grief. Quietly, he packed his bag and returned home to his mother. If his heart ached, he did not speak of it to her.

Friends and well-wishers of the family informed Krishnadevi about the upcoming post of the assistant collector of customs, Karachi. 'It is tailor-made for your son!' they told her. Woodenly, he consented to his mother's wish to apply for the position.

He did not tell his mother of his anguish at leaving his master. He did not protest at being pushed into a worldly career which held no interest for him. He did not even argue or plead with his mother to let him return to where he felt he belonged – at the feet of his Gurudev.

But a mother is after all a mother. A sensitive and caring woman, Krishnadevi could see through her son's silence. She acknowledged that her son's future belonged with his uncle. On the morning of the third day after his return, she called him to her side and gave him the approval he had been longing for, 'Son, I know your heart is not here. I give you the freedom to follow your wish. You may return to your revered uncle with my blessings.'

Jashan felt he could fly! But he knew that his master would never accept him if he returned then and there. So, he entreated his mother to express her consent in writing, to pen a letter to Sadhu Vaswani, intimating her whole-hearted approval to him.

The mother obliged readily. She wrote a letter to Sadhu Vaswani stating she was handing over her beloved Jashan in his care, wholly and completely. Her brother-in-law could carve his nephew's future as he desired.

When Sadhu Vaswani received the letter, he folded it carefully, putting it away in safe-keeping. He instructed that the letter be preserved for him with great care. Even today, the indispensable consent of Krishnadevi penned out in the form of a letter is part of his carefully preserved collection in the sacred *kutiya* at the Sadhu Vaswani Mission in Pune.

They were back in Hyderabad now. Jashan was overjoyed as he had reached the land of his heart's desire. Nothing could separate him from his beloved master. The journey was even more blessed now, thanks to the gracious consent of his mother.

Every project that he took up, whether in relation to academics or to a task assigned to him by his master, Jashan did it with deep sincerity and perseverance. Abiding by the teaching of his master, he had perfected the fine art of doing whatever he did, as an offering to the lord, and therefore, poured into it his very best.

Even while he was working for his master's degree, he had been deeply influenced by the worldview of Sadhu Vaswani. The world and its allurements, his academic career, his friends and family, all paled into insignificance. Sadhu Vaswani became his life and goal. The hunger for acquiring further degrees was replaced by an insatiable longing to serve the master.

Jashan had almost completed his thesis, 'The Scattering of X-rays by Solids', when he was drawn to the master. Now that he knew this is where his future lay, his thesis and its completion slipped into oblivion.

A friend and classmate noticed how Jashan's brilliant thesis was gathering dust. He requested Jashan to give it to him so he could complete it and submit it as his own and acquire a master's degree without much effort on his part. Jashan readily agreed and handed over the thesis to him. He was simply thrilled! The friend immediately narrated the entire incident to Sadhu Vaswani happily.

In the evening, when Jashan came to Sadhu Vaswani, he found displeasure writ large over the master's face and enquired about it. 'Not only are you cheating yourself, but you are being a party to untruth and falsehood by allowing another to submit your work as his own. Only after you have submitted your thesis and completed all the formalities for your MSc,' Sadhu Vaswani said firmly, 'can you return to me.'

Jashan had to be away in Karachi for fifteen long days, during this time, he pieced together his thesis and completed the formalities of submission; it was assessed by none other than Sir C. V. Raman, who went on to become a Nobel Laureate.

The revelation of the assessor's identity cast a doubt in Jashan's mind. He had a momentary misgiving about passing his MSc; for the hypothesis he had formulated in his research project was exactly the opposite of the famous Raman Effect. His misgivings, however, turned out to be uncalled for. C. V. Raman, in true scientific spirit, appreciated and encouraged Jashan's independent bent of mind and ensured that he qualified for the MSc degree. The degree came in handy a few years later when St Mira's College, founded by Sadhu Vaswani in Pune, needed a principal who held a master's degree. Naturally, Jashan fit the bill perfectly.

Sadhu Vaswani's influence indeed helped shape the disciple.

One morning, when Sadhu Vaswani had come out of his meditation, Jashan confided in him, 'Why do I feel such restlessness? I have met several holy men and have tried to live by their many teachings, yet I remain restless.'

'Seekers on the spiritual path remain restless for different reasons,' explained the master. 'One type of seeker, the *Arta bhakta*, is the distressed devotee who, in bad times, yearns for the grace of God to find relief from his suffering. Another is the *Jigyasu* who is a seeker of knowledge, who seeks the grace of God to attain wisdom. *Artharthi* is the seeker of wealth who longs for earthly possessions for a happy life. Therefore, he propitiates God so that he may amass wealth.'

'Such seekers are either distressed, dissatisfied or filled with craving. All of them experience restlessness because their devotion is of a lower type.'

'What is the highest form of devotion, then?' Jashan wanted to know.

'The *Jnani* is the wise one, who is satisfied and contented with the self, desiring only the self as the all-inclusive God. He has attained self-illumination. He experiences the supreme peace of the highest, which puts an end to all the restlessness. He becomes one with the self where he sees nothing else, where he hears nothing else. He experiences that he and the Beloved are one. The Jnani is one who has gained a perfect identity with the Lord.'

'So, what does freedom from restlessness imply?' asked young Jashan.

'It implies freedom from desire and fear.'

'And what must one do to attain that state?'

'One must take refuge at the feet of an enlightened one, a holy one. The guru's grace is needed to attain that state.'

Jashan became silent. The conversation continued the next day.

'Please, talk to me about death. How does one overcome grief?' asked Jashan of him, who was now his mentor and master.

'Grief is due to attachment,' replied Sadhu Vaswani. 'And attachment is due to ignorance. Why is man sad? Because he clings to forms. The essence is not the form. The wise man does not grieve because he understands that, at death, only the form departs, the *atman* lives on. The wise man knows that the departed ones are still alive in another sphere of consciousness.'

'Does the wise man, then, never feel grief at all?'

'He does, but he also understands that overcoming grief is the way to develop spiritual power and win the battle of the spirit. He thinks, "Krishna walked, and Jesus walked through the valley of the shadow of death. Who am I to say that I must escape sorrow and anguish? I too, must bear my cross, bear and bleed; only let me remember that when I bear and bleed, the will of God will be working through me: and through suffering and pain, the will of God will be purifying me and preparing me for the vision of transfiguration, the *vishva darshanam*, the vision of the one Lord of life and light and love in all that is around me, above me, below me, within me!"'

Sadhu Vaswani paused for a moment. Jashan remained still, waiting for him to continue. 'Grief, then, is sacred,' continued Sadhu Vaswani. 'It is God's gift to the seeker; it is the benediction he pours upon him to whom he would reveal the meaning of his infinite mercy, to reveal himself, his wisdom, and his love.'

It was a balmy night in Hyderabad-Sind. Jashan sat in his room, with his eyes closed in meditation. His mind was at peace and he felt he was in communion with the Divine. He felt an inexplicable happiness springing forth from within him.

Suddenly, as a swarm of locusts swoops upon a field, undesirable thoughts attacked him from all sides. Only a moment ago, he seemed to be in the Divine presence and now, he was perplexed!

Fighting the overwhelming negativity, Jashan was unable to sleep all night. Early in the morning, he left his room quietly and sought the company of nature in the garden. He felt enthused as he saw the master sitting on a bench underneath a tree. Jashan quietly went up to him and sat at his feet. He was struggling to subdue the storm raging within him.

His eyes half-closed, the master sat in silence, his mind pondering on the eternal. He was the very picture of peace that defies description. Jashan couldn't stop staring at his face. Out of it flowed a current which seemed to soothe his distracted mind.

After a while, the master opened his eyes. He smiled and asked Jashan, 'What ails you, my child? You seem to carry a tremendous load on your mind!' Nothing, it seemed, escaped his notice!

A great weight seemed to be lifted off Jashan's mind. He told the master of the disturbing thoughts that troubled him as he sat in silence. 'From where do these thoughts come?' he asked Sadhu Vaswani. 'And pray, tell me, what may I do to check the restlessness of my mind?'

The master attempted to put an end to the dilemma confronting his disciple. 'My child! Do not feel worried! Let evil thoughts come: let them pour out! The more they come out, the purer will your mind become!'

'Teach me a simple discipline,' begged Jashan, 'by which I may cleanse the mind of these negative thoughts.'

The master asked Jashan to clap his hands. As soon as he brought his hands together to clap, the birds resting on the tree flew away.

'See how the birds fly away at the clapping of your hands! So do the evil thoughts fly away as you clap your hands and sing the Name of God. Sing the Name as often as you can. And as you sing, meditate on the form or some symbol of the great one whose name you sing. Sing the Name Divine in love and longing for the Lord. Sing the Name with tears in your eyes. Sing it aloud. Sing it in the silence of your room or as you walk on the street. Sing it alone or in the company of other *bhakta*s (devotees). And evil thoughts will disturb you no longer,' he said to his beloved nephew.

'But, Master! How can one sing the Name all day long!' asked Jashan, puzzled.

'Therefore, learn to live and work for the good of others, but see that your work is free from all taint of egoism. Work as an instrument of the eternal, knowing that he is the one worker! Such work will purify you and prepare you for a life of contemplation. The important thing is to keep the mind occupied,' continued the master, 'for the mind is restful only when it is occupied. Keep the mind occupied either in singing the Name or in doing some work devoted to the welfare of others. For, verily, an idle mind is more dangerous than a car in the hands of a drunk driver.'

Jashan bowed his head in reverence and clung to the feet of the master. 'Give me, I pray, a few simple rules to which I may adhere in all my work and aspiration.'

The master looked lovingly at his nephew. He stretched out his hand and said, 'Even as the hand has five fingers, so let your life of daily deeds be built in five simple rules.' And he enumerated them, 'First and foremost, return love for hate. Like the great mystic, Rabia, let your heart be so filled with love that not a corner may remain for any thought of hatred. And, remember, when a man does you harm or cheats you or slanders you, he does it out of ignorance. He needs your loving prayers. The more evil he sends you, the more good you must send out into the world! How beautiful is the prayer of Jesus for his persecutors: "Father! Forgive them, for they know not what they do!"'

He then shared with his disciple the second principle of goodness, 'See the good in all. Each one of us is a mixture of good and evil. If you have eyes to see, there is not a man so drenched in evil that he has no goodness which you may not learn of him. See the good in everyone you meet and bow down to it.' As Jashan listened intently, he was enlightened with the third, 'Walk the way of acceptance. Know that all that happens, happens according to the will of God. And in his will is our peace. Meet every situation in life with the prayer, "Thy will be done!" Many things will happen which you, with your puny intellect, will not be able to understand. Complain not, but in the simple faith of a trusting child say to yourself: "I know nothing, lord! Thou knowest everything. And thou art my father, my mother, my guardian and my guide! Thy will be done!" At every step, in every round, thank him and praise him! For whatever happens, his will is always for the best.'

Sadhu Vaswani concluded with the last two lessons, 'Give compassion to all – men, birds and animals. The Qur'an speaks of God as Al-Rahman, the compassionate one. If at his doorstep we stand and ask for compassion, we must first give compassion to others. So, feed birds and cows and dogs every day and give them water to drink. And in your dress and diet, keep clear of violence. Abstain from meat-eating and wearing silken garments which cost millions of silkworms their precious life. And see that no needy person is turned away empty-handed by you. Above all, give the compassion of your heart to those whom the world condemns as thieves, criminals, gamblers, drunkards, sinners sunk in wickedness and vice. Fifth, each day pray for all – all men of all nations, all birds, all beasts, all animate creatures, and all inanimate objects. Pray for friends and strangers, for the sick and disabled, for lunatics and lepers, for all who are in the agony of pain – physical, mental, spiritual. Pray that all may be happy, full of bliss!'

Tears of joy and relief flowed from Jashan's eyes. This was heaven! This was light! This was true wisdom!

Another incident that was etched in the mind of Jashan, was later published in one of his articles:

I returned from an errand on which my beloved master had sent me. On the way I saw several of my brothers and sisters absorbed in speaking to each other. I paused to listen. I gathered that they were discussing, in the severest language, a sister who had been 'caught' in sin. And a voice within me whispered, 'Move on! This is not the place for you!'

When I met Sadhu Vaswani, I spoke to him of what I had seen and heard on the way. And Sadhu Vaswani said, 'My child, remember, there is no sin greater than the sin of separateness. When you sit in judgment upon a brother or a sister, whose sin has been exposed, you indulge in a worse sin, an inexcusable crime. And in judging another, you but condemn yourself. Is it not true, that if you strip yourself of all "coverings" you will find that within you lurk all the sins man is capable of committing? Alas! The shadow of your passions darkens your eyes!'

'If I am not to condemn a brother who has sinned, how shall I help him to change his ways?'

'Let the sin of your brother teach you to turn the searchlight on yourself. It will reveal to you your own sin. And as you endeavour to cleanse yourself and to expiate the sin, you will know how deep are its roots and how oppressive it is to keep up the good fight. And through your experience you will know how great is your own need for sympathy and love, in your struggle against sin, how when this sympathy and love flow to you, you are strengthened in your efforts to find a lasting cure. The best way to help an erring brother is the way of sympathy and love!'

After a brief pause, Sadhu Vaswani continued, 'As you sit in your morning meditations and your evening prayers, and as you move about during the day, send out loving thoughts to all who have fallen into the dark abyss of sin but would fain climb out of it to greet the light of the morning sun. And pray for them who lie fettered in prison houses and for all who are on beds of illness groaning in the agony of pain. For the sinner, too, is a sick man; he needs the loving treatment of a great mother heart. Nothing else will cure him, nothing else.'

Once, the master was in Karachi for a few weeks. 'This letter must reach Hyderabad today, Jashan,' he said to his nephew. 'Will you see to it at once?'

'Of course, it will be done,' replied the devout disciple. 'We will find someone to carry it for us by today's train.'

Back then, the postal services functioned at a snail's pace and letters would take forever to reach their destination. Often, people would go to the station, find an acquaintance or a friend travelling on the train and hand over the letter to him for personal delivery. This would save them the hassle of posting the letter.

So, the master and his disciple went to the Karachi cantonment station on the day. But events took an unexpected turn. While Jashan was walking down the platform, trying to find a familiar face on the train, the master, on the spur of the moment, boarded the train. He had made up his mind to travel to Hyderabad himself! The train began to move and to Jashan's utter surprise, he saw his master waving at him from one of the moving compartments! The other devotees who had accompanied the master, had also got into the train with him by now! Imagine Jashan's predicament when he found himself waving goodbye to the master, standing all alone on the station platform!

Jashan returned to Krishta Kunj, which now seemed to wear a deserted look.

It was past lunch time now and Jashan's stomach was growling with hunger. But asking someone for food would be awkward, he felt. 'I shall go to my house to eat,' he decided.

Jashan's mother did not ask him if he was hungry or wanted to eat something as she usually did. It was late in the day and she assumed her son had already eaten lunch. Jashan, being the sensitive, gentle and undemanding person that he was, did not ask his mother for food either!

That day, Jashan discovered for the first time in his life, what it was to experience hunger pangs. Characteristically, he made this experience his teacher. The spasms of hunger that he suffered made him empathize with the plight of countless brethren who go without a meal every day.

Dada, therefore, always insisted later that no one who came to the Sadhu Vaswani Mission leave without prasad. No one, absolutely no one, would ever go away hungry from the sacred premises where Dada lived. Dada insisted that self-improvement, ideals, values and the teaching of profound spiritual truths could wait until the poor and hungry are provided with life's most basic necessity – food.

One day, when the master was enjoying a rare moment of leisure, his beloved nephew said to him, 'You have written so many books concerning so many things. And in your wondrous ways you have unfolded many truths of the spirit. Tell me, in a few simple words, the essence of all that you have taught.'

Sadhu Vaswani smiled at this eager request. With the humility characteristic of him, Jashan's uncle replied, 'I do not know if I have taught anything. But this is what I have learnt: Be a little one. Be a child. Be unknown. Live the hidden life in the hidden God.'

Jashan was struck with these profound but simple injunctions. He ruminated: He who has become a little one hath broken the fetters of power and prominence, of ambition and authority, of honours and greatness and all that the world values greatly. He is truly free, he abides in heaven. And the one infallible mark of such a one is love! He loves God, he loves his neighbours. He loves all men of all communities and races and religions, all men of all types, rich and poor, young and old, beautiful and unpleasant, saint and sinner. He loves all creatures, birds and animals, fish and fowl, insect and ant. He loves all things created, stone and star, sun and moon, tree and flower, river and rock. He becomes the very picture of love. He becomes love itself. Love flows out of him in an endless stream blessing all the world, all the universe.

Jashan recalled the words of St John that he had read sometime earlier. 'Let us love one another,' urged St John, 'for love is of God; and everyone that loveth is begotten of God, and knoweth God: He that loveth knoweth God: For God is Love.'

Jashan learnt through his master that love gives and love forgives, asking nothing in return. He who would walk the way of love must be prepared to give, give, and ever give!

'We are proud of our power and inventions; yet what are we?' asked Sadhu Vaswani of Jashan one day, out of the blue.

He proceeded to answer the question himself, 'We are grass that floats on a stream. For infinite are the worlds, and the universe is a river: Ever full, ever flowing.'

'In such a world how must one be?' asked Jashan in a soft voice.

'The world was built in beauty and man was meant to live as a songbird, unfettered and free. But alas, he has become a bird in a cage. It is the cage of self-centredness. Not until self-centredness goes may man become truly free and full of the joy of life. And the prison of self-centredness opens to the key of humility.'

'What is the mark of him who has attained true humility?'

Taking a pencil, Sadhu Vaswani drew a zero and said, 'This is the mark of him who has attained; he becomes a zero.'

Sadhu Vaswani paused for a while, and Jashan held his breath. 'Blessed be thou, if thou bend until thou break, becoming nothing: a zero. In the yoga (union) of two zeroes is the one infinite,' he told Jashan, whose eyes grew wide with amazement.

An incident had spiralled Jashan into despondency. He was deeply dejected at what had happened.

In the interim, he appeared before his beloved master, who looked at his wretched face but once, and then did not look at him again. Nor did he say a word to console the young man. Jashan was dismayed at being ignored by his uncle. In the next few days that followed, there was no interaction between them. It seemed to Jashan as though the master was consciously keeping a distance from him.

Jashan was in anguish. Living under the same roof, he was denied the privilege of seeing the master whom he loved beyond any earthly love. Jashan could not fathom the cause of what seemed like his master's callous indifference to him. Evil thoughts reared their ugly head once again and jibed at Jashan, 'See how much the master loves you!'

It took Jashan five days to realize that he had to wipe the sad expression off his miserable visage before he could become worthy of being admitted to his beloved uncle's presence. Jashan forced a smile upon his face and drew near the master.

The master was loving as ever. As he enfolded his nephew in a warm embrace, unbidden tears rolled down Jashan's cheeks. The master spoke to him affectionately, as though nothing untoward had happened.

Much later, Sadhu Vaswani told Jashan of St Francis and the sufferings that the prince among men had to undergo. 'And yet,' the master pointed out, 'St Francis never renounced the smile on his lips. He was free from melancholy. He looked cheerful. He retained his sunny serenity and he maintained his humour. To his brothers, he said, when laying down for them the rules of discipline: "Ye shall take care that ye do not behave outwardly like melancholy hypocrites. But ye shall behave in the Lord, fresh and gay and agreeable."'

Ever since, St Francis had been one of the inspirations of Dada's life. Dada would say, 'I have meditated on him, again and again, and on his love-lit eyes. And often, I have recalled to myself one of his wonderful sayings: To the devil belongs to be sad, but to us ever to be glad and rejoice in the Lord.'

'What is God?' Jashan once asked his beloved master as the two of them sat amicably in the peace that prevailed in the little garden of Sadhu Vaswani's house in Karachi. Together, they sat underneath the canopy of the clear, starlit skies of Sind as the disciple raised the question. A gentle breeze blew over them and the air was fragrant with the scent of the rajnigandha. They were enveloped in a wondrous silence that was shaken off gently by Jashan.

On that beautiful, unforgettable night, the master spoke to Jashan of several things, of the kingdom where neither sun nor stars do shine, of the rebirth of man, of the treasures of wisdom, of the beauty of the Beloved whose vision emancipates the heart, of the love which travels from God to man and is reflected back from man to God. And drinking in the wisdom that was poured upon him so abundantly, Jashan asked him, 'Pray, tell me, tell me, what is God?'

The master replied, 'God is truth. And God is good, absolute good. And God is beauty. And God is holiness. The human soul has somehow lost him, and he may not be found again until, in his infinite grace, he comes down and touches the human soul. For it is true, too true, that behind man's search for God is God's search for man. God seeks man. God seeks every one of his children who have turned away from him. And God will not rest until all have returned to him. Therein lies our deepest hope.'

'What is it that stands between man and God?' Jashan asked curiously. The master told him, 'Veils have fallen on man and he remains sunk in ignorance and apathy. He is unable to see God. Man, under the influence of his gross physical environment, is blind to the beauty of God and runs after the vanities of the world. Man is a victim of the one great veil – that of appetite or desire: of the flesh; it is a very great veil. Desires dominate man and he turns his face away from the light.'

'Man may turn to Him again and behold the beauty of God. This may be achieved by God's mercy and grace. Beholding him in his grace, we may see him as light. Not until the seeker travels to the realm of light may he become truly a "man". Most of us are no better than animals, excommunicated from the city of light. Man, tied to a life of the senses, is no better than a brute–beast. Man's destiny is to be a divine bird, to grow wings and fly from this world of darkness to the radiant world of light.'

Jashan sat at the master's feet, spellbound. He felt uplifted by the wisdom of his uncle and could listen to him forever.

As soon as his uncle finished answering the question, Jashan put up another, 'What may I do to grow wings and fly to the realm of radiance and light?'

The master smiled and answered, 'Realize, first, that you live in a state of banishment from the Beloved. Then know that you must die to "selfhood" in order to live in the Beloved.'

'What is the path that leadeth to the city of light, the city of God?' Jashan persisted.

Thus spoke the master, 'Many be the paths that lead Godward. The essence of them all is in two things: One, when the little self, the "ego" dies, we enter into the limitless; two, the limitless is love – the all-living love. When the heart is pure, love glows in the heart within.'

Jashan was left wanting more. 'How should a man prepare to behold the face of love in the heart within?'

'Concentrate on the heart! It is a mirror in which you may behold the face of love. But the mirror is soiled, is greasy, and the reflection of the Beloved is blurred. Cleanse the mirror of your heart. Wipe away the impurities which stain the heart. The one great cause of impurities is "ego", "self". When the "ego" is annihilated, the face of the Beloved is seen shining in the mirror of the heart.'

Jashan could never run out of questions in the presence of his master, 'How may the "ego" be annihilated?'

'As the seeker makes progress on the path, he finds that sometimes he prides himself on his efforts. Sometimes, he thinks he is achieving success. Sometimes, he loses the joy of existence. It is so difficult, he says, to be spiritual. Then comes to him a realization that his efforts and endeavours are not pure, but tainted, spotted. The darkest spot, he finds, is the little "self", the "ego", "I". And he begins to realize that of his own accord he can do nothing. Then he learns to accept whatever comes – abasement, criticism and contumely – as the will of God.'

Sadhu Vaswani showered infinite wisdom upon his nephew. He spoke at length about the most supreme love there is on earth, 'The love of God gradually fills him, his "egoism" dies. A higher stage is still to come when he realizes that God loves him and hath awakened love in his heart. Then he realizes that divine love and divine grace encompass life from beginning to end. Then all desires, appetites, allurements, attachments, depart: he is free: he is calm!'

On the path of his quest, the disciple is subjected to loneliness and despair. Only a great master can submit his disciple to this very essential spiritual catharsis and then release the disciple from this state of dejection.

During one such period of testing, Jashan, a novice, felt that his revered master, Sadhu Vaswani, no longer loved him. 'I enter and leave the room unnoticed. He ignores my greeting,' he lamented to himself. His heart pined for sympathy. The intensity of his suffering was so great it had become a burden difficult to carry. Jashan resorted to rebellion and made up his mind to run away that night. He spent the night in a garden nearby, shivering in the bitter cold, yet obstinacy got the better of him. He was not going to return to the master ever.

The lack of sleep sapped the agility of his mind and magnified his torment. There he sat, dejected, miserable and lonely, sulking in pain.

Early next morning, his cheeks were still stinging from the torrent of the salty tears that had flown from his eyes liberally the previous night. He retraced his steps to go back home to the master. The drifter was finally home. He knocked at the door and it was opened by the master himself.

Dressed in all-white as usual, he was aglow with ethereal light. The light from his countenance enveloped everything that surrounded him. A guilt-ridden Jashan threw himself at the feet of the master, like a swallow diving in flight. For a split second, there was a moment of most perfect, unbelievable bliss, which overwhelmed him.

'Do you think you can run away from me?' the master asked Jashan, who clung to the feet of his guru, begging for forgiveness.

Jashan was being burnished in the cleansing fire which would purify him and transform him into gold that shone with incredible lustre.

The master expected more of Jashan than of any of his other disciples. The tests that Jashan was put through bear witness to his gigantic struggles, but perseverance was no stranger to him. He emptied his heart of all else, except for the grace of his guru.

Somewhere in the Upanishads, our quest for spirituality has been summed up rather strikingly, 'If you want truth as badly as a drowning man wants air, you will realize it in a split second.' But who wants truth as badly as that? It is the task of a guru to set the heart aflame with an inextinguishable fire of longing; it is his duty to keep it burning until the ego is reduced to ashes.

The sentiment echoed in the religious text resonated with Sadhu Vaswani, who subjected his dearly loved disciple to a rigorous method of training and discipline in a bid to deflate his ego, 'Go! Go away!' said the master to the disciple, one night. 'If you dare to come here again, you will be turned out.' When one or two other disciples tried to plead in favour of Jashan, the master said they could leave as well. The guru, it seems, was unconcerned.

All through the night, Jashan sat outside the entrance to the premises. How his heart ached! Where could he go? Wasn't his home at the feet of his beloved Gurudev? He prayed, 'Where can I go? How can I live without you?'

In the early hours of the dawn, he saw the master standing in front of him. 'How are you?' he asked in a friendly way, his kind smile lighting up his face. How beautiful the master looked in the golden light! His skin seemed to glow from within! His hands held a cup of hot tea, his eyes beamed with affection – the look the disciple knew all too well and loved with all his heart; Jashan broke down into uncontrollable sobs as the master drew close to him. 'Thy will be done!' The prayer in the Bible had been lived by Jashan.

Sadhu Vaswani had been invited to address a very important gathering. In the days leading up to the meeting, Sadhu Vaswani repeated almost every day, 'If it be God's will, none except Jashan will accompany me to the meeting.'

On the morning of the meeting, the master reiterated, 'God willing, only Jashan will come with me this evening!'

The much-anticipated evening came. The master asked everyone except Jashan to accompany him to the meeting. He thought the master had inadvertently forgotten to call him. The party moved out. Jashan stood behind a door, peeping through a chink, hoping he would be called at the penultimate moment. A ray of hope shone through when he heard someone mention his name to the master. Alas! The master brushed it aside.

Jashan returned to his room with a broken heart. He wept bitter tears of anguish. He said to himself, 'Hereafter, I shall have nothing to do with the master!'

At night, the party returned in high spirits. They discussed the beautiful events that had transpired at the meeting. Jashan felt miserable. He was called by the master. But he revolted and shed woeful tears all over again.

Jashan's mind was as restless as a storm-tossed boat. He lost his appetite and was sleep deprived. He wanted to run away to some distant, remote place, where even the thought of his master would not touch him. This went on for three days.

On the evening of the third day, the master entered Jashan's room and said to him, 'My child! Until you become nothing, you will gain nothing. You may stay here for years together, but you will gain nothing, until you have become nothing!'

Jashan clung to the master's feet, shed tears of remorse and cried, 'Never leave me, Gurudev, though I am but an inadequate servant. Make me thine! Make me nothing!'

The master lifted him up and held him in a loving embrace.

'You are so loving,' Jashan sobbed. 'How could I ever doubt your love?' From then on, he resolved to walk the way of unquestioning obedience.

To be with the master, to serve him, was Jashan's sole aspiration. In the course of his travels with his master, Jashan paid scant attention to his own needs and comforts.

Once, Sadhu Vaswani was on a lecture tour of Sind. He was invited to stay with a humble devotee, whose lodging consisted of just two rooms. The family occupied one room, while the other was offered to Sadhu Vaswani for the night. Where could Jashan possibly sleep? The question did not bother him. He laid a wooden plank close to the fireplace, and slept like a baby even on the hard surface of the plank.

It was the year 1944. A few devotees were fortunate enough to accompany the master to the holy city of Varanasi, known to pious Hindus as Kashi. The city is held dear by thousands of Indians as here flows the sacred Ganga. If Varanasi is the heart of India, the Ganga is its artery.

Almost every Hindu aspires to take a holy dip in the Ganga in the holy city of Kashi. Jashan cherished the same dream. He had always wished to take a dip in the waters, hoping some of its holiness would rub off on him. And now, here he was in Kashi, with the sacred river flowing right outside the accommodation where his group was lodged.

Every morning, Jashan would get ready for the *Gangasnaan*, (a bath in the Ganga) but each morning, some work would come up. Oh! The Ganga was so near, yet so far.

He did try, again and again, to slip out quietly for a few minutes, to take the ritual bath, but he simply couldn't make it.

Soon it was time for the group to leave Varanasi. Their train was to depart at 12:30 p.m. The long overdue moment had arrived, 'Today, I shall take the holy dip!' Jashan said to himself, looking forward to realizing his dream.

Many friends and relatives had earnestly told him to utter their name and think of them while he bathed in the sacred river. Remembering their fervent entreaties, Jashan grabbed a towel and prepared to go for his bath.

He had walked a few steps towards the river, when a sister called out, saying that Sadhu Vaswani was looking for him. Jashan promptly retracted his steps and went to the master's room. Sadhu Vaswani wanted a letter to be sent out on an important and urgent matter and Jashan had to take the dictation. Once again he had to forego the opportunity.

As their train chugged out of Varanasi station that day, Jashan's heart was filled with a strange sadness. He was in Kashi, the land of river Ganga. But he had not been able to bathe in the mother's sacred waters.

Jashan was seated next to the master in the train and felt somewhat comforted by his luminous presence. But somehow, he continued to be restless.

That night, as he fell into a disturbed sleep on the train, he had an unforgettable dream. Lord Shiva appeared before him, resplendent in his leopard skin, holy ash on his forehead, his *trishul* held majestically by his side. He smiled enigmatically, holding up the palm of his hand as though to bless Jashan. But Jashan was taken aback to see that the gentle Ganga was not flowing from his intricately knotted locks.

'Dear Lord!' Jashan gasped, even as he gazed at him with folded hands. 'What is this I see? Where is the Ganga? Why is she not flowing from your locks?'

'Don't be so shocked, dear Jashan,' the Lord said, smiling. 'True, the Ganga used to flow from me, but now, she has changed direction.'

'Changed direction?' Jashan repeated, astonished. 'But Lord, how can the Ganga continue to flow in Kashi, if she has not emerged from your sacred locks?'

'I will tell you, dear Jashan,' the Lord replied. 'The Ganga emerges from the sacred feet of the saints and *satpurkh*s of this holy land. You need not be disappointed and upset. Were you not at the feet of your beloved Gurudev the last few days in Kashi? The Ganga was flowing right there, at his feet. Why then are you so dejected?'

Jashan awoke with a start. He saw Sadhu Vaswani sleeping peacefully, as always, with a beautiful smile on his angelic face. Instinctively, Jashan touched his feet and bowed his head in reverence.

Often Dada would say: 'Are not Kaaba and Kashi, Mecca and Mathura, Ganga and Jamuna, at the feet of the guru?'

STORMY CLOUDS OF PARTITION

The year 1947 was the year that carved out an important chapter in Indian history. India's independence was close at hand, but the dark clouds of Partition too were gathering ominously. There was communal disharmony all over the Indian subcontinent. Sadhu Vaswani deeply grieved at the strife and tension that had replaced the brotherhood and amity between Hindus and Muslims, who had fought shoulder to shoulder for India's freedom. Sadhu Vaswani's towering leadership had garnered admirers from both the communities. To the Hindus, he was a *sant*, a sadhu; to the Muslim brethren, a *pir*, a dervish.

The worst fears of the people came true. India was being split, and Sind, with its majority Muslim population, became a part of Pakistan. Then began a mass exodus of the Hindu people from Sind.

For the Sindhis, the landmark event of the nation's freedom became synonymous to the loss of their homeland. The Hindus of

Sind felt that, if they were to be true to the faith of their fathers, they could no longer stay in the land of their birth. Leaving their properties and possessions behind, they bade farewell to their motherland and sought a new home in India. While most migrated to India going into cramped and overcrowded refugee camps, others chose to settle in distant parts of the world, where families and friends had established roots. True, Punjab and Bengal were also partitioned, but Punjabi and Bengali refugees from Pakistan still had a homeland in India, where their language and culture continued unchanged. Unfortunately, for the Sindhi Hindus, there was no place they could call home; no 'space' to call their own in geographical, cultural, and linguistic terms. The state of affairs continues to this day as Sind belongs entirely to Pakistan.

Indian independence was hailed by many as a 'triumph of non-violence'. A 'bloodless revolution' was supposed to have taken place. Unfortunately, the orgies of murder in the wake of freedom, shattered the hopes of the great apostles of non-violence, including Mahatma Gandhi himself. Massive looting, plundering, arson and killing in broad daylight sullied the holy land.

Sadhu Vaswani and a small group of his followers remained in Sind for a little over a year post-Partition. The master felt he should stay on and that the St Mira's School should continue to serve the children of those who had newly arrived in Sind. However, prevailing circumstances compelled them to leave the land of their birth.

Utter lawlessness prevailed in the cultured cradle of civilization called Sind, the land where Hindus, Muslims and Sikhs had lived in harmony for centuries. The Partition turned the peaceful land into an inferno haunted by assassins, murderers and looters. An unruly mob set their sights on the capture of St Mira's School and a storm of vilification and vicious propaganda ensued. At a meeting of about thirty thousand people, a lie was fabricated. It was announced that at the time of Jinnah's death, *halwa* (a type of sweetmeat) had been distributed at Sadhu Vaswani's satsang, in reality, what had actually been distributed was the *karah prasad* of the satsang. But the incensed mob refused to listen. They cheered the mob leader who declared his intentions aloud. Said he, brandishing a pistol in his hand, 'This Vaswani shall not live!'

Jashan stayed close to his beloved master throughout the days of anarchy. The editor of a local daily paper came to meet Jashan and narrated the whole incident. 'It is for me to warn you, dear Jashan,' he said. 'It is for you to see that Sadhu Vaswani does not move out for a few days.' Then, with a knowing look in his eyes, he added, 'See that you broach the matter with Sadhu Vaswani very tactfully.'

Experience had taught Jashan not to use 'tact' in dealing with the master. So, when evening came, Jashan truthfully related all that he had been told and entreated the master, 'I pray, Master, that you keep indoors for a few days. For all I know, the man may be prowling somewhere near, looking out for a chance to use his pistol.'

He smiled and placed his gentle hand on Jashan, 'Actually, today I felt rather tired and I had thought of resting at home instead of taking the regular evening walk. But after hearing you and seeing you frightened and perturbed, I feel I should definitely go out for a walk. My child! Remember one thing. Life is a gift of God. What he hath given, only he can take away. When it be his will, this body will mingle with the dust. And when the moment arrives, no power on earth can hold me back. Until the hour hath come, no pistol-shot can touch a single hair of my head. Blessed be his name.'

With those words, the master moved out on his evening walk, as usual. His nephew followed him wordlessly. True to the prophecy of the master, he returned home safely.

FAREWELL, SIND

Sadhu Vaswani and a few devoted ones, including Jashan, stayed on in Sind, braving rumours and allegations of riot and conspiracy. The St Mira School and other welfare institutions founded by Sadhu Vaswani continued to serve people of all castes and creeds, even when faced with opposition and aggression. He still considered Sind his homeland, and here, he did whatever little he could, to alleviate the suffering and hardships of the desolate, starving Muslim refugees who were pouring into Pakistan from India. Accompanied by Jashan, he would make frequent visits to refugee camps; he spoke to the uprooted; he gave them food and clothing; but above all, he showered his love and grace upon them.

But alas, in November 1948, one of the members of Sadhu Vaswani's satsang was brutally murdered. The master became anxious for the safety of those who stayed on in Pakistan solely for his sake. He finally decided to leave Hyderabad, the city of his birth, and move to India, where he could continue with his humanitarian work. Accompanied by his nephew Jashan, his adopted daughter, Shanti, his sister Hari and his devoted disciple Dadi Sati, and a few close followers, he landed in Bombay on 10 November 1948.

FOUR

New Beginnings: Pune, the Chosen City

'New beginnings are always disguised as painful endings.'
– Lao Tzu

In the first few days following their 'exile' from Sind, Jashan spent much of his time accompanying Sadhu Vaswani on visits to refugee camps. The plight of the refugees was indeed wretched, and the master's heart moved out to them in love and compassion. He urged his devotees and followers to do as much as they could for the thousands of refugees who lived in the camps. He personally met them and offered them the comfort and consolation he alone could give.

The refugees, who were once prosperous citizens in their homeland, were now forced to live in appalling conditions of deprivation. In one stroke they had lost homes, lands, buisnesses and enterprises, secure employment, civil service positions, material possessions and, in the case of many, even their loved ones. Sadhu Vaswani urged them to be strong within. He exhorted them to be self-sufficient and refrain from soliciting government help. Again and again, he repeated those magical words which became a mantra of positive thinking for all his followers: 'Within you lies a hidden shakti; awaken that shakti and all will be well with you.'

Dada Jashan later grew emotional as he recalled the master's unforgettable call to the shattered community, 'Believe and achieve.' Devotees were urged to do whatever they could to serve these unfortunate people who lacked virtually everything. Whatever offerings Sadhu Vaswani received were spent in their service. Above all, he poured out his love and benedictions on them. Jashan was both a witness to and a participant in the healing process. So totally was he a part of his master's ministrations to one and all that he unconsciously absorbed the same demeanour, tone of voice, and words of comfort.

However, the frenetic pace and hectic lifestyle of India's commercial capital, Bombay, did not suit the contemplative, reflective life chosen by Sadhu Vaswani. Devotees who realized this suggested two alternatives: Pune or Bangalore.

Bhai Mulchand Uttamchandani, a sincere devotee, arranged to rent an apartment for Sadhu Vaswani at Panday Cottage, Pudumjee Park, in the city of Pune, not far from Bombay. He knew the master well and felt that Sadhu Vaswani would certainly prefer the calm and quiet atmosphere of Pune.

On 13 February 1949, three months after he landed in Bombay, Sadhu Vaswani and his group arrived in Pune by the Deccan Queen. A sizeable crowd of Sindhis had collected at the Pune Railway Station to welcome their beloved master. History was made when Sadhu Vaswani alighted on the sacred soil of Pune, for the city would speak of his name and fame in the years to come!

First thing after his arrival, the master started his daily satsangs at Panday Cottage, marking the historical commencement of the Pune satsang which still continues to draw thousands of Sadhu Vaswani's devotees from the world over. As the word of the satsang spread, Sindhis thronged to join the gathering. Soon thereafter, the satsang had to be shifted to the bungalow of a devotee, Bhai Ramchand Daryanani, to accommodate the ever-growing number of aspirants.

Sadhu Vaswani, along with Jashan, visited the Pimpri Refugee Camp near Pune, where thousands of homeless, penniless, displaced people were temporarily accommodated. Sindhis are known to be self-reliant, generous people, used to giving rather than receiving. They are recognized for their munificence and generosity in aiding worthy causes. Here, in post-Partition India, many of them were reduced to abject poverty. Sadhu Vaswani helped these displaced people as much as he could and also urged his wealthy devotees to look after their brothers and sisters in distress.

Soon, invitations began to pour in for the master to visit other Indian cities where his devotees resided. Many service and educational institutes invited him to give talks and preside over functions. Sadhu Vaswani would always travel by third class, accompanied by Jashan and a group of disciples. All the way on their journey, the devotees would sing *bhajans* and *kirtans*, making the train journey one long, joyful satsang.

Pune became Dada Jashan's *karma bhoomi* now. In 1954, he started the *East and West Series*, a monthly magazine devoted to publishing the writings of Sadhu Vaswani, with the purpose of reaching a wider audience. Soon, the construction of the Gita Bhavan, a spacious hall for prayer, kirtan and gatherings, also got underway. In 1962, St Mira's College for Girls was started and affiliated to the University of Poona. Of this institution, the master made Jashan the principal, a post that he was to retain for fourteen years.

THE GOOD WORK GOES ON

On Guru Nanak's birthday, Sadhu Vaswani set up a grocery store, where the affluent purchased grains and other basic necessities and donated them to the poor and the needy. To this day, the *modikhana* is a part of the Guru Nanak birthday celebrations at the Mission.

Sadhu Vaswani's presence soon began to be felt by the cultured citizens of Pune. At a crowded gathering in Gokhale Hall, he shared the dais with Maharishi Karve, the eminent social reformer and educationist, who introduced him to the citizens of Pune as the Saint of Sind. He said that it was the city's good fortune that a holy man of Sadhu Vaswani's stature had come to live here.

In his moving address, Sadhu Vaswani said:

> I am not a stranger to Poona. I have come here as a pilgrim. When I reached Poona on 13 February, I bowed to the memory of Sri Lokmanya Tilak, Sri Gokhale and Chhatrapati Shivaji. In Maharashtra, my thoughts have turned, over and over again to her saints – Ramdas, Tukaram, Eknath and Jnaneshwar. They realized the purpose of life and they imparted teachings which the world has yet to understand … With folded hands, I greet you. I am your brother and a servant of the sages and saints of humanity. May the benedictions of my master and your master shine upon you forever and forever more!

THE TEMPLE OF TREES

The Sadhu Vaswani Mission, as we know it today, is not just a brick-and-mortar institution, nor a conglomeration of departments. It is a saga of service founded on the *tapasya* of people who dedicated their life and effort to the master's mission.

Wherever Sadhu Vaswani went, he was followed by his devoted band of disciples. Under his guidance and inspiration, it was not long before they resumed in full earnest their good work of service and aid to society at large. What Hyderabad–Sind had lost, Pune had gained.

On 26 January 1950, a charitable dispensary was started. It was followed by a modest working centre for women, Kalyan Nari Shala, where needy sisters could earn their livelihood by sewing and tailoring. Service of the poor and the *sufed posh* (needy families) continued as before. Soon, devotees began to express the desire that Mira School should be restarted in Pune. For Sadhu Vaswani, too, the cause of education was dear and close to his heart. When he gave his consent, his earnest devotee, Sri Gangaram Sajandas, took up the task earnestly.

Sri Gangaram had given up a promising career with the Electric Supply Corporation in Hyderabad–Sind, to devote his life in service of the master. He was an able administrator who later became the chairperson of the Sadhu Vaswani Mission, to be known as baba, as affectionately called by Dada J. P. Vaswani. Education was Baba Gangaram's passion. He was the man with the Midas touch; it was he who ensured that donations were received and routed for the right purpose, at the right time.

To start with, the school began functioning on temporary premises at the Council Hall in Pune. This was something rare and unheard of, that a private school should be allowed to function on government premises. The Council Hall, in those days, was used as the state secretariat for four months in the year, during the monsoons. Therefore, the chief minister of Bombay, B. G. Kher, who had heard of Sadhu Vaswani and his noble work, freely gave permission for Mira School to function for a few months, while the secretariat was not functioning there. But soon, the monsoon session would begin, and the secretariat would have to be vacated. However, God had better things in mind for the noble cause of education that Sadhu Vaswani had undertaken. Around this time, Jeejeebhoy Castle, a beautiful heritage building, located in the heart of Pune, not far from the station, fell vacant. It was occupied for several years by the Deccan College and Research Institute, which now shifted to its own spacious premises in Yerwada, near Pune. The Government of Bombay promptly requisitioned Jeejeebhoy Castle and handed it over to Mira School in June 1950.

Now, Lady Jeejeebhoy tried to annul the acquisition so that the family could reclaim possession of the building. But Baba Gangaram, the Master's trusted aide and administrator, persuaded her to sell the heritage building to the Brotherhood Association, as the Sadhu Vaswani Mission was called at that time. The price of rupees five lakhs and forty-five thousand was negotiated for the building. It seemed enormous but was nevertheless regarded as a fair price for the huge structure. The money was raised, thanks to the generous donations from numerous devotees and admirers of Sadhu Vaswani. Jejeebhoy Castle became the official premises of the Brotherhood Association from the year 1950.

Jeejeebhoy Castle seemed to be the perfect fit for all the Mission's activities. On the ground floor of the building was a spacious hall, quite suitable for the satsang. In this hall was put up the beautiful portrait of St Mira, which Sri Gangaram had managed to bring with him, all the way from Hyderabad-Sind. In due course, this hall came to be known as the Mira Hall.

The grounds of Jeejeebhoy Castle were spacious and filled with shady green trees. Sadhu Vaswani loved to sit beneath those verdant shades for his reading and writing, referring to the shady compound as his Temple of Trees.

In the meanwhile, the apartment at Panday Cottage proved to be insufficient to accommodate the growing number of devotees who thronged to meet their spiritual mentor. Sadhu Vaswani was persuaded by the devotees to come and live in a small section of the newly acquired building. He took up his residence on the first floor and began to live in the room which is still revered by thousands of devotees as the sacred kutiya. Typically, he insisted that he would pay a monthly rent to the institution for his personal accommodation.

A new and blessed chapter had begun for the devotees of Sadhu Vaswani.

A LIFE OF SIMPLICITY AND SERVICE

Whatever assets had been built up for the Brotherhood Association in Karachi and Hyderabad–Sind had been lost, left behind during Partition; whatever little remained was always shared with the needy. In those days, there was just one bicycle on the campus and anyone who had work outside the Mission took turns to use this healthy and clean mode of transport. Jashan would take the bike and go around Poona Camp, to attend to a variety of tasks: To meet printers and publishers, get master's books printed, run errands for Sadhu Vaswani and attend to other Mission-related work. It was much later that devotees pooled money to donate a car for the use of the master and the Mission's administrative work.

Life in the Sadhu Vaswani household was exceedingly frugal and simple. The members ate their meals seated on the ground, with Dadi Sati Thadani serving the members. Dadi Sati came from a family of devotees. Her father had in fact donated a bungalow, Sati Lodge in Karachi, on 18 June 1936, where Sadhu Vaswani held his satsangs for a few years. Like so many other devotees, Dadi Sati offered her life in dedication to Sadhu Vaswani, becoming part of his household in the early days at Hyderabad. Dadi Sati's memory is held sacred today as the first biographer of Sadhu Vaswani. Her book in Sindhi, *Dadal Shah*, is still a source book for the life of the master. She was also the editor of *Shyam*, the newspaper started by Sadhu Vaswani in the year 1938. She was blessed with the privilege of rendering personal service to both Sadhu Vaswani and Dada J. P. Vaswani all her life.

Sadhu Vaswani always ate separately. The family lived from day to day, practising complete trust in the guru and God. Sadhu Vaswani would tell them to empty all the water containers at night, for God would provide them what they needed for the morrow.

In those days when twenty-four-hour water supply was unheard of, this was indeed unusual. Only two hours of water supply were available from the municipal corporation; and water had to be filled in several containers and *matkas*, not only for the household but for the entire *sangat* to be used after the regular satsang and prasad distribution. Every night, Sadhu Vaswani would insist that all the pots be emptied on the flowerbeds. Members of the sangat who knew about this would fill their flasks and bottles and take the water home, treating it like prasad. And, Sadhu Vaswani proved to be right. Never once did the sangat or the household ever run out of water.

'SHAPE ME, MOULD ME!'

Jashan had the privilege of being the master's own nephew – the eldest son of Sadhu Vaswani's brother, who was loved dearly by the master. In the prime of his youth, he had brushed aside all thoughts of worldly advancement just to be with his beloved uncle and Gurudev. Such was the divine will, such was the master's grace that his mantle would fall upon his dear nephew, who would become his favourite disciple and his spiritual heir.

Jashan and Sister Shanti were brought together by divine destiny at the lotus feet of a guru they both venerated. She had come to Sadhu Vaswani as a little girl of ten, to stay with the guru, who was to her, a spiritual father. So blessed was she that he actually adopted her and gave her the name Shanti T. Vaswani. Loving, pure, simple and innocent, she made her entire life an offering at the feet of the master.

Dada often speaks of Sister Shanti as his *upa-guru*.

High words of praise come from the inheritor of a great spiritual tradition about the dearly beloved sister who shared the privilege of *guru seva* with him.

Everyone who knew Jashan as a young man saw him as an intellectual. Widely read and highly perceptive, he had a logical bent of mind that questioned, rather than blindly accept anything he was told. The master himself said of Jashan that he had an analytical mind. In fact, the early days of his discipleship were given to many an argument with his master. The other devotees would be concerned and apprehensive about the physical toll this tussle of wits was taking on the master. But it also made Jashan realize the towering intellect and wisdom of his master, whose knowledge and intelligence far surpassed his own.

It was Shanti who urged him not to argue, but to accept. Intuitive and emotionally sensitive, she herself was a living example of absolute faith and acceptance, and she instilled in young Jashan the spirit of submission to the master's will.

When Jashan had been a college student, he was acquainted with a holy man of God, who developed a great affection for the young man, who was so unlike others of his age.

Looking into Dada's deep, luminous eyes, the holy man said to him one day, 'I would like to grant you a blessing. From now on, when you look at anyone's palm, I shall speak through you. You will be able to read accurately, the past and the future of people you meet.'

Strangely enough, the blessing came true. Though Dada made no study of palmistry, whenever he saw anyone's palm, he would tell them precisely of their past and would also predict things about their future, which always came true.

In the early years in Pune, when troubled devotees came to Sadhu Vaswani, he would often refer them to Jashan, who would read their palms and guide them accordingly. However, one day, Sadhu Vaswani called Jashan and said to him, 'My child, reading others' palms is an obstruction to your spiritual evolution. It will hamper your growth. It is a practise you should avoid in the future.'

From then on, it was as if the gift of reading palms was taken away from him. People would show their palms to him, but he could not speak a word about their past or future.

Later, when Dada was asked what he thought of palmistry and astrology, he would reply that astrology is a science, but it needs to be interpreted right.

As for Dada's own gift of palm-reading, he would remark that it was given to him by one saint and taken away by another.

Accompanying the master on one of his evening walks, Jashan saw a stone obstructing the path. Eager as always to be of service to the master, he rushed ahead and kicked the stone aside, lest it should hurt the master's feet.

Sadhu Vaswani reproved of his loving action. With characteristic insight, he asked him, 'If God dwells in the scripture, does he not dwell in the stone?'

Dada had imbibed the master's lesson so well that today he teaches us to treat everything, everyone, with respect, love and reverence. In a beautiful prayer, he says: 'O lord, teach me to regard all life as sacred. There is but one life that flows into all – men and birds and animals, living and non-living things.'

'May I touch everything with love, treat everyone with respect!'

Grand words alone do not reveal a saint's life to you. It is a minute, day-by-day account that shows you how a saint is made. Laymen thus learn that God's men, too, have to go through the same difficulties, trials and tribulations that we do, but where we hassle under pressure, they grow stronger in purpose. They make temptations their stepping stones to lofty goals and nobler pursuits in life.

Engrossed in his own thoughts, Jashan was once accosted by a traffic policeman for cycling along the wrong side of the road. Thinking that he could take advantage of the situation, the policeman said he would oblige him and let him off if he pays a small amount of money to him.

'I'd rather go to the police station with you,' said young Jashan, politely but firmly, making his point. He would not encourage bribery. Incensed by what he regarded as the young man's stubborn refusal to pay up and leave, the policeman asked him to walk by the roadside while he wrote out a receipt for the fine.

But he simply ignored Jashan, while he stopped other cyclists, motorists, deliberately letting the young man sweat it out in the sweltering heat of the sun.

Jashan despaired of trying to catch the constable's eye. But, unwilling to waste any further time, he drew out the proofs of Sadhu Vaswani's monograph on Tukaram, which he was carrying in his bag and began to go through them once more. As a matter of fact, he had been cycling to the press to hand over the proofs, when he was caught by the constable.

Intrigued that his victim was absorbed in reading, the constable came over and took the proofs from Jashan. The cover page photograph of Sant Tukaram startled him.

'What is this?' he demanded suspiciously. 'It is a book on Sant Tukaram, written by our guru, Sadhu Vaswani,' Jashan replied politely. 'I was taking the proofs to the press and I was pre-occupied with the task, which is why I must have swerved to the wrong side.'

'Who are you? And who is your master? Which part of India do you come from?'

'We are from Sind, which is now in Pakistan. We came over to Pune after the Partition.'

'You are Sindhi refugees in Pune and you venerate our Sant Tukaram,' said the policeman, a lump forming in his throat, 'Do you know my name is Tukaram! I would like to see your master.'

'Oh, you are always welcome to visit us,' Jashan warmly said to him. 'Sadhu Vaswani will be happy to meet someone who bears the name of Sant Tukaram. And let me tell you, we will offer you prasad when you come to our ashram. But right now, I will not part with a paisa unless you give me a receipt for it.'

Police constable Tukaram let Jashan go, waving him off with a broad smile. 'No fine, since you are doing God's work and spreading the word of our saints,' he called out in parting.

When Sadhu Vaswani decided to build the Gita Mandir at the Mission's campus in Pune, Jashan was put through a tough experience – and once again, with the grace of God and the guru, he passed the test.

It happened this way. All the volunteers at the Mission had been allotted different duties in respect of the plans to build the Gita Mandir. Dada was assigned the duty of raising ten thousand rupees for the construction of the mandir.

Jashan, who was still in his early 30s, had his own qualms and reservations about asking people for money. He cringed at the thought of going to friends and begging for donations. But he had promised himself to walk the way of obedience. He thought of the master walking the way of the fakir all those days ago in Sukkur. If Sadhu Vaswani could take the lowest place, was it not incumbent upon his dear, devoted disciple to do the same?

The next morning Jashan presented himself at the house of Mr Boolchand. The family welcomed him warmly, and as they were just about to sit down for breakfast, they earnestly requested Jashan to join them.

Jashan only looked at the sumptuous breakfast placed before him and it seemed to have choked his throat. He lost all his appetite, thinking of the ordeal ahead.

The meal was over, and Mr Boolchand invited the young man to join him in the library. Jashan was grateful that he could do his 'begging' in private, away from the family members. He cleared his throat and made mental preparation to begin, when Mr Boolchand sat down at his desk and said to him, 'Dear Jashan, it is God's grace that has brought you here today. Last night, the thought came to me that I must make a small contribution to Gita Mandir that is being built by Sadhu Vaswani. I have written out a cheque, and I request you to hand it over to Sadhu Vaswani as my humble offering.'

Saying this, he placed the cheque before Jashan, who could not believe his eyes when he read the figure on the cheque – it was for the sum of exactly ten thousand rupees.

Once Jashan said to the master, 'You always suggest that we think of God even as we attend to our daily work. How is that possible? When we do our duty, we need to focus all our concentration on it to do the work well. How can we continue to think of God at such times? It is impossible to focus on two things at the same time!'

Sadhu Vaswani listened patiently but did not reply immediately to his nephew's impatient query. Jashan repeated the question, thinking it had gone unheard. Sadhu Vaswani remained non-committal and did not give any response. Instead, he asked Jashan to take him for a drive. Putting aside his doubts, Jashan joyfully took his master for a long drive.

On the way, as they enjoyed the beautiful breeze, Sadhu Vaswani started an interesting conversation with Jashan. Jashan, with his hands placed firmly on the steering wheel and driving expertly, continued to participate animatedly in the conversation. Suddenly Sadhu Vaswani said, 'Now did you get an answer to your question?'

'Which question?' asked Jashan, startled. The question he had raised earlier in the day had completely escaped his mind.

Sadhu Vaswani answered, 'You have been wholeheartedly immersed in the conversation with me, and yet you have been driving with full focus and attention. Why can you not do the same with God? We can easily continue to chat with him, while doing our worldly chores. His presence can always be in our consciousness. We can carry his fragrance and aura with us even as we cope with our daily lives.'

Those were indeed unforgettable days when the master lived and walked and moved amongst his devotees, blessing every moment of their lives with his physical presence, even as he inspires and moves thousands of us today, and touches every aspect of our lives with his spiritual power.

The senior devotees would recall those bygone days with nostalgia and tell us that it is difficult to recapture the zeal and spirit with which all volunteers worked. The Mission was, at that time, not the huge organization which it is today. There was no organizational structure or hierarchical administrative set-up. All the work was done by dedicated volunteers.

One day Jashan found himself attending to a routine maintenance job in the Morris car he used to drive then. There was a wire that had to be soldered. Jashan had an old-fashioned soldering iron. He used an extension wire to connect it to a plug point in the main building and began to attend to the job.

Halfway through, someone called out to him to attend a phone call. As he went in to the office, he took care to switch off the power at the plug point.

A few minutes later, he returned to the car. He only had to check that the point was in place. It seemed fine, so he decided to take his equipment inside, and close the bonnet.

No sooner did he put his hand on the soldering iron than he saw stars – he saw a void brighter than the sun confronting him, overwhelming him, drawing him within.

Dada recalls that maybe, he cried out; perhaps his whole life flashed before him in an instant – in a microsecond he saw thirty odd years flash by. Within that microsecond, he thought of his beloved master, his loving mother, his brothers and sisters ... how he wished he had the chance to bid them all a final farewell.

This was the end, he thought to himself. He thought of the master, and he begged for his grace to lead him across the void, safely to a life beyond death.

But he would live to tell the tale. As God had other plans for him!

What had really happened was: Jashan had switched off the power to the extension box when he went in – for he was always a careful worker. But it was a huge, old-fashioned switch board with several switches and power points. Someone had switched the power on by mistake. And when Jashan tried to detach the soldering iron from the extension, he got an electric shock.

Those days, Sadhu Vaswani spent much of his time in silence and contemplation. He was not keeping well at that time, and was unable to sleep at night; whenever he was overcome by exhaustion which kept the pain in abeyance, he would fall into a light sleep. Devotees would close the door of his kutiya to ensure that nobody disturbed his much-needed sleep, and it was Jashan's task to ensure he was not disturbed.

One day a young man, who had resolved to travel across the country on his bicycle, came to get Sadhu Vaswani's blessings for his venture. Full of ambition and excitement, he was certain that he would get to meet the master right away and have a private conversation with him.

He was greeted by Jashan outside the master's kutiya. Jashan pointed to the closed door of Sadhu Vaswani's room and informed him that he could not be disturbed; when the master was ready to receive visitors, he would open the door himself.

The young man could not take such a response from one whom he considered absurdly young. Enraged, he shouted, 'Who do you think you are? How dare you stop me from meeting Sadhu Vaswani? Do you know who I am and what a tight schedule I have? I will not be kept waiting.'

'Dear brother, the master's door is closed and we cannot disturb him now,' Jashan replied, firmly but politely.

In sheer rage and frustration, the impudent young man slapped Jashan on his face. Completely unperturbed, Jashan remembered the words of Jesus Christ that his master so often quoted to him, 'If someone strikes thee on the right cheek, offer him the left,' and so, he offered him the other cheek. The man, even more enraged, thinking that Jashan was being impudent, he slapped him even harder. Jashan spoke not a word nor did he remonstrate; he remained calm and silent.

Shortly thereafter, the door opened and Jashan invited the young man into Sadhu Vaswani's room. The master saw the red marks on his dear disciple's face, but he uttered not a word; he only raised a hand to his own cheek, as if he were in pain! Only master and disciple knew what passed between them. Sadhu Vaswani received the visitor in his usual warm and loving way, giving him generous gifts as prasad.

A devotee who had watched all the commotion created by the visitor reported the matter to Sadhu Vaswani when the man had departed. The master was moved to tears and warmly embraced his dear Jashan. He felt fulfilled at having a disciple who was a man of true humility, for only such a one can be a man of forgiveness.

Even as a youth, Jashan's tender heart was always on the lookout for ways and means by which he would be able to alleviate the sufferings of people. In those days, homoeopathy was gaining popularity as an alternative therapy with fewer side effects. Ever ready to learn something new, he took a keen interest in it, and with his sharp intellect, mastered this therapy. He then started administering the sweet pills with sympathy to those who suffered. He blended sympathy and love to his homoeopathic medicines. No wonder that his medicines worked miracles for those who took them!

Dada's prescription for good health has always been to consult the four 'special' doctors:

One, Dr Quiet: Spend some time in silence every day and sing the Name of God.

Two, Dr Diet: See that your food is simple and nutritious and free from violence.

Three, Dr Sunshine: Go for long, brisk walks every day.

Four, Dr Laughter: Develop a healthy sense of humour.

In 1958, Sadhu Vaswani expressed the desire that the occasion of Jashan's 40th birthday (2 August) be celebrated in a fitting manner. This was not only the first official celebration of Dada's birthday by the sangat; it was also an indication to many that their dear Jashan was being chosen to continue the master's work. In this way, the master also established the tradition whereby Jashan's birthday celebration would become an annual celebration for the sangat.

A year later, on his 41st birthday, Sadhu Vaswani read out to the sangat the message that he had written for Jashan:

How blessed are we to have one such as him in our midst! And on this auspicious day, I breathe out an aspiration that my dear Jashan may go from heart to heart, home to home, nation to nation, carrying with himself the message of the rishis and sages of India.

And today, I have been saying to myself, 'My reverential salutations to those who seek the Beloved in the temple of the heart!' Most of us are busy running after wealth and possessions, hankering after name and fame. Only a fortunate few seek the Beloved. Only a blessed few seek to enter the shrine of the heart. To this category belongs my dear child, Jashan! He has sought to find the Beloved in the cave of his heart. In quest of the Beloved has he undertaken the journey within!

It was clear to an elated sangat that Jashan was indeed the chosen one. They felt safe and secure, knowing that the mantle of the master would one day rest on his young and able shoulders. And the sangat loved their young leader. He had been the exemplary disciple who, in the flower of his youth, when he had talent, success, personality, acclaim, and a brilliant future before him, had chosen, instead, to walk the straight and narrow path to the temple of the Beloved. Uncompromising in his quest, and steadfast in his devotion and service to the guru, he had reached his destination. Having attained that, he continued to serve the master with utmost humility and love. He retained his discipleship. Therefore, he was worthy of becoming, eventually, a master in his own right.

'CHILD OF MY TEARS!'

In 1960, on his 42nd birthday, Sadhu Vaswani wrote the following message for Jashan:

Child of my tears and prayers; Child of destiny!

This day I give thanks to him, the builder of destiny, that I have seen your face again and touched your feet and been blessed once more. I know I soon must quit this scene and rise from flame to flame and seek the stars. India, alas, is broken and the world is sad and lonely. A prayer rises in my heart, today, that you may still trust the rishis, the seers of the secret of life; that you may always have a heart of sympathy and love; that you may always seek your joy in communion with the common life and in the songs of children; and that, in the tumult and noise of modern life, you may still bear witness to the city of saints and sages.

Rich is your spiritual inheritance from your revered father. Compassion is the crowning aspiration of your life. Is not compassion the Ganga, which flows on, gently pouring in the heart the water of healing that the sad world needs? Is not compassion the key to that freedom which we find in the hearts of the noblest and the purest among mankind? Far from my home am I today. Blessed be the name of the Lord that, in my exile here, I have been blessed by you and taught by you the great lessons of compassion and sympathy. To him, I bow down with a prayerful heart. May he grant you strength and illumination to fulfil your mission in life.

Last night I went afar from you: I know not where I wandered in homeless space. Methinks I saw God lonely, standing in a corner, and dreaming his dreams and saying, 'Dreamers I need!' You are one of his dreamers! May your life be richly blessed in the holy service of sympathy and love! And may you bear witness, wherever you be, to the tree beneath which the Buddha sat to receive enlightenment – the Bodhi Tree of brotherhood and love, of fellowship between all nations, all races, all religions, all countries, all communities, fellowship between the East and West.

This was indeed a veritable roadmap that the master set out for his chosen spiritual heir and successor. 'Child of tears' and 'Child of prayers' refers to the great tapasya that the master and disciple had gone through to be with each other and shoulder the burden of their spiritual journey. It is also an expression of deep gratitude and joy, for, as Jesus Christ said, 'Many are called, few are chosen.' For the sake of these fortunate few, saints take interest in several seekers after truth, but only a few chosen ones will rise to the pinnacle of glory. For the sake of these few select ones, saints draw innumerable souls in the hope that the former will fling asunder their worldly fetters and devote themselves solely to God.

'Child of tears' also refers to all that the master invested of himself in nurturing the one who came to him as a tender sapling, raising it into a powerful, majestic tree that was now ready to offer shelter to many. Tears, according to Sadhu Vaswani, are of great significance in the spiritual journey. 'For without tears,' he says, 'there is no real yearning.' He believed that it is only when you shed tears of longing, the tears of yearning for the Lord that you draw close to him. 'Radha,' he said, 'shed tears, and only then did she get her Shyam.'

In this message are also spelt out the concerns of Sadhu Vaswani, which he was directing his disciple to address. The first was the state in which India found herself. She had indeed gained independence but had yet to attain true freedom: Freedom from want. It was the master's firm belief that more than political leaders, men of sacrifice and service were needed to lead India out of poverty, injustice, and divisiveness into a future era of glory and greatness. It would be the life mission of his 'child of tears' to awaken young India to the timeless wisdom of the rishis; to the understanding that only through sympathy and love, service and sacrifice that India could be uplifted.

Thus, did the guru publicly anoint Jashan. The disciple had become an instrument, tuned to perfection, and fit to render any melody composed by the master from the earthly plane or from beyond the stars.

A spiritual teacher is always a source of comfort and moral support to distressed souls. He is a fountain of love and sympathy, a reservoir of inner strength, a beacon of light to whom we turn to in hours of crisis. When our hearts crave for love, when we are wretched and miserable, it is to the guru that we turn for grace and guidance.

People of all classes and communities flocked to Sadhu Vaswani. With broken hearts and tearful eyes, they turned to him for comfort and cheer. He received them with love and compassion and they always went back with renewed spirit and faith. Jashan, who was in the constant company of the master, was both a witness and a participant of the healing process. He would lead the distressed to his master's side; he would make the appointments; he would watch the master comfort them.

When the master was confined to bed from 1960 to 1966, his fragile health made it impossible for him to personally meet the hundreds who flocked to see him every day. And so, it was up to the disciple to undertake the master's responsibility. How well he did it! The wretched in spirit, the poor and the miserable, the orphan and the widow – he comforted and consoled them, wiped away their tears, bringing a ray of hope into their lives.

Dada continued to do this noble service. In the true spirit of the master, he dispelled gloom and darkness, spreading the sunshine of hope and joy.

As a young seeker, Jashan had argued, discussed and debated freely with his master. If the questioning spirit had dominated one phase of his spiritual growth, there came, later, a phase of absolute and complete acceptance.

At that time, Sadhu Vaswani was ailing and in severe pain. All night long, Jashan had been awake, administering whatever comfort he could give to the master. Finally, overcome by exhaustion, both guru and disciple drifted into sleep, in the forenoon on the following day. When Jashan woke up with a start, it was midday. The master was awake too, and enquired, 'What is the time now?'

'It's just past twelve in the afternoon,' Jashan replied. 'Should I bring you something to eat?'

'You're mistaken,' said the master. 'It is past midnight now.'

Without hesitation, Jashan agreed. 'The master is always right,' he said to himself.

Dada told later that with faith in the words of the master, he went out to the verandah and looked up at the sky. In his mind there was no doubt that it was midnight, as his guru had said.

And believe it or not, on that memorable cloudy afternoon, Jashan did, indeed, behold the stars.

A NEW CHAPTER BEGINS

St Mira's College was established in 1962 despite great opposition from the sceptics (some of them, actually well-wishers) who felt that an exclusive girls' college would not survive for long in the academic environment of Pune. They cautioned Sadhu Vaswani that similar attempts had been made before by other local institutions, but their endeavours had failed.

Sadhu Vaswani was undeterred. With the master's blessings and inspiration, the Brotherhood Association launched this ambitious project.

Professor K. N. Vaswani, a senior professor from Sind, who had written extensively on Mahatma Gandhi and Indian thought, was appointed as the first principal of the college. However, he could not continue for long. The vacancy had to be immediately filled in by someone. A few applications had been received and candidates were interviewed by the board, but none was found suitable. The college could not be entrusted to people who were not in tune with the high ideals and values that Sadhu Vaswani had placed at its core.

Sadhu Vaswani then requested Jashan to accept the post. Thus began yet another phase in the young disciple's life. He accepted the request in what had become his life's motto now: Thy will be done.

When the master decided to establish St Mira's College, the Brotherhood Association had to pay an affiliation fee of rupees 25,000 to the University of Poona – an exorbitant sum in those days! This amount had to be deposited every year, for a period of four years. The first 25,000 rupees came in the form of a humble offering by the renowned barrister, Mr H. G. Advani, who was the founder-president of the Hyderabad–Sind National Collegiate Board in India. The next 25,000 rupees had to be paid the following year. How could they come up with the next installment?

Sri Gangaram, who was the Secretary of the Brotherhood Association and looked after all educational and financial matters of the Association, was in a quandary. He had to fill up a form with the stipulated information, namely the bank where the college had its account. Sadhu Vaswani filled up the details, 'Our account is with the Bank of Providence,' he wrote, and he smiled at Baba Gangaram, saying, 'The Bank of Providence never fails; it will give us the right amount at the right time.'

Anxious about deadlines, Baba Gangaram came to Sadhu Vaswani and said that there were only fourteen days left before which the money had to be paid to avoid disaffiliation. Every day he met Sadhu Vaswani to remind the master of the deadline. Sadhu Vaswani would listen to him patiently and only give his enigmatic smile as a reply.

And the countdown went on. Finally, Baba Gangaram came to him and said that there were only three days left before which the affiliation fees had to be deposited. On that day, around 2 p.m., a lady came to meet Jashan. She was from an affluent

Sindhi business family and had come to offer her respects to Sadhu Vaswani. She was delighted to see Jashan, as many years ago they had been classmates in college. She was in fact, one of the young ladies, whom Jashan had tutored in Karachi. Maya B. Ramchand would later become the chairperson of the Sadhu Vaswani Mission, Mumbai, and offer yeoman services to the Mission. Eagerly, she said to him, 'Can you please advise me on an important matter? I would like to offer the association a small sum that I am carrying for a good cause. Can you suggest something worthwhile?'

Jashan smiled and said to her, 'I know a good cause that needs your help.' He took the lady to Sadhu Vaswani and told the master about her generous offer. Sadhu Vaswani sent for Baba Gangaram; as Secretary, he was asked to receive the donation from the lady, and requested to count the unspecified amount – it was exactly 25,000 rupees.

A PRINCIPAL OF PRINCIPLES

As a principal, Jashan also taught in the college. He gave lectures on civilization science. Usually, college students are given to bunking lectures. But when he was in the class, everyone loved to be present. One of the students in his class recalled at an alumni meet much later that principal Jashan's lecture on the early civilizations of the world, with his vivid accounts of people and their cultures, was so eloquent and captivating that the students felt they were watching a motion picture.

Jashan too, was not the kind of teacher who would deliver his prepared lecture as a set piece and go away; he was very particular that each and every student was involved in the class, and each one understood what was being taught. Once, he was explaining the structure of the atom to his class; some of the students could not grasp the lesson easily. He saw expressions of bewilderment on a few faces; he redrew the figure on a larger scale on the blackboard and repeated his explanation. When this too, could not help the last few students, he took a piece of paper and created a three-dimensional model, which took the point home to all students. The class was indeed thrilled.

His lectures were always very interesting and illuminating because he blended anecdotes, general knowledge and jokes along with teaching the scheduled syllabus. His lecture always started with a short prayer. He was very punctual and expected his students also to be on time.

However, there was one student who would always come late to class. Principal Jashan would be so absorbed in his lectures that he would hardly notice her quietly slip into the lecture hall and sit in the last row.

One day, he noticed her entering the class late and did not approve of her late arrival. Later, the girl went to the office and explained to him the reason for her delay. She was the mother of a small child and had to drop the child at school before she came to the college. Her delay was therefore unavoidable.

Next time, when principal Jashan noticed her entering late, he stopped his lecture, welcomed her and explained to all the students the reason for her late arrival.

Time and again, he would bring snacks and other eatables for his students. His tender love and concern, his spirit of understanding and helpfulness endeared him to one and all.

Eager patrons and devotees had by now contributed to build a hostel for college students and M. K. Hostel was inaugurated in the year 1965. At that time, there were just seventeen students in the college hostel. Their principal cared for the hostelites as he would care for his own younger sisters. If one of them fell ill, he would pay a personal visit to the sick room with the doctor. When a visiting devotee/donor/patron offered dinner to the senior members of the satsang, he would always make sure that the hostel girls were invited to the feast. The seeker-turned-academician always retained his humane and best human traits.

As the principal of St Mira's College for Girls, he was deeply loved and admired by the staff and the students alike. Being a saintly soul, his spirituality was never of the holier-than-thou variety. On the contrary, he specialized in the art of making others feel at ease and welcomed, regardless of whether he was with visiting dignitaries, professors, doctors, peons or children. The college students adored him because of the sympathy, guidance and understanding he gave to them, they found it so easy to approach him with their personal problems. They always found a kind and sympathetic friend and mentor in him.

We speak big things, make grand statements about women's empowerment today. But Jashan practised the ideal in his day-to-day work as a principal.

Two Muslim girls, who found it difficult to pay the college fees, once approached him with the request to extend the last date of payment. When principal Jashan probed a little further, the girls spontaneously unburdened their hearts. Theirs was not at all an easy, carefree life. They came from a poor family which lived from hand to mouth. They were first-generation learners and the family had to make sacrifices to afford their higher education; the parents had consented to make this effort, only because they had complete trust in the safety and security of Mira College, and its saintly founder, Sadhu Vaswani.

To help pay their college fees, the girls had hired a sewing machine and had stitching clothes to earn a living. When their principal heard this, his compassionate heart was moved. An instant decision was taken and promptly conveyed to the office. Not only were they exempted from paying fees thereafter, but all the fees paid by them earlier was reimbursed. He even went a step further and got them a new sewing machine so that they could save on the rent of the hired one.

Times have changed since the halcyon days of the 1960s, but Dada's devotees have proved to be benevolent donors, offering freeships, scholarships and other forms of financial aid to such genuinely needy students, who, for one reason or the other, are not entitled to government scholarships. Books, notebooks, food, clothes and even transport costs are provided to many of them. What is more important, all help was extended to them discreetly, without fanfare.

New recruits who were privileged to serve the college under Dada recall that the moment they met him was indeed a transforming occasion. They felt elevated and inspired; it was no routine job they were getting, but a vocation to teach and serve and become a part of a noble Mission and vision. Here, they soon realized, there was no room for petty prejudices and negative attitudes; only a great ideal to follow, and a spiritual luminary who was always available to show them the way forward.

Humour was never absent when principal Jashan was around. Once, a young English teacher came with a complaint to him that girls from the vernacular medium were insisting on joining the optional English class which required a high standard of comprehension and writing skills. Gently, he explained to her that the girls' ambitions deserved to be respected, and no opportunities should be denied to them for their advancement. The teacher, whom he knew to be capable and caring, should take extra efforts with these students and bring them at par with the rest of the class. With a twinkle in his eyes, he added, 'You know very well that they will add much needed ballast to your class.'

On another occasion, a local inquiry committee from the University of Poona was visiting the college for the purpose of extension of affiliation. Looking at the plan of the college building, one of the members asked the principal, 'Which is the largest room in the college?' Without a moment's hesitation, he answered, 'The room for improvement, of course.' After a moment's startled silence, the committee broke into a hearty laugh.

The Sanctuary, a daily early morning period devoted to the Art of Living (a name chosen in the 1930s) was first conceptualized and put into practise by Sadhu Vaswani from the earliest days of Mira School in Hyderabad–Sind. It was a compulsory period for all the classes. It was the first period of the day and all the students sat on the floor, in the moment of humility and reverence, to share thoughts on living life the right way. This practise is continued till this day in all the Mira institutions which are named after Sadhu Vaswani from 1966.

The principal addressed the Sanctuary every Tuesday and Friday. Students would flock to sit in the first row, to be able to see him and catch his every word and expression. His brief but powerful reflections on the thought for the day, or on a great one of humanity, were not only heard attentively, but also appreciated deeply and inscribed on the hearts of the students.

St Mira's College had a unique aura. Anyone, regardless of the hierarchical order, was free to walk to the principal's room and discuss their grievances. The principal was always accessible, and always ready to lend a sympathetic ear to them. At the outset, candidates who appeared for interviews were daunted by his presence, but his warm demeanour made them feel at home. He would begin by telling them quite disarmingly, 'I am not an expert at your subject. But I am here to learn something from you.'

The concept of learning-by-doing is highly recommended for school children. At St Mira's, the idea of learning-by-watching prevailed. Watching the principal go about his daily work and do small deeds of humility served as an inspiration to the onlookers.

Principal Jashan led from the front, participating in all the activities of the college. He was what we would call a hands-on leader today. When a teacher could not make it to her class, he would gladly step in for her, handling English or Civics with effortless ease. He participated in the mandatory staff events on the annual sports day too. Here, he excelled in slow and fast cycling. He took the lead in the social service programmes. Bands of young girls used to carry eatables cooked with their own hands and other useful articles, and distribute them in the cottages of the poor.

He urged the students to hone their skills and develop their overall personality, because they were the builders of the future. The woman-soul, he urged, quoting his beloved master, would lead us upward.

This is the philosophy which persists in St Mira's institutions even now. Every day the girls of St Mira's undertake some act of *seva* (service) – it could be feeding the birds, or serving poor children, or the inmates of a blind home. The point is, they do it all, in the spirit fostered by the founder.

And the result? More compassionate students, who are sensitive to the reality of hardships and sufferings around them. The education imparted in St Mira's College does not aim at developing the intellect alone, but also the hand and the heart; above all, it is meant to cultivate the soul.

His humility has always been profound. Even at the close of an interview for a vacancy in the college, he would say, 'I am not a principal. I am but a labourer commissioned to work by my master in his vineyard.' The smoothness and efficiency with which the college functioned was a testimony to his administrative abilities. He brought to his work a single-minded devotion which no training could offer. To him, each individual staff member, student or peon, was equally dear and so he treated each and every one with love and consideration.

In those days when there were practically just a few colleges in Pune, he was not only a distinguished professor and principal, but also a member of the University Senate. He would drive to the University campus at the other end of the city to attend Senate meetings regularly. Every aspect of the university related matters was personally attended to by him, for he did not wait for office staff or others to brief him. Whether it was affiliation or examination related work, he ensured that he was apprised of all matters related to the college administration.

He would often tell his colleagues, 'The plane of action is also the plane of friction.' Differences of opinion and clashes of ideas were bound to crop up, as also complaints and protests. Carrying tales, gossip and backbiting were firmly discouraged with the words, 'You are mine and so is the other person.'

He was indeed a wonderful leader and educational administrator.

As a hands-on leader and principal, he had his finger on the pulse of the institution. With remarkable intuition and insight, he could sense the problems faced by his teachers and students and would solve them immediately.

In those days, the sanctuary of the college was held in the first-floor hall. As the college began to grow, the hall would fill to its maximum capacity with students and teachers. One professor, who had arthritis, sat outside the hall every morning, so that her chair would not occupy precious space which was so sought after in the sanctuary hall.

The principal noticed her sitting outside the hall and said to her, 'Dear sister, why don't you join us inside the sanctuary?'

The professor explained that due to the pain in her legs she was constrained to sit with her feet outstretched. 'How could I stretch my feet in a place of worship where God is present?' she asked Dada, with humility and sensitivity.

'Tell me where God is not,' the principal said to her gently.

Those simple, kind words so gladdened the professor's heart that from the very next day, she took her place inside the sanctuary hall, enjoying her favourite prayer sessions every day.

Even though he was a principal burdened with administrative responsibilities, he was also much loved as a professor at St Mira's

College. His way of teaching was uniquely his own. When he had to teach his class the law of gravity, he began the lesson by distributing juicy, red apples to the students. Needless to say, the students would never ever forget Newton!

Once, a professor of English requested him to teach a lesson from her English text to the class. It was a lesson on radio receivers and transmitters; not being conversant with science, she found it difficult to get the lesson across to her students, and therefore sought his help. He readily agreed to help her and engaged the class in English. There are no prizes for guessing who his most attentive student in class was that day! It was the senior professor herself, who listened to his masterly exposition with rapt attention. Later, she would recall the incident and talk of Dada's outstanding versatility as a teacher.

For him, the rule book was not the rigid arbiter of what was right. Once, a young English lecturer got engaged to be married, and within a short while, her marriage was solemnized, and she left for Canada with her husband. He and the staff members bid her a fond farewell and did not hold her back for the mandated three-month notice. But when no substitute could be found to teach her subject, linguistics, he did not allow the final BA students to miss classes in what they regarded as a difficult paper. He felt that the students should not be made to suffer, or their best interests compromised in any manner; he called up one of his own former students who had just passed her MA and requested her to take the class. He did not allow formal interviews and appointments to come in the way of a situation which required quick action. The end of the academic year was approaching, and the formalities would only be a hindrance. The young, new teacher who was understandably nervous, was encouraged to share her knowledge of the subject with her juniors of her alma mater. 'You are just out of your MA and the subject must be fresh in your mind. Go to class and share it with the students who are eager to learn from you.'

It was 100 per cent pass results in the linguistics paper that year!

An erstwhile student of St Mira's College, Neena, had a rebellious streak in her as many youngsters tend to have. She decided to just keep away from the Sanctuary period, the first lecture of the day, which all the students were expected to attend. It came to the notice of the teachers that she had avoided it for about a month. The vice principal of the college asked her for an explanation. Neena was always ready with an excuse. This time too she came up with one, but the authorities felt it was not good enough. She was asked to meet the principal.

Neena had great reverence for him and felt ashamed as she sat before him. She gave him a lame excuse that she had an outdated alarm clock that failed to function. She expected him to be furious and reprimand her for her behaviour. Instead, he heard her seriously and presented her with a brand new alarm clock. He requested her to attend the sanctuary period regularly. What followed was astounding. The recalcitrant student realized her mistake and from that day onwards, never missed a single day's sanctuary. The reformed truant, Mrs Neena Daryanani is now the chairperson of the Sadhu Vaswani Centre, Hong Kong.

ALWAYS THERE FOR THE MASTER

Building an institution is a tough task. And this is especially so when there are special ideals and values one wishes to uphold. Jashan's responsibilities as a principal were onerous; but he had taken on the task in the spirit of *arpanam* or offering to the master. It did not stop him from devoting his energy and efforts towards guru seva, as he had always done earlier.

The task of principal and professor of St Mira's College took up considerable time, as did the editing of the *East and West Series*. Handling it all with energy and dedication, brother Jashan continued to offer his personal seva to the master, day and night.

His duties included taking dictation from the master, attending to his correspondence, representing him at various meetings, and attending to all his personal needs.

Ever since he had had a fall in 1959, the master had been unable to walk. He would be carried outside his room on a chair by four disciples. When visitors came to meet the master, he wrote out beautiful thoughts for them on cards. Jashan would be asked to read these messages and interpret them. Gradually, Sadhu Vaswani withdrew more and more from outer activities, devoting a greater amount of his time to the inner life.

It is difficult for most of us to imagine the beauty of the relationship that exists between a true disciple and his master. The Hindu scriptures say that both the teacher and the disciple must be wonderful. In Sadhu Vaswani and Dada J. P. Vaswani, we have both the wonderful teacher and the wonderful disciple together, a perfect blend.

A true disciple ever aspires by conscious, deliberate actions, to spend all his time in rendering some personal service to his master, unconditionally. He weaves the fabric of his life with the threads of his master's will. Dada Jashan had the special privilege of living with his master. He watched him waking, eating, working, dreaming, sleeping, serving, chanting, meditating, ever-loving, denying himself to none.

Under the protecting wings of his master, Dada Jashan lived a life of undaunted courage, determination and fortitude, content to be able to serve him in the humblest capacity.

He attended to every need of the master. He would take everything out of his hands, into his own; carry all he needed, to his room; help in kindling the sacred *havan*-fire and, at the same time, attend to many other duties. Wings grew upon his heels at the sound of his master's dearly, loved voice.

These small acts were, to him, outer symbols of the deep devotion of his heart, little rituals that thrilled him as nothing else could have. To look at his beloved master was meditation for him. With immense gratitude and unspeakable reverence, he nourished his very soul at all the opportunities that were offered to him to live and learn in the master's presence. His real treasures were the gracious glances that the divinely loving master bestowed on him from time to time; a hand of blessing placed upon his head that sent a sensation throughout his body; a warm embrace that thrilled him; a word said or written upon a card that sank into his heart and was never lost or forgotten.

On one occasion, when the master was confined to the bed and Jashan served him day and night, the master said, 'I am reminded of my father when I see you looking after my needs with such tender concern.'

Through his example, Dada made it explicit that once a spiritual aspirant has set his foot firmly on the path, he must channelize all his energies exclusively to serving the master in every way possible. By attuning himself to the needs of the guru, he opens the door of receptivity to the divine grace that flows to every sincere disciple.

It was the 14 January 1966. Sadhu Vaswani expressed a desire to meet the sangat. Many thronged to receive his blessings. Among them were some who were poor in the wealth of the world. Sadhu Vaswani called Jashan and said to him, 'Jashan, bring me all my clothes. Keep only two for me. I shall distribute them among these pictures of God.'

How was one to know that the master would be a guest with them for only two more days?

On the 15th evening, Sadhu Vaswani again expressed a desire to be at the satsang. He met each and every one with the tenderness of a mother's heart.

After having his light dinner, he called Jashan and said to him, 'My head is in a whirl. Jashan, my child, be by me.'

These last words spoken by the master are so significant. The whole night the nephew sat close to him. Around 3 a.m., Dada and Sister Shanti felt that Sadhu Vaswani's breathing was not normal. Immediately, the best doctors of Pune were called up.

Dr Grant and Dr Wadia examined the master and expressed their considered opinion that he has had a brain haemorrhage. There was little that could be done for him. They advised that a nurse should be called to attend on him in the night.

For Jashan and Shanti, the grim vigil continued. Sister Shanti noticed that the twitching in the master's legs had stopped altogether, and brought it to Dada's attention. The two had to face the worst now, and offered their silent support to each other as the end seemed to draw near.

At about 8:20 a.m. on the morning of the 16th, the nurse advised Dada that they should turn over the master on to his other side, as lying on the same side would lead to congestion in the lungs. As the three of them gently turned the master over, he breathed his last.

A great hush seemed to descend on the world. Quietly, abruptly, Jashan left the sacred *kutiya* to go to his own room. He felt strange, forsaken, forlorn, as if he had been left in a terrible vacuum.

But this dark mood was instantly dispelled when he recalled the master's last words to him: 'Be by me!' Was he not with the master even now? Was not the master by his side? How could he ever think otherwise?

Devotees who were beginning to flock to the kutiya saw that Dada was calm, peaceful and actually had a radiant smile upon his lips as he came out of his room, shortly thereafter. The momentary feeling of loss had been replaced by the certainty that death could not touch the spirit. The master had neither left them nor had he gone away; he was with them, he would always be with them in spirit. Jashan knew the burden of responsibility that had been left upon him, and he was ready to bear it, in the certainty of his master's blessings.

'Be by me' – the master's last words of promise that echoed in his ears, kept Jashan going. Yet nothing could substitute for the radiant physical presence of his beloved master.

Hundreds of people poured into the Mission campus to bid their final farewell to the master. They were despondent at the departure of the blessed one, but Dada Jashan's composure gave them a reason to keep hope alive. The master's devoted disciple was now Dada Jashan to the members of the sangat.

THE LIGHT CONTINUES TO SHINE

The disciple's heart ached with pain when Dada Jashan lit the master's funeral pyre – the same spot where Sadhu Vaswani sought shade under the canopy of trees. Today, this is his sacred *samadhi*. From here, he continues to bestow his grace upon those bereft of hope.

Dada recollected that he had asked the master a question once, 'What is the happiest moment in the life of a guru?'

'When he loses his disciple,' Sadhu Vaswani had replied promptly.

Taken aback, Dada asked, 'But ... how is that?'

The master replied with a heart-warming smile, 'The guru works day in and day out so that the disciple may be led to the *sadguru* within his heart. And when this happens, the disciple himself becomes a guru. The guru loses a disciple. It is to him a day of great rejoicing. His work is over! His task is fulfiled!'

The day had arrived; the world had gained a guru in the same moment that a disciple was lost! Many years later, when writing about the *guru–shishya* relationship, Dada stated, 'The guru and the shishya do not live apart, they are one in consciousness, in function, and transmission of the spirit. A shishya, indeed, cannot live apart from his guru, for a disciple to be torn from his roots in the guru is suicide.'

Yes, Sadhu Vaswani had left the world, but a precious trace of him was still alive in the shape of Dada Jashan, who describes himself as the 'guru of none, disciple of all.'

'ANJALI' — AN OFFERING TO THE MASTER

The initial period after the departure of his guru was one of immense pain and grief. But Dada composed songs that were born out of love and reverence for the guru. The songs of separation that played on Dada's lips during this period are heart-wrenching. He invokes his master as a magician who coloured him with his magic and then one fine day, simply departed. Dada laments the fact that it took the master just one moment to withdraw, leaving his loved ones bereft and shattered. He simply slipped away, wounding many hearts. The disciple describes how his eyes can now only rain tears for his beloved.

Verse after verse, the anguish pours out. 'O beloved,' says he, 'You were like a swan bird that has left behind imprints for us to follow. Fragrant was your life, full of beauty, as the *leela* of the lord. You captured every heart with your leela and, then, you flew away. Your earthly span was like one brief night. How could I know that it would be so brief? The times we spent with you were sheer ecstasy. Now the thought of your departure plunges me in sorrow. What can poor hapless Anjali (Dada's nom de plume) do? She can merely go from pillar to post asking where she may find you again.'

Ever since, Dada has remained a minstrel. When in the midst of nature or when ecstatic, Dada's eyes close and his lips part to hum songs abounding in love, joy and peace. Devotees immediately write down the lyrics on a piece of paper lest they forget them.

Many of these songs in Sindhi have been compiled as the *Anjali Sangraha*. Dada bears the name Anjali when he writes. Anjali, the word that has a beautiful ring to it, means offering. And Dada's every word, every breath, each drop of blood, his entire life itself is an offering at the feet of his master.

TAKING ON THE MANTLE OF LEADERSHIP

The beloved of the sangat now came to be addressed as Dada Jashan or Dada J. P. Vaswani, but he was most fondly known as Dada. The sangat, drowned in loss and grief, requested Dada to be the Sole Life Trustee of the Brotherhood Association so that the multifarious service activities set up under the master's guidance would continue uninterrupted. On 21 February 1978, the association was renamed as the Sadhu Vaswani Mission. To the many thirsty ones who were eager to call him their guru, Dada would reiterate, 'Sadhu Vaswani can have no successor; for he lives and will continue to live, age after age. He has no need of a successor.'

Dada also shared with his fellow disciples what Sadhu Vaswani had said to him before he passed away: 'I can do greater things through you than I have done through this body.' And that was exactly what the disciples, led by Dada, resolved to do.

The passing away of Sadhu Vaswani took an emotional toll on Dada. He could not bring out the monthly magazine *East and West Series*, which had carried immortal monographs and brilliant sketches by Sadhu Vaswani centred around the great saints of all faiths. After a hiatus of six months, Dada finally brought out an issue. Significantly, it featured the last days of great ones, such as Chaitanya, Buddha, Father Damien, Sri Krishna, Jesus, Guru Nanak, St Francis, St Mira, Saint Tukaram, and Abu Hassan. Dada's own sister, Dadi Hari, who had been the headmistress of St Mira's School in Hyderabad–Sind, and had devoted her life to the cause, contributed a moving article on the last days of the master's earthly pilgrimage. She was also the author of Sadhu

Vaswani's biography in English, entitled *A Saint of Modern India* (Mira Union, Pune, 1975).

The numerous activities and service programmes of the sangat that Dada introduced after the departure of his guru bore the sacred name of his master. They were all consecrated to him and continue to be so. Repeatedly, Dada urged the sangat to practice experiencing the presence of the guru, to carry his name on their lips, his image in their hearts and his message in their deeds of daily living. As for Dada, his life was dedicated to serving his master, by upholding his ideals. After his early morning meditation, he would go into the kutiya of his guru to seek his blessings and receive his guidance. His evenings would also conclude with some moments of silent communion with the master.

A ten-feet-high bronze statue of the master was erected at the chowk (crossroads) near the Mission campus, now renamed as Sadhu Vaswani Chowk.

One of the first things that Dada laid emphasis on was *kaar seva*. He would motivate all the devotees to do seva with their own hands. He would personally join in the collective effort of cooking for and serving the poor, conceptualizing and carrying out projects for social welfare and rural development. Upon insistence, Dada also began to deliver regular talks during the satsang. The talks were initially restricted to Sundays when he spoke on the thought of the day. This would be drawn from the book of 365 thoughts written by Sadhu Vaswani in Sindhi, entitled *Prabhat ji Parde Mein* – In the Veil of the Dawn. Gradually, a pattern developed: On Thursdays and Sundays he would discourse in Sindhi, while on every fourth Thursday of the month, he would speak in English. The last Saturday of every month was especially devoted to addressing the youth.

Shanti, Sadhu Vaswani's adopted daughter, was devastated when the master passed away. She had come to the master as a ten-year-old girl battling a severe illness. Sadhu Vaswani had extricated her from the jaws of death when all doctors had given up hope. Thereafter, she refused to leave Sadhu Vaswani, who, she felt, had given her a new lease of life. Moving out of her parents' home, she became a member of the guru's household. Sadhu Vaswani formally adopted her as his daughter. Her purity, gentleness, single-minded dedication to Sadhu Vaswani and her immense compassion for all beings, were her special qualities that endeared her to everyone in the master's circle. Dada too was no exception! While Dada was intellectual, highly perceptive with a logical bent of mind, Shanti was emotional, deeply devoted, mystical in temperament and the embodiment of love. Just as it was for Jashan, there was absolutely no life, no world, nothing beyond Sadhu Vaswani for Shanti either.

Dada had always shared a very special bond with Shanti for two reasons: One, she was close to him in age and two, they were both extremely close to the master's heart. Dada often thought of her as a mother figure. In trying times, when the master was annoyed with him, Shanti would come to his rescue. She would soothe him and gently stress on the significance of investing unwavering faith in the guru. She would often tell him, 'Whatever happens, don't look left or right. Just look straight at your guru. Ultimately, victory will be yours.'

Sadhu Vaswani had always known that Shanti would never be the same after he would pass away. So, he entrusted his adopted daughter to Dada's special care in the days preceding his death. 'You must ensure that she is looked after well, Jashan,' he had said to his chosen disciple, 'for she will not be able to bear separation from me.'

It was Dada's considered opinion that Shanti had an ancient karmic link with the master, which had enabled her, at the tender age of ten, to abandon all ties of kith and kin and dwell at the feet of the master. For her, to live was to serve him, to love him, to draw nearer to him, all in utter devotion and self-surrender. She basked in the sunshine of his love and grace until she herself became a picture of love and compassion.

Shanti was afflicted by a cardiac problem that left her weak and exhausted. Dada did everything to fulfil the promise he made to his master. Every morning, after his period of prayer and silence, he would come down from his room on the second floor and bow down to her and greet her. In the evenings, he would sit by her side. Other devotees would often join him and a little satsang would ensue at her feet.

Dada Jashan treated Shanti with great love and reverence. And why not? She was like a flower whose fragrance would enchant those around her.

Since she had a heart problem, she could not accompany Dada anywhere. So, he would seek her permission before stepping out of the premises, whether it was for a daily walk, a satsang, or some errand. For Dada, everything Shanti said was a divine law.

Every evening, Dada would stroll around the Mission campus and Shanti would accompany him outdoors. However, she could not walk for long as her knees would give up on her too soon. Instead, she would sit on a bench and watch Dada continue his walk.

One evening, she told Dada that she would not be able to accompany him for the walk. 'I would like to rest for some time,' she said, 'you take your walk and come back. I will be waiting for you.' Ten minutes later, while Dada was still walking, someone rushed out to inform him about Shanti's health was taking a turn for the worse. Dada immediately rushed to her room and found her lying on the bed with eyes closed. A doctor was hastily summoned. He examined Shanti for a while and declared, 'There is no pulse and no sign of breathing.'

Dada was alarmed, 'Shanti, you can't do this to me,' he reproached his friend, fellow-disciple and upa-guru. 'You promised to wait for me.'

And then, the unimaginable happened! Shanti opened her eyes and looked at Dada. Perhaps she had been listening to him all this while, watching his despair. She smiled and gently placed her head in Dada's lap. She looked at his glowing face and closed her eyes once again.

Shanti survived the master by merely four years, giving up her body on 15 May 1970. Her ashes rest by the side of the master at his sacred samadhi. Every year, 15 and 16 May are observed as Shanti Mahayagna days in remembrance and honour of the great soul.

GOING THE EXTRA MILE

Until 1976, Dada served as the principal of the St Mira's College despite his hectic schedule and extensive travels. But a time came when he decided he had to give up the position.

Mrs Ratna Atam Vaswani was to be his successor. She was born into a family of Sadhu Vaswani's devotees. Incidentally, she also married into a family close to the master. Notwithstanding the pressing duties upon her as a mother, housewife and daughter-in-law in a joint family, she had been persuaded to do her MEd and MA in Philosophy by Dada. In 1972, she took charge of the Department of Education at St Mira's College. Later, she was made the vice principal of the college. She and her colleagues had the great privilege of serving under the stewardship of Dada as principal of the college, thereby imbibing the true spirit of Mira education derived from personal experience.

Mrs Ratna Vaswani recollects how Dada would save her the hassle of looking around for a substitute when a teacher was late for examination duty. Dada would step in unasked and distribute the answer sheets and question papers, so that the exams could begin on schedule. That aside, Dada would humbly do the duties assigned to a peon. He would himself ring the bell to mark the end of a lecture when a peon was not around.

Mrs Ratna Vaswani was astounded when Dada called her for a private meeting and requested her to take over as principal of the college, as the Mission and the satsang required all his time and effort. To Mrs Vaswani it was unthinkable, almost undoable to step into Dada's shoes as a principal. But Dada not only managed to convince her; but he even offered to be the vice principal for a year until she developed the confidence and acumen to take over the reins of the college. Mrs Vaswani was stunned by his magnanimity. She protested that it could not be, but eventually relented in obedience.

Their names on the muster exchanged places; from the position of vice principal, Mrs Ratna Vaswani's name went up to the first spot as principal; Dada's name followed as vice principal. But by no means was this a nominal change. For one whole academic term, Dada stood by the new principal and her band of teachers, attending meetings, taking on his administrative tasks as vice principal and ensuring that there was no vacuum when he demitted his office as professor and moved out of the day-to-day administration.

We live at a time when people are fussy, egoistical and very particular about their designations and appellations. We can only marvel at the humility and true greatness of someone like Dada, who, actually, stayed on to help the new principal settle into her role!

Principal Jashan Vaswani was now truly the man he had always wanted to be: The disciple carrying on the mission and the message entrusted to him by the master. The perfect disciple had been thrust by providence to take on the mantle of his guru, although, to the end of his days, Dada never ever allowed people to refer to him as their guru. He would respond to all such attempts firmly but kindly, 'I am the disciple of all, but guru of none.'

FIVE

In the Footsteps of the Master

'He has not left us. He has not passed away. He is with us, within us, by us, beside us, guiding us, guarding us, inspiring us, leading us on. And his voice says to us, "If you will grow, be humble as grass, patient as the tree, and prayerful as the daisy that turns its face to the sun!"'

– Dada J. P. Vaswani

For six years after the master departed, Dada made it a point to never stay out of the Mission campus overnight. His travels were restricted to visiting devotees in Mumbai or the surrounding areas of Pune, which would allow him to return on the same day. Sadhu Vaswani's sacred ashes were encased in urns placed in the kutiya. Dada verily believed that the urns containing the master's sacred ashes represented the physical presence of the guru.

Dada was the beloved one, the representative of God and guru to the devotees, who yearned to hear him address the satsang. Only he could effectively communicate and enunciate the master's message to them.

Invitations had started pouring in from devotees from different parts of India, and Dada now took on the mantle of the *yatri* – a traveller, a pilgrim – who must carry forward the message of his master to every nook and corner of the country. Dada began moving out on his pilgrimages 1972 onwards. He travelled extensively and regularly to cities and towns, where devout disciples and numerous followers of Sadhu Vaswani yearned to connect with him as well as the Mission. With Dada's unwavering commitment and tireless labour, numerous Sadhu Vaswani centres were set up all over India, where Dada was called out of love and reverence to perform *bhoomi puja* – consecration ceremony.

With devotees by his side, the journeys turned into spiritual sessions enlivened by kirtans, question-answer sessions, peals of laughter and, not to forget, storytelling events led by Dada himself. Plenty of wholesome prasad was available for all.

During those early days, Dada made it a point to visit many small towns and villages throughout Saurashtra, Gujarat and Maharashtra, where many Sindhis were settled. Akola, Miraj, Kolhapur, Sholapur, Junagadh, Adipur and Gandhidham were often on his itinerary. At many of these places, the devotees lived in humble dwellings, often without basic amenities. But this never discouraged Dada, who was used to putting himself and his comforts last.

People would wait at stations en route for Dada's train, just to speak to him once or catch a tiny glimpse of him!

In many places where Dada stayed, makeshift toilets were erected and Dada's own room often had nothing more than a hard bench or a charpoy. But none of this daunted Dada, who would halt for a day or night just to be able to hold an informal satsang with the local communities! Dada was a man on a mission to spread the message of his master among the devout and thirsty souls.

Once when he was in Baroda, Dada was invited to visit the jail and address the prisoners. The prisoners rejoiced at the thought of having a holy man amidst them. One prisoner, who had been given life imprisonment, requested that Dada meet him alone for a few minutes. Dada readily agreed. The prisoner sobbed and narrated with overwhelming emotion, the crime he had committed.

Falling at Dada's feet, he said to him, 'You are a holy man of God, I pray, give me your grace and ask God to forgive me.'

Dada, with his own handkerchief, wiped the tears that flowed down the prisoner's cheeks and lifted him up, saying, 'Brother, there is still hope even for the worst among us. For God is our divine mother and will wash our stained souls. Let us go to God as the universal mother in the spirit of a child, fallen and bruised, and say to her: Divine mother, cleanse me!'

During one of Dada's frequent visits to Gujarat, a group of poor villagers from the drought-stricken areas of Kutch had assembled to receive help in cash and kind. As a gesture of thanksgiving, they started singing kirtan and Dada readily joined in the chanting. At the close of the kirtan, Dada personally spoke to each one of them, enquired about their source of livelihood, looked into their needs and gave them the help they needed.

Suddenly, Dada noticed the torn and tattered shirt of one of the villagers seated at a distance. Dada went up to him and without a moment's hesitation, took off his own shirt and put it around the shoulders of the villager. The poor man's eyes lit up. He trembled with emotion at this personal service rendered by the saint's own hands. Dada patted him on the shoulder as if to soothe away his fears and comforted lovingly, 'You are my brother. Why should you not wear my shirt?'

Several invitations from the East and the West poured in and Dada agreed to visit a few far-Eastern countries, in addition to Sri Lanka.

A World Hindu Conference was to be held in Colombo in 1982 and an invitation was extended to Dada to address the delegates. Although Dada's health was not in the best shape ever since he returned from a yatra in December 1981, the devotees were assured of a miracle — and so it unfolded. On the day that the final decision was to be taken, Dada was fit enough to be permitted to undertake the yatra.

In a session presided over by Mr C. Rajadurai, Dada spoke on 'peace is your birth right' at the Ramakrishna International Hall, Wellawatte, Colombo. In his quest for service, Dada went among the poor folk of Colombo, who lived on the footpaths, and distributed food packets to them. He fanned some of the people sleeping on the roadside in the scorching heat. Taken by surprise, the poor folk couldn't help but wonder where the good samaritan had come from.

From Sri Lanka, Dada flew out to Hong Kong.

One day, the car in which Dada and his followers were travelling accidentally hit a cat which had swiftly darted across the road, seemingly out of nowhere. As soon as they reached home, Dada suggested that a prayer meeting be dedicated to the cat that had just been run over. In that solemn moment of the night, he asked for forgiveness and offered a moving prayer for the cat. The prayer elicited tears from many devotees. Dada skipped his dinner that night and was unusually quiet.

Alas! Many of us thoughtlessly take away the life of insects. It is Dada's belief that even if done unintentionally, we become an instrument of death, which only adds to our karmic burden.

At all the places Dada travelled, the followers found in his speeches new horizons opening up for them. They found Dada's views and teachings universal, encompassing all religions and all faiths.

'Noor-e-Illahi is what lights up everything, because there is not an atom which does not contain it,' Dada once said. 'To perceive this light within us and within all that is, is the purpose for which we are born on earth. However, we are unable to see the Noor-e-Illahi because we are not pure enough. When a man grows in inner purification, he sees within him a point of light which keeps on growing until it becomes a conflagration. Only then does he see this light in all that is! He becomes a servant of all, for he realizes that though the Noor-e-Illahi is in everyone, very few are aware of it!'

'What is your ambition?' someone asked Dada during a press interview at Jakarta.

'I have no ambition,' Dada answered. 'Every ambition is a chain that binds us to this earth. I but aspire to be a servant of my master, whose name my lips are not worthy to say.'

During his trips to the West, Dada spoke on various platforms and addressed the cosmopolitan audiences in the US with his trademark humility and wisdom. Dada's natural gift as an orator enthralled his audiences wherever he spoke.

Addressing diplomats at the Dag Hammarskjöld Auditorium of the UN, Dada said: 'Even if all the statesmen signed a declaration of peace, we would not have peace. Peace does not depend upon governments. There can be no peace in the world as long as the hearts of men are a volcano. Even if the governments were to ban the bomb, it would not lead to peace. For the bomb is only a symptom of the disease. We must treat the cause. So long as selfishness and hatred exist in the hearts of men, so long would wars continue to mutilate humanity. Therefore, if you would have peace, begin with the child.'

Among the volley of questions that came his way, one deserves mention, 'Why is there so much destruction? Is there any hope for this agitated age?' Dada smiled and said, 'Yes! Our hope is in our education. Begin with the child. If only we can bring up our children to blossom into men and women of the right type, who will bear witness to the ideals of universal brotherhood and peace in daily living, we will have contributed to the building of a new world order!'

Even during his hectic tour programme, Dada ensured he added service activities to his busy schedule every day, which would breathe a new hope and courage into people, regardless of their religion, nationality, gender or age.

As Dada's whirlwind tour continued, a lecture was organized in Florida on a subject dear to Dada's heart: The power of prayer.

An expectant crowd had gathered to hear him as the topic offered all kinds of interesting avenues for reflection.

A hush descended over the crowd as Dada rose to speak on how prayer is power. This power lies locked up within each one of us; it is up to each one of us to use this power wisely and well, he reminded the listeners.

After the talk concluded, there was a minute-long silence as the people were absorbed in the atmosphere created by Dada's words. One young girl, who was part of the crowd moved slowly towards the front and stood hesitantly near Dada. Dada looked at her lovingly and asked, 'My child, what is troubling you?' Tears streamed from her eyes and she told her story. She lowered her eyes as she admitted that she was a drug addict. She said, 'I want to rid myself of this terrible habit, I want to come out of it but I don't know how. Your words have inspired me and given me some hope. Is there a way out of this morass? Do you think prayer can help an offender like me?'

Dada immediately answered in the affirmative and then said kindly, 'Let us sit down here and pray together.' Dada sat beside the girl and prayed with her for half an hour, at the end of which she tremulously said, 'I think I feel strengthened. I don't think I will touch drugs again.'

The next day, someone who had witnessed the whole transformation praised Dada on changing the girl's life in such a dramatic manner. Dada's humble response was, 'I didn't change her life. She changed it herself by tapping into the power of prayer.' Such is the potent power of prayer.

At another instance, in Los Angeles, Dada spoke to a spellbound audience at the Balaji Temple. After his invigorating talk, a Sikh gentleman came and met Dada, pleading with him to accept him as a disciple. 'I have been deeply moved by your words and humility. Please accept me as your disciple.' Dada quietly answered, 'I seek to be a disciple myself.'

The next day, the man and his wife accompanied Dada on his morning walk. They plied Dada with several questions, and one of them was, 'Is the physical presence of a guru necessary for the spiritual advancement of a disciple?'

'Yes, in several cases,' Dada replied. 'When the disciple is in the physical proximity of the guru, all the negative aspects of the disciple are drawn out. The guru cleanses the inner *dosha*s of the disciple merely through his presence.'

'Dada,' the lady asked, 'if I, as a householder, grow in the spirit of detachment, will I be able to care for and love my children in the same manner as I am doing now?'

'Yes!' Dada answered without a trace of doubt in his voice. 'When you grow in the spirit of detachment, you will be able to do your duties better and in a more fulfilling manner. As a parent, you will not be attached to the child, and so, will have a better and greater perspective of the welfare and growth of the child.'

In Los Angeles, an American woman, Barbara, felt drawn to Dada and his teachings. She would accompany Dada for the morning walks. During her conversation with him, she told him, 'My dream has come true. I had been looking and longing for an Indian guru. And how fortunate I am to have met you. Seeing you, listening to you, touches a hidden chord in me. I long for God and want to realize him. But I have my duties towards my husband and children. How can I realize both?'

'There is no conflict between God and duty,' Dada explained to her. 'The very first step to God, affirms the Bhagavad Gita, is the performance of one's duty to the best of one's ability. Never stray from the path of duty, but offer every little thing you do to God. Practise his presence in your daily life. As you attend to your daily chores, let this aspiration spring from your heart: For thy sake, o Lord! For thy sake alone!'

At the Tenth Hindu Conference organized by the Vishwa Hindu Parishad of America in 1984, Dada delivered a fiery speech.

Among other stalwarts of Hinduism, seated on the dais were Dr Karan Singh, Swami Chinmayananda, Sri Keshavdas and Dr Gopal Singh. Speaking on the occasion, Dada said, 'In spite of the ravages of time, the Hindu faith lives on, for it has a message to give to the modern world – the message that there can be no true freedom without spirituality. The Hindu faith is not a creed or a dogma or a ritual. It is a *darshana* and a *marga* – an insight and a way of life.

'For the rejuvenation of the Hindu faith, three types of architects are needed,' and he went on to enumerate: 'The seer, the rishi, who alone can give us the right vision of freedom; the leader, whose essential qualities are unselfishness, simplicity, right judgement, and love for the poor and broken ones; the social servant, whose most important task is education of the true type. For building a universal creed of Hinduism, begin with the child. Take care of your children, for the nation walks on the feet of the little ones.'

At St James Independent School, London, where Dada was invited, his joy knew no bounds when he found that in a school where over ninety per cent of the students were of British origin, Sanskrit was being taught to the students. He learnt that the students also studied the great Indian scriptures – the Bhagavad Gita and Upanishads. Meditation was taught to them and vegetarian meals were provided too. Speaking to them, Dada exclaimed, 'In you and such as you lies the hope of a new tomorrow.'

He further narrated to them the story of heaven and hell. The students listened to him in rapt attention. The next day, he received a large package containing drawings, in which the students had depicted the story he had narrated to them. Some of them even corresponded with Dada when he returned to India.

At Bharatiya Vidya Bhavan, London, a citation was presented to Dada that referred to him as *Ajatashatru*, 'friend of all, enemy of none', 'one of the most distinguished sons of Mother India', and 'a citizen of the world'.

In India, once the dedicated secretary of the Mumbai Humanitarian League, Mr Mankar, revealed to Dada that he had been selected by the Animal Welfare Board of India to receive the Prani Mitra Award for the year. 'What have I to do with awards?' Dada asked in a matter-of-fact manner. 'I have done nothing to deserve the award. Awards and titles are chains. What has a seeker of God to do with them?' From then on, citations and awards for Dada were often announced as a fait accompli in his presence at public functions. On such occasions, Dada would accept their tributes in a spirit of humility, with the words, 'All glory to the master.'

Dada was always empathetic towards his followers; not just in his lectures but also in the way he touched lives through his actions. At a town hall in Ahmedabad in 1987, Dada was to deliver a lecture on life after death. He was requested to bless the people of the city as this was the fourth consecutive year that a drought had struck Ahmedabad. The words touched Dada's heart. In his lecture, he addressed the grief-stricken listeners: 'The people of Ahmedabad are passing through a difficult period. They do not need lectures but food. I request my friends to bring me wheat and other groceries and dry goods which I may send to the drought-stricken people in the villages.' Within a matter of minutes, large sacks of wheat were brought, which Dada passed on to the workers to be distributed among the poor. It was only after this that Dada proceeded to deliver his talk.

Everyone who ever saw and heard Dada, simply fell in love with him. 'Our hearts need to be saturated with love, for love is the light which will illumine the world. More than developed brains, we need enlightened hearts,' mentioned Dada at the Global Conference of Spiritual and Parliamentary Leaders on Human Survival held at Oxford in April 1988. His universal vision, his non-sectarian approach, his avoidance of any religious bias and his refusal to impose dogma or propagate rituals of any religion endeared him to the diaspora. Invited to inaugurate the St Thomas Orthodox Syrian Church at Kirkee, Pune, on 20 February 1993, Dada made a passionate defence of true religious faith, 'Today, in the name of religion, we have fights and feuds, sectarian strife, hatred and violence. Religion came to unite, to reconcile, to create harmony among men. Little wonder that young men and women today are turning away from religion. It is not religion which has failed us; it is we who have failed religion.'

Following his master's precept, he proclaimed, 'Let us talk of religion less and practise it more.'

'What humanity needs today is not merely philosophy or theology, but a message of assurance. People need to know that they are not alone, that they have not been abandoned; but that there is One who loves them for what they are, who cares about them. Philosophy and theology have so much to tell us about God, but people today want to experience God. There is a difference between eating dinner and merely reading the menu.'

'Peace does not depend upon outer things but resides within the soul. Before we can find a human balance for modern mechanized society, man must first find peace within himself. The key to human balance is reverence for nature and kindness towards all living beings,' affirmed Dada addressing the Fourth International Conference at the Global Forum of Spiritual and Parliamentary Leaders held at Kyoto, Japan in April 1993.

'*Vedanta* teaches that there is but one life in all,' Dada said at the World Vision 2000, a conference organized at Washington D. C., 1993. 'The one life sleeps in the mineral and the stone, stirs in the vegetable and the plant, dreams in the animal and wakes up in man. Creation is one family, and birds and animals are man's younger brothers and sisters. It is man's duty to guard them and protect them from the cruel knife of the butcher.'

He continued, 'The time has come when we must decide, once and for all, that all types of exploitation must cease. We must recognize the moral inviolability of the individual – both human and non-human. All types of human tyranny must cease if we are to have peace on earth.'

'Every animal has some fundamental rights', Dada pointed out, saying that the time had come when we must formulate a charter of rights for animals and a charter of man's duties towards the animal kingdom. The very first fundamental right of an animal is the right to live. No man can take away that which he cannot give. And since we cannot give life to a dead creature, we have no right to take away the life of a living one.

Hinduism is not just a religion, but a way of life. Dada's address emphasized that the Hindu way of life embraced God's creation in its entirety.

In his powerful and captivating address to the Parliament of World Religions, Chicago, in 1993, Dada traced the history of India's spirit of tolerance and harmony. He said, 'India has always stood up for religious harmony and understanding. Today, India is passing through a difficult period. But this is only a temporary, transitional phase. The history of India bears ample testimony to the fact that through the centuries, the truth and the message of religious harmony have influenced the Hindu people, Hindu society, Hindu political thought, Hindu state policy, both of large empires and small states, all over India. Unroll the pages of the past and you will find that among all the nations of the earth, India alone has greeted and welcomed with love and respect every foreign religion that entered the country. Judaism, Christianity, Islam, Zoroastrianism, Baha'ism, have all become naturalized in India, have become religions of India, and have been influenced by the Indian environment. When they first entered India, they were all received with respect and love. This is an outstanding example of history.'

Dada also delineated details of the conditions under which the early Jews, Christians and Zoroastrians first came to India and their warm reception by the Hindu people. He elucidated, 'India has become the land of many religions and has always respected every religion. For India has profoundly believed, through the centuries, that God is one, but the ways to reach him are many. The Hindus not merely tolerate, but accept every religion, praying in the mosque of the Muslim, worshipping before the fire of Zoroastrians and kneeling before the cross of the Christians, knowing that so many religions are but so many ways for the human soul to grasp and realize the infinite.'

Once, an American lady met Dada in Key West, Florida. She had read the Bhagavad Gita and was so inspired by it that she wanted to declare herself a Hindu. Dada's advice to her was truly significant, 'You must never do that. You will not draw closer to the heart of Krishna just by labelling yourself a Hindu. What the Gita offers, the Bible also offers. You must make an attempt to find it out and be a good Christian. A Christian can be equally dear to Krishna as a Hindu. For in the kingdom of God, there are no labels.'

According to him, true conversion was not just a change of labels. Converting a Hindu into a Christian or vice versa was not a change. Dada pointed out that by 'conversion' Jesus meant not change of label or conformity to a creed or dogma, but a change of mind and heart. True conversion can thus lead to a change of attitude, which can ultimately result in the transformation of one's life. In the kingdom of God, we will not be judged according to our labels, but according to the life we have lived.

In his inimitable way, Dada tells us that our religion is like our mother and all religions are sisters. So, if Hinduism is your mother, Christianity is like your aunt. He would himself often say, 'If Krishna is my father, Christ is my uncle!'

As we do not choose the family into which we are born, even so, we do not choose the religion into which we are born. For the choice made by God is surely for our highest good. We cannot give up our mother and adopt another's.

Dada once met an American Christian brother in New York, who said to him, 'Why do our missionaries take the trouble of visiting distant lands and converting people to Christianity? Why can't they convert the Christians in America to Christianity?' 'All great religions are equally true,' Dada said. 'Humanity is the greatest religion, so instead of converting from one religion to another, we should rather strive to be better human beings.'

It is difficult to imagine a saint with an outlook as liberal as Dada's. Hindus call him their own; Muslims consider him a brother; Christians marvel at his knowledge of the Bible; Parsis join Dada as he celebrates days special to them; Jains regard him as an apostle of non-violence and ahimsa; and the Sikhs rejoice to see Dada at the Modikhana, selling articles for the service of the needy. At the Mission satsang, 'multi-faith prayers' are often held, with priests, rabbis, *maulvi*s and pandits reciting from the scriptures of their respective faiths. The atmosphere is electric and the huge satsang hall is thronged by the devouts.

Dada's universal outlook is beautifully expressed in his famous fellowship song:

The whole earth is our Country,
And the sky is its dome;
The nations are as mansions
In the Heav'nly Father's Home!

We of, China and Japan,
Of, 'Merica and Ind,
We all are brothers, sisters
Of, Soviet and of Sind!

Hindus, Muslims, Christians,
all! Buddhists and Bahais
We share each other's friendship,
And th' love that never dies!

One is the faith we live by;
One is the song we sing!
With little deeds of service
We worship Him, our King!

We feed those that are hungry,
We work for no reward;
We help the poor and the needy
For Love of Him, our Lord!

We're friends of all the friendless,
Servers of those in pain!
We're brothers of the voiceless.
The cow, the dog, the hen!

We trust in God, His mercy,
And in ourselves believe!
All what today we hope for
We shall one day achieve!

Hand in Hand we march on still!
A better World to build,
A World of love and laughter,
With peace and plenty filled!

('Tear drops' by J. P. Vaswani, 1967)

For Dada, all religions were one and he had the greatest respect for each one of them. He would be deeply impressed by our Muslim brethren, including little children, who fast for forty days during Ramzan.

Mr S. Zaki Haider, an associate of Dada, invited him to bless his daughter on her first Id Roza (fast) at his residence. Dada gladly accepted the invitation. He reached the Haider residence during the Namaz time when all the men rushed to an allocated spot and started their ritualistic prayers. Unfazed, Dada joined them. He knelt and bowed just like they did and prayed in the same respectful manner as the others. Mr Haider, and all those present, were not only deeply touched but also impressed by Dada's demonstration of kinship. One gentleman was heard whispering to his neighbours that he felt as though a *pir* (Muslim saint) had come to bless them that evening and make it unforgettable.

Dada also regarded Sind as sacred: Here, on the banks of the Vedic Sindhu river, flourished one of the world's greatest ancient civilizations – the Harappan civilization. It is also the land of Sufis and mystics, dervishes and fakirs. Here, saints and sages, poets and prophets lived together, contributing to its rich heritage of culture, literature, art and religion.

As an uprooted and dispersed community, the Sindhis were in danger of becoming a rootless and alienated people, who needed spiritual guidance to foster their sense of identity and culture. They had also suffered the angst of losing their language and culture after their beloved motherland. Therefore, wherever he travelled, Dada urged Sindhis to keep alive their language, for language, according to Dada, was the great marker of cultural identity.

Cheti Chand is an important Sindhi festival which ushers in the new year in the month of April and coincides with the Maharashtrian festival Gudi Padwa. On this auspicious day, devotees would flock to Dada to receive the twin gifts of neem leaves and sugar candy (*mishri*). The leaves of neem symbolize life's bitter experiences and the mishri, the pleasant ones. Each devotee dreads the bitter neem leaf and implores Dada to select the tender leaf along with the sweet mishri. Once, after Dada had finished distributing the prasad, naturally, quite a few neem leaves were left over in the plate. To everyone's surprise, Dada gathered the neem leaves in a bunch and ate them all. Someone in the gathering likened his act to Lord Shiva, who took upon himself all the bitterness and poison of the earth so humanity could live in peace and blessedness.

During his yatras, Dada would thus urge his distinguished audience to unite in the task of building a new world, one of love, sympathy, compassion and service.

Addressing the Interfaith Symposium at New York in 1995, Dada said, 'My vision of the twenty-first century is of a world without wars and without want: a world in which every human being, irrespective of his country, colour, creed or race, receives the necessities of life, a world in which every human being can hold his head high, a world in which the right to live is accorded to every creature that breathes the breath of life.'

'Wars will not cease,' Dada said, 'until all killing is stopped. No sentient creature must be killed. For, if a man kills an animal for food, he will not hesitate in killing a fellow-man whom he regards as an enemy. We must grow in the spirit of reverence for all life. All life must be regarded as sacred.'

Dada's gentle yet firm voice drove the message home. Dada proceeded to point out that a brave, new world would be built not in the senate or parliament, but in the home and the school, for the children of today would be the builders of tomorrow. Put the child right, he said, and the world would come out right!

During Dada's visit to Nepal in 1996, his hosts urged him to visit the Neelkanth Har Har Shrine.

As they entered the splendid temple, keen to offer prayers to the Lord, Dada's eye caught sight of an emaciated figure. It was huddled in a corner of the place of worship. Curious, Dada walked towards it. He noticed a crouched leper, wailing in pain. The affliction had spread to all parts of his body and hundreds of flies seemed to hover around him. Though he was in excruciating pain, the leper lay still.

Dada was overwhelmed with emotion. He knelt close to the leper and did the unimaginable; bringing out his handkerchief from his pocket, he began to fan the leper gently. 'My temple is right here, at the feet of this leper!' he exclaimed to the devotees around him.

Dada sat by the side of the leper and refused to leave him. He did not have the heart to abandon a suffering brother. To him, offering a helping hand was the highest form of devotion to the Almighty.

As the day drew to a close, a local boy willing to take care of the man was finally found. The boy demanded a sum in exchange for his services, which was duly compensated by Dada without any apprehensions. However, Dada sought a promise out of him, of looking after the man afflicted with leprosy.

That day, Dada's wish to worship Lord Shiva was unfulfilled. However, he had paid devotion to the Gods in the most illustrious way by offering devotion to a neglected sufferer, the sight of whom repelled onlookers.

At a civic reception organized in Miami, Florida, on 14 September 2007 a commendation from the Mayor of Miami was presented to Dada. The words of the commendation were significant: 'In recognition of your invaluable contribution to the brotherhood of mankind, it is a privilege to welcome to our city a man who expressed his noble belief when he said, "Individuals and nations alike must either love each other or perish. There is no other choice." By virtue of the authority vested in me as mayor, and on behalf of the city commissioner and our citizens, I do hereby tender this commendation.'

In all humility, Dada responded, 'In giving me this honour, you have honoured my beloved master, Sadhu Vaswani, and my great country, India. I came to you as a stranger, and you have treated me as a brother. My Master taught that we must build a bridge of brotherhood between East and West; that life and all the bounties of life are given to us as a trust to be spent in the service of God and the suffering children of God. It is neither the will for power nor the will to live, but the will to become an instrument of God's help and healing in this world of suffering and pain, that will lead to the fulfilment of man's Divine destiny.'

East and West, black and white, are but barriers that divide humanity. Where the mind is open and the spirit is free, such distinctions dissolve and the unity of mankind prevails in its essential truth and beauty.

So it was that the State of Georgia conferred its Honorary Citizenship on Dada on May 18, 1996, at a memorable function held at the Gwinnett Civic and Cultural Center. Mr Terry Slayton, Assistant Secretary of State, who conferred the Citizenship on Dada, said that he felt indeed 'awed, blessed and uplifted' on seeing Dada.

Miami or Mumbai, Georgia or Johannesburg, New York or New Delhi – Dada's message of universal love is always welcomed by receptive hearts.

Religion today has been made a convenient scapegoat for all the atrocities perpetrated by man. Terrorism, bloodshed and the killing of innocent men and women are widespread today, unfortunately, all in the name of religion. It takes a great spiritual leader with courage and conviction to defend true religion from such malicious intent and wanton abuse. Dada has always been one such staunch defender of true religion.

The gift of inner harmony is given only to God's chosen few. Dada was one such rare, harmonious being. In him, mind, heart and spirit are harmoniously united to emanate the cosmic music of divine love. It was fitting for the Inter-Religious Harmony Movement to honour Dada as the Harmony Man of the year 1997 at the St Joseph Auditorium, Bangalore, on 15 February. Introducing him to the audience, revered Ronnie Prabhu said, 'If one has to look for a model human being, thoroughly blending with nature, in harmony with every living being and spreading the gospel of love and peace across all barriers, then we have Dada J. P.

Vaswani. He is the epitome of piety, purity, humility, compassion and peace.'

His profound humility echoed in his words as he responded by saying, 'I have done nothing to deserve this honour. I take it as an honour to my beloved master, Sadhu Vaswani, who indeed was a prophet of harmony, in every sense of that term.' He added, 'The great task that lies ahead of us is that of building a new nation, an India of the truly strong and free. This new India will not be built in the Lok Sabha or the Rajya Sabha. It will be built by men and women of character, of harmony and understanding, of vision and love, of self-control and self-effacement. My hope is more in education than in politics. The youth of today are the builders of tomorrow. Give them the right type of education and the work you do will not easily fade away.'

'There is no Hindu, no Muslim, no Christian and no Jew. We all are children of the one heavenly father, the one divine mother of the universe.'

With this resounding message of unity and brotherhood, Dada greeted a distinguished audience of international ambassadors who had gathered together at St Bartholomew's Church in New York, on 25 April 1997. The gathering had been organized by the United Nations Community to felicitate the newly elected secretary-general, Mr Kofi Annan.

In keeping with the character of the international community present at the function, Dada urged, 'Let us forget all sense of separateness and join hands together in the one great task of building a new civilization of peace, sympathy and service.'

Ambassadors to the UN from various countries were delighted to meet Dada. They warmly invited him to visit their respective countries.

When the most prestigious institutes of the world were inviting Dada to invigorate audiences with his powerful words, Smithsonian Institute, Washington D. C. – the fountainhead of American culture – invited Dada in 1997, to the inaugural series of lectures on Sufism.

Dada described a Sufi as one who has seen the face of God unveiled; who has a direct knowledge of God; who lives and moves in his radiant presence; who works and offers all his labour to God; who possesses nothing but is himself God-possessed; who lives day by day, intoxicated in the love of God. Sufism, Dada added, is a way of life that reaches God through love. The Sufi believes that the best way to worship God is to serve people. Service without any thought of reward is love-in-action.

Pointing out the similarity in different religions of the world and the teachings of their great founders, Dada once observed in the course of his address: 'I have found a beautiful similarity in their message. To study different religions in the spirit of sympathy and understanding is to know that each one of them emphasizes the same fundamental truth. I wonder why people say that some religions are true and others are not.'

With his capacity to consider all religions as his own and all men and women as his brothers and sisters, Dada was the very epitome of *sadhbavana* (good-will) and *samadrishti* (equanimity) wherever the pilgrim path took him.

SIX

Everyone's Beloved Dada

'With royalty he is regal,
With the poor he is simple,
With scholars he is learned,
And with children, he is disarmingly childlike,
And radiantly happy.
The perfect master is perfect at every level.'

– Rick Chapman

It was difficult for anyone not to be drawn to Dada's ever-smiling face. His large, luminous eyes, shining with compassion, expressed more than words could. In his voice, there was a music that soothed and healed lacerated hearts. His tender, loving touch could transport a person to another world.

The aura around him was spiritually charged and one felt blessed to be around him. Clad in a simple khadi *kurta* and pyjama with a shawl loosely hanging from his shoulders, his impressive yet humble personality would get entrenched in the mind. His magnetism, none could resist.

Dada always poured tremendous love and affection on the sangat.

Whenever Dada entered the satsang hall, he bowed down to all the brothers and sisters with his hands folded. Once, even as he was greeting the sangat, his eyes fell on a little boy dressed in rags, sitting outside the hall, listening to the kirtan. Dada went out and leading the boy gently by his hand, brought him in, made him sit beside him and said, *Aap to mere bhai hai.*

The little boy was moved to tears. How true it is – for the one who sees the one-in-all, there is no difference between the good and the bad, the rich and the poor, the Brahmin and the outcaste.

In the early days, he would often go out for long walks in the wide open, uncongested roads of Pune Cantonment accompanied by the sangat. Dada was a brisk walker, so much so that people who could not keep pace with him followed his entourage in an auto-rickshaw. Often, he would drop into the homes of friends and devotees for a cup of tea, breakfast, or an evening snack depending on the time of day. The route of the walk or the areas to be visited were never planned in advance. Dada would go wherever his steps guided him and stop unplanned, without notice at the house of a volunteer or devotee. Tea would be served not just to Dada, but to all who accompanied him. The hostess would not be put through any trouble at all; members of the sangat would gladly assist her; milk, tea and sugar would arrive as if by magic, as well as biscuits and snacks and any number of teacups from neighbours and friends. (These were the days before paper cups and plates were not heard of.) Amidst fun, laughter and a festive atmosphere, as many as a hundred people would be comfortably served tea and snacks.

Sometimes, he would hold impromptu satsangs that began with a 'thought of the day'. Then, there would be a brief kirtan, followed by a question-answer session. Often, the host would invite the sangat to have lunch, and in a jiffy, the ladies would get together and cook a simple but tasty meal for the gathering. At the end of the day, none of them could explain how the food was cooked and served to so many people in their humble abode.

And who were the 'chosen' people on whom this blessing was bestowed? Not just the rich and the influential, the well-connected and the well-known, but anyone. From the simplest and the humblest, to the professionals and the regulars, the hosts were chosen at random and Dada simply would brighten their day. But there was a condition – if anyone begged, pleaded or persuaded Dada to visit their home, he would not go to them. So, people learnt their lesson the hard way. They prayed in their hearts for his arrival but took care never to vocalize their wish.

For over five decades now, the Sadhu Vaswani Mission has offered the seva of serving early morning tea to the homeless and the destitute on the streets of Pune, even before the city wakes up. Passengers alighting from early morning trains at Pune station are often surprised to behold poor, homeless people sleeping on platforms being served steaming hot tea by the volunteers of the Mission. The poor are also fed two meals a day by the Mission's *bhandara*, and on special occasions and feast days, they are treated to a hearty meal even before the guests and devotees sit down for their *langar* (fellowship meals).

No task was too low for Dada; no service too humble. His humility was not just in words and deeds; it arose spontaneously from his heart. In his presence, one seemed to absorb humility and discard the inborn pride and arrogance.

Once, in his younger days, Dada had decided to carry cooked food to a needy family in the neighbourhood. As he drew near the cottage, a harrowing sight greeted his eyes.

'Mother! We are hungry! Give us food to eat,' wailed little children. Their eyes were full of tears, their stomachs gnawingly empty.

'Just wait a while, my dear ones. See, your food is cooking over the fire. In a few minutes, we shall all sit down to have a meal.' the mother soothed her children.

She was, in fact, lying desperately. There was not a grain of food in the cottage. In hopes of comforting her little ones, the poor mother had placed water to boil. The starving children fell asleep while waiting for food that was not going to arrive. As for the mother, she grieved and wept bitter tears at the plight of her little ones. Was not the God she worshipped called Deena Bandhu – a friend of the weak and the unprotected? Would he not come to their rescue?

'Sister! Sister!' Dada called out in a soft and gentle voice from the doorway.

The poor woman had wiped away her tears, covered her head and opened the door. The person in the doorway seemed a total stranger. He carried a basket of rations – a gift of love and service. At the time, Dada was fulfiling his vow to perform at least one good deed a day and providence had brought him to the doorstep of the hapless woman in the nick of time. For her, the young stranger was God's own messenger.

This incident was etched in Dada's heart. He determined to do his best so that no one would go hungry while it was in his power to feed them. Dada's loving compassion inspires the Mission's ongoing seva of feeding the poor.

The first week of August is a period of great rejoicing for all Mira institutions for it is Dada's birthday week. Dada would assign a special day to visit each institution dedicated to Sadhu Vaswani and spend some time with the staff and students on the day.

Time and again, Dada requested the devotees not to celebrate his birthday in a grand way. The schools and colleges, therefore, performed special social service activities during the week to show their love and regard for him. Sometimes, however, they would get carried away by their love and enthusiasm. A special cake would be baked and everyone insisted that Dada cut it. What then could he do? He was simplicity personified and shunned all worldly offerings. And yet, he was an embodiment of kindness and could never have the heart to say 'no' to his children.

Dada solved this problem effortlessly. He would accept the cake graciously and then ask the students, 'Is there anyone here who is celebrating a birthday today?' Invariably, out of a gathering of 3,000 odd students, someone's birthday was sure to fall on that day. Dada would invite them, present the bouquet that would have been offered to him, and ask them to cut the birthday cake while the entire gathering sang 'happy birthday'.

Who else but Dada could think of such a simple, yet beautiful and selfless gesture?

Once, Dada was about to board a train from Pune on one of his yatras. On the platform, there was a small, crippled boy who gasped for breath as he limped to board his train. He experienced great difficulty as he struggled to hold a bunch of packages under his arm and his crutches at the same time.

Many people rushed to and fro, unmindful of the little boy, while others accidentally bumped into him, knocking his packages from his hands. A few even scolded him for being clumsy and getting in their way.

The plight of the boy did not escape a pair of observant eyes. Ever-loving, ever-compassionate, ever-ready to help, Dada quickly stepped forward, picked up the boy's scattered belongings, and said to him softly, 'I am sorry, my child.' He then helped the boy to get on the train and find his seat. A box of *mithai* and a few fruits brought by one of the devotees was offered lovingly to the boy.

The child, who had seldom seen such tender concern, was overwhelmed. All he could do was wave out his hand in gratitude even as the train pulled out of the platform.

While he was being driven to Solapur in a devotee's car, Dada saw on the road a man tottering under the weight of the cart he was pulling. Ahead of him was a steep bridge over which he had to pass. Moved by the sight, Dada got down from the car to lend a helping hand to the cart-puller. All the others accompanying Dada rushed to offer help and together they effortlessly pulled his cart up the bridge.

The poor man was overwhelmed and rendered speechless by what had just happened. He folded his hands in admiration but was at a loss for words. Dada bowed to touch his feet, passed on some money to him and left, not lingering a minute longer to give the cart-puller a chance to express his gratitude.

When Dada was in Delhi during the sacred festival of Deepavali, he willingly participated in the festivities. The devotees were overjoyed. It was for the first time that Dada was with them in Delhi on the sacred day. In a moving speech, Dada said, 'The right way to worship Goddess Lakshmi is to share one's wealth with those in need.'

At night, Dada visited a slum area and served food to the needy folk of the locality. Outside a hut, a few men sat together in front of a picture of Sri Rama. With great devotion, they sang the sacred Name. So lost were they in remembering him that they were hardly aware of the group that stood around them. Dada joined in the singing. The kirtan gathered momentum. Suddenly, they noticed Dada among the crowd and flocked to seek his blessings. Dada generously distributed gifts to them and showered his blessings upon them.

An ardent lover of animals, Dada genuinely felt for the defenceless creatures and regarded them as his younger brothers and sisters in the one family of creation.

Once, very late at night, Dada was taking a walk around the slumbering streets of Pune city. Suddenly, a cry of agony broke the silence. The night was dark and not a star shone in the sky. It seemed like the cry of someone in intense pain. Dada followed the direction from where the shriek seemed to be emerging. He soon found out that a dog had been run over by a passing vehicle and it was yelping in pain. There it lay, wounded and bleeding profusely. Dada's eyes moistened.

Realizing that the dog's end was near, Dada knelt beside the dying animal, picked it up from the middle of the road and laid it on one side. He recited a few slokas from the Bhagavad Gita and caressed the dog with his gentle hands. It was not long before the dog breathed its last. The look of gratitude that the dog wore in his eyes as Dada knelt beside it haunted him for days together. It seemed to say to him, 'Am I not your brother?'

A stray cat would often stroll through Dada's house and room. One day when Dada entered his room, a soft mewling was heard. After having looked high and low, it was found that the cat had delivered kittens underneath Dada's footrest. Dada asked everyone not to disturb his feline guests as the place was theirs for the taking until they were ready to depart. He also asked them to place a bowl of milk near them and ensure it was filled up regularly.

On one occasion, Dada went to the Bund Garden by the riverside in Pune with a group of brothers and sisters. How happy and excited were the devotees at the prospect of spending an enjoyable time with their dearly loved Gurudev! However, when they reached the garden, Dada's eyes mirrored the melancholy in his heart. His eye had caught notice of a few fishermen who had cast their nets in the waters and were waiting to catch the fish. When their nets grew heavy enough, they hauled up a sizeable catch.

Dada looked at the fish gasping for breath. He could not hold himself back any longer. He hurried towards the fishermen to make an appeal, 'How much will you charge for the entire lot?' Though the price quoted seemed exorbitant to the other devotees, Dada paid the amount without giving it a second thought. He owned over a hundred fishes now. Without a moment's delay, Dada released them into the waters, giving the fishes a new lease of life. He implored the fishermen not to catch any more fish at least on that one day.

Having done a noble deed to the best of his ability, Dada made his way back feeling content. As he walked away from the garden, Dada slipped on some grime and fell on the rocks, spraining his foot and ankle.

The minor hairline fracture which ensued had to be put in plaster for about three weeks. But Dada had no regrets whatsoever, 'No price is too high to save a life.' he told his devotees.

All you need to do to dispel darkness is to light a candle, and Dada lit an endless number of candles every day to usher light where it was dark. 'Love, love, love; love even thine enemy and though he hates thee as a thorn, thou wilt blossom as a rose.' was Sadhu Vaswani's message to his followers. Dada followed this precept in letter and spirit.

On one occasion, organizers of a major annual festival in Pune requested Dada to be their honoured guest and accept their felicitation. Dada refused the invitation with folded hands.

'Call me to sweep the floor of the auditorium,' he said, 'and I shall do it willingly. But pray, do not offer me honours. I am a servant of all.'

Can we find a better precept of the master's teaching: 'He is truly great who greatly serves.'

'Do you have a special desire?' someone asked Dada once at a press conference.

'Yes', he replied. 'My one desire is to help each and every one of you to experience God.'

'Make God a reality in your daily life,' Dada urged his people again and again. 'Awaken divine love within your hearts. A human being without love is as a beehive without honey. Love God with your mind, heart and soul – for the way to know God is to love him.'

A man once said to him, 'I have never heard you say anything ill about anyone. I believe you would say something good even about the devil.' Dada's eyes twinkled and he replied, 'I certainly admire his perseverance.'

'Fold your hands in obeisance to the God who resides within everyone,' Dada would preach, and not just to greet the outer form.

One day, after a discussion with his devotees regarding some administrative tasks, the moment Dada got up to leave, one of the devotees rushed to get his slippers and placed them before him. Dada put them on and expressed his gratitude to the brother who brought them. One good turn deserves another so they say, but

Dada lives it. He brought the shoes of the devotee who had got his. He placed them before him saying, 'I am your servant.'

The brother, with a lump in his throat, exclaimed, 'O, Dada, how could you do this?'

Dada said, 'Can there be a higher privilege than being a servant to the devotees of the Lord?'

He would reinstate faith in the creator through small acts. Once, a lady had a beautiful idol of Lord Krishna which she would lovingly worship every day. One day, as she was carefully cleaning it, it slipped from her hands, and its legs were broken. She looked at it with dismay and wondered if the broken leg would portend some harm or misfortune to her or the family. She did not want to have anything more to do with the idol. Now, it was merely a damaged idol for her, and no longer a representation of Lord Krishna himself.

She brought the idol to Dada saying that she was superstitious about the broken idol and did not want it in her house. Dada looked adoringly at the beautiful idol of Lord Krishna and gave his *pranaam*s to it. Then he turned to the lady and said, 'Suppose you have a child in the house, who breaks his leg, will you throw him out? You will naturally take him to the doctor to get his fracture fixed. Similarly, you must try to get the idol repaired in such a way that no one will even realize the damage. It can be done. If you wish, I could do it. Lord Krishna is your Lord. You would not give your child away, then how can you abandon the Lord?

'In school, I was good at arts and craft and I guarantee that the leg can be mended in a way where you will not even feel that it had been broken. You must realize that they are not mere idols, they are living entities. Your faith breathes life into them, and then it is your faith which comes back to you through them.'

The woman was ashamed and repented. She gratefully took the idol back home.

One of Dada's favourite prayers was, 'I love you, God! I want to love you more and more. I want to love you more than anything else in the world. I want to love you to distraction, to intoxication. Grant me pure love and devotion for thy lotus feet. And so bless me, that this world-bewitching *maya* may not lead me astray. And make me, blessed master, an instrument of thy help and healing in this world of suffering and pain.'

A journalist once remarked to Dada, 'Your engagement diary must be filled with many pressing commitments you have to attend to every day!'

Dada said to him gently, 'I do not plan anything. I just let the will of God guide me.'

With this faith, Dada moved from one schedule to another effortlessly. At the end of the day, everything had been attended to.

A great believer of leading an active life, Dada never allowed himself to indulge in idleness. His daily schedule was so packed with events, activities and things to do that he often put into twenty-four hours what most of us would take a week to accomplish.

'Do not remain idle even for a single moment,' he would urge. 'Time is the most precious of all possessions. Therefore, take care of your minutes, your moments.'

Busy and active, Dada was always ready to give a patient hearing to the people who thronged to see him. Time management came naturally to him.

Everyone who came in touch with Dada was invariably enchanted by the magic of his love.

One day, while a *satsang* was in progress in Pune, a drunkard came and fell at Dada's feet. Sobbing uncontrollably, he said, 'Try as hard as I may, I am unable to resist liquor. Pray, show me the way to overcome this terrible addiction. I can do nothing on my own. I feel so helpless! You alone can save me from slavery to this habit.'

Dada looked at him with compassion-filled eyes and embracing him, said, 'Will you do as I say?'

'Yes, blessed master, command and I shall obey!'

'Just do this one thing, Every time you get an urge to drink, come to me. I will accompany you to the bar and drink with you as many glasses as you do.'

Shame was writ large on his face. 'No, beloved Dada, I will never touch alcohol again,' he promised.

Dada had his own endearing ways out of a difficulty.

Everyone tried to capture the magic of his presence only to find that language was inadequate to put Dada's glances and smiles into words. An American calls him the world's magnet who drew people towards him irresistibly. One captivated admirer calls Dada a smile millionaire, for his million-dollar smile could chase away all blues. Another remarked that he held in his hands the helm that steered humanity.

'To hear Dada speak,' avows an enthralled listener, 'would move even one with a heart of stone.'

An inspiring speaker, Dada would sometimes touch upon a thought in his talk and then proceed to elaborate on it spontaneously. In a ten-minute *ruh-rihan* (an informal, heart-to-heart talk), he could melt the hardest of hearts. On more formal occasions, he could speak fluently for over an hour and hold his audience spellbound throughout. His command over language was impeccable and words and images seemed to dance to his tune! The richness of his vocabulary, the scientific precision of his knowledge, and the electrifying spiritual power of his ideas have made his speeches unforgettable. How did he do it, again and again?

Not only that, Dada even wrote lucidly. Having authored more than 150 books in English and Sindhi, translated into seventeen world languages, Dada's commentaries on the stories and the sacred scriptures of different world faiths cover an array of topics right from life after death to tips for daily living; from spirituality to love and laughter; from education to stress-control; from karma to child psychology. They act as a guide from which one could read and re-read to draw inspiration and spiritual strength. They are an inexhaustible source of wisdom and faith for countless readers.

A devotee who once came to spend the day with Dada said how his only wish was that the day would never end!

Dada was hardly affected by the praise lavished on him. He took in his stride the admiration and adoration that was poured upon him wherever he went. He remained unmoved by the kind of adulation that might have overwhelmed one, usually.

'What prompted you to take up the path of service and sacrifice?' Dada was asked once.

Dada replied:

It all happened in the most natural way – neither by design nor by choice. When I finished my college education, friends and relatives tried to persuade me to study for the ICS examination. It was then that my master, Sadhu Vaswani, entered my life. He awakened my slumbering soul and I realized that life is given to us not to make money or to acquire positions of power but to be poured out as a sacrifice unto the eternal. It was my master's doing. His love was like a magnet that kept pulling me and in comparison to his love, everything else seemed so pale and insignificant. All glory unto him!

For this, Dada was thankful to his master. Every day, following his simple and song-like routine, Dada would start his day in the holy hours of dawn, meditating in silence towards union with God. He would then get ready and come out to Sadhu Vaswani's kutiya to seek blessings and inspiration from his master. After the salutations, he would proceed to cleanse the box in which the sacred urns containing Sadhu Vaswani's ashes have been placed, before he greeted the sangat with his first darshan.

Once, a man who was keen to learn to meditate came to Dada in desperation and poured out his heart's longing. Dada explained to him that meditation is a very difficult thing as the mind is like a monkey that is drunk and bitten by a scorpion. The man, however, begged Dada to help him out. Dada, showing infinite mercy, agreed and requested him to clean out his bookcase – to wipe all the books and put them back in their right place. The man thought that Dada had misunderstood and assured him that he was not looking for a part-time job but had come to learn meditation. Lovingly, Dada replied, 'I know, I know, but do as I say; and please be quick about your job as you have a lot more to get done. If you finish all the work by nightfall, I will tell you about meditation.' The man hastened and finished the work assigned to him. No thought of food or water entered his mind. At the end of the day, feeling famished yet triumphant, he went to Dada. Dada welcomed him with a smile and listened to the man, who excitedly shared how he had spent the day. Dada then asked him what he had been thinking about all this time. The man looked stunned for he had not thought of anything. Dada concluded, 'This is exactly what meditation is, and you have achieved it without even realizing! Once you bring about one-pointed focus and concentration, you are into meditation. Your focus and concentration was so deep that it drove out all thoughts. So, meditation is not impossible.' The man took home the most precious lesson on meditation that day.

Each day in Dada's life was different from the other. His infinite vitality, warmth, gentle unshakable strength, never-failing sense of humour and effervescent joy added a new colour to every minute one spent with him. A man with no possessions, he had the greatest possession of all – the peace that passeth, surpasseth understanding.

Those who got a chance to spend a day with him could only exclaim, 'It is simply so wonderful!'

'What is the most surprising thing in the world?' someone once asked Dada.

'The most surprising thing in this world,' Dada replied, 'is that every day so many people leave this world, but still we feel that we are immortal, that we shall never die.'

'The greatest tragedy of man,' he added, 'is that he thinks he has plenty of time.'

We receive countless reminders every day, telling us that we are here on earth, but as pilgrims. Sooner or later, the call will come when we will have to bid adieu to all that we hold dear and cross over to the other shore.

Dada would constantly ask, 'What will we carry with us? Are we gathering the treasure imperishable, or are we frittering away our precious lives in vain pursuits?'

Dada pointed out that youth, beauty, wealth and power are all transient as they will all pass away. Therefore, what are we proud of? 'Let me be humble as a blade of grass,' Dada prayed.

Dada bore testimony to the ideal of utter simplicity in his daily life. His needs were simple, his wants were few.

What a lesson for each one of us!

Once, it was time for Dada to leave for an important meeting. He began clearing away his table, arranging his books and papers neatly and methodically in place. This took quite some time and the volunteers noticed that Dada seemed to be searching for something.

'What are you looking for, Dada?' they asked him respectfully.

'My pencil,' Dada replied. 'It was a tiny pencil that I was using, to make notes for the meeting tonight.'

Eager to save him time and trouble, they took out a new pencil, sharpened it and offered it to him. But Dada would have none of it.

'No! No!' he said. 'I would like to have my old, small pencil. I can't just take a new one and forget my old pencil. It was given to me with a lot of love and it has served me so well for such a long time.'

And so, Dada and all others hunted together until the tiny pencil was found! Dada was very happy and left for his meeting on time.

Another time, when Dada was ready to leave for a conference where he was to give a talk, it was brought to his notice that there was a stain on his shawl. It was suggested that he wear another shawl. He refused and chuckled, 'I will change the very same shawl.' He turned it inside out and the stain was no longer visible!

It was one of those cold and rainy days in Pune when most people prefer to stay indoors. Yet there was a spring in Dada's step as he moved out, raincoat clad, to take his daily walk. As he turned around the corner of a long lane, Dada's gaze fell upon a poor old man, who was shivering and wet. He was seeking refuge from the rain under the porch of a house. Reaching him in a few strides, Dada leaned down to touch his shoulder. 'Brother, you must be terribly cold out here in this weather.' said Dada with tender concern.

It was as though a transformation came over the old man. His face softened, the wrinkles seemed to disappear. He looked straight into Dada's eyes, and giving him a beautiful, endearing, toothless smile, said, 'I was, before you came here!'

His few simple words uttered quietly and sincerely, spoke volumes even as his countenance was aglow with joy! Has it not been said that the best and most beautiful things in the world cannot be seen or touched, but are only felt in the heart?

'I've had enough! I can't take it anymore! I am going to end my life!' exclaimed a dejected, dispirited young man who had once come to see Dada. He was suffering from severe depression and no therapy had succeeded in relieving him of his misery.

Quietly, Dada handed over a pen and a sheet of paper to him, saying, 'Brother, take this and write down each and everything for which you should feel grateful to God.'

'Feel grateful to God? What for?' wailed the young man. 'Look at me! I am so miserable, and you ask me to feel grateful to God? If you ask me to write down all the things that God has failed me in, let me down, not given me, I can do that very quickly,' he retorted.

Ever so gently, Dada persuaded him, 'There are countless blessings that God has bestowed on you. You have parents who love you; friends who care for you; above all, you have an able body. Are not all these great blessings for which you should be grateful to God? Go and list all your blessings; and don't forget to write on every sheet "Thank you, God. Thank you, God. Thank you, God."'

A couple of days later, the young man returned. His step was buoyant and there was serenity upon his face. Dada's therapy of thanksgiving had worked miracles for him!

'Love can change the world,' was Dada's inspiring message to his followers.

Aware as he was of the multifarious departments of the Mission, Dada kept himself abreast of all the developments in the various activities undertaken by them. The devotees and volunteers who carried out the tasks were only human and naturally, mistakes might have been committed inadvertently. Dada noticed them but never ever pointed a finger at or condemned anyone.

He often said, 'Never look at others' faults. By focusing your attention on people's faults, you only draw negative forces to yourself.'

And how did he himself handle others' mistakes? He was blessed with a remarkably sunny temperament and a delightful sense of humour. He had a mind like quicksilver and with a repartee here and an appropriate anecdote there, all wrongs would be set right!

There was an instance when an aggrieved volunteer approached Dada to complain against her co-worker. She had brought proof to show how the person had acted wrongly. She was sure that Dada would pull her up for it.

Dada listened to her complaint patiently. At the end of her recital of grievances, he said to her gently, 'When you find fault with someone, you only draw that fault to yourself. Fault-finding and magnifying other people's mistakes are poor ways of changing the world. Is it not better to light a candle than to curse the darkness?

You will be able to win over your co-worker with the power of your love.'

Love can, indeed, change the world for the better.

A young boy who came to meet Dada asked him, 'How can I believe in God when I have never seen him?'

In response, Dada led the child to an electric plug point, plugged in a gadget and switched it on. Pointing to the electrically operated machine, Dada asked, 'Do you believe that this machine is working?'

'Of course!' answered the boy.

'What makes the machine work?' asked Dada.

'Electric power,' answered the boy, as a matter of fact.

'You do not see electric power, do you?' asked Dada. 'Yet you believe in it because you see what it can do,' he explained patiently, in a manner the boy would understand. 'Likewise, you must believe in God because of all he does. What makes the universe work? What makes the sun rise and set? What makes the stars shine? A super power, which, for want of a better word, we call God!'

On one occasion, a call had come during a live radio interview that Dada was giving in Puerto Rico. It was a phone-in programme in which listeners could dial the radio station and talk directly to the guest speaker for the evening.

'Dada, please help!' said a frantic voice over the telephone. 'I am an utter failure in life and I do not know where to turn for help!'

As the programme host watched anxiously, hundreds of radio listeners waited with bated breath to hear Dada's response to the unknown caller's cry of anguish.

In a gentle, soothing voice that has been a balm for many a wounded heart, Dada said to the nameless, faceless soul in distress, 'You are not alone! God, our heavenly father, is always with you – guarding you, guiding you, protecting you, leading you on. He is the source of all strength, wisdom, success and prosperity. All we have to do is to turn to him in childlike faith, and he will never fail us! Turn to him, and you will see miracles happen in your life!'

The man's uncontrollable sobs could be heard as Dada spoke. Dada continued to comfort him. At the end of the conversation, the man thanked Dada for lifting his spirits.

Everyone has had some experience of love – a beautiful feeling that warms your heart and makes you happy, content, and at total peace. That one moment when you feel most alive, when you feel more than yourself, more than the body and the mind, what is that, but love?

In general, we feel happy when we receive something – gifts, honours and titles. But in love, 'giving' makes you supremely happy, perhaps even more than 'receiving'. Love makes the journey easy; it helps you bear burdens and accept challenges of life with a smile.

Dada was a perennial, everflowing, stream of love. He would often say, 'What is it that makes the world look as beautiful as paradise? Being in love!' And again, he would remark with a smile, 'Love is the spoonful of sugar that makes the medicine go down.'

Love transcends the boundaries of mind and reason, it fills you with unknown strength and courage, it shuns darkness and reveals the light of true knowledge and wisdom. What textbooks struggle to teach you in a thousand pages, love may teach you in just one experience. Even such an experience Dada offered, to each aspiring heart that gravitated towards him.

Dada lived love; love was his essential nature. 'Wake up love in your heart,' he would say again and again. 'We can kindle our inner light by waking up love within our hearts. The true light of life is love. If you want to kindle the light, you must wake up love: love for all, love not only for those who are good, or the so called good, but love for all, love for the saint, love for the sinner, love for everyone.'

During one of his yatras a reporter asked him, 'What do you teach?' Dada answered, 'My life is my message.'

SEVEN

Dada: The Man for All Seasons and Climes

'No great man lives in vain. The history of the world is but the biography of great men.'

– Thomas Carlyle

HIGHLY SOUGHT-AFTER

Dada was a class apart as a spiritual leader, even in a country like India – often referred to as a home of the gurus – where every city, every state, every segment of the population has a special mentor or teacher. What made Dada unique in this galaxy of gurus was his non-sectarian, non-controversial and non-judgmental nature, one that transcended all political divisions.

His warm, friendly and magnetic personality, the ability to connect with people of all ages and the gift of holding listeners enthralled by the power of his thoughts and words had all made him a well-loved speaker and a much sought-after guest at prestigious gatherings. Honours and awards have been conferred on Dada from several quarters: Social, cultural, humanitarian and spiritual. Associations deemed it their honour to felicitate him. Reluctant to take awards, Dada would accept these special honours conferred on him solely in humble acquiescence to the master. His innate kindness and goodness made him bow down to the love and regard with which people treated him.

U THANT AWARD — NEW JERSEY, 1998

'For his many years of God-loving, man-inspiring and heart-expanding services to the seekers of the ultimate truth', the prestigious U Thant Peace Award was presented to Dada at an impressive function held at Alpine, New Jersey, USA, on 23 April 1998, on the day of the sacred Rama Navami.

Named after the distinguished former Secretary General of the UN, the U Thant Award carries a distinction that is unique in nature. The recipients of the award are individuals and institutions reflecting U Thant's lofty spiritual ideals. Dada would join such luminaries as Mother Teresa, Nelson Mandela and President Gorbachev, who were also recipients of this coveted award.

Presenting the award to Dada, Sri Chinmoy, Director of the Peace Mediation Center at the UN, paid a tribute to him, 'Dada Vaswani is one of the brightest jewels of our Mother Earth. His presence amongst us is a great blessing for humanity.' On a personal note, he added, 'I am one of those who dearly cherishes his life of constant compassion, sympathy, oneness and equality.'

Dada, who was convalescing after his open-heart surgery, made a brief, moving speech. 'The greatest need of humanity is peace and unity. The Gita tells us in unequivocal terms that if you want peace you must become anchored in that which is changeless and which, for want of a better word, we call God. Chasing the shadow-shapes of possessions, pleasure and power will not give you peace. Peace belongs to those who have settled in the Self, the *atman* within. Therefore, keep awake at night and meditate and during the daytime, help as many as you can to lift the load on the rough road of life.'

WORLD PARLIAMENT OF RELIGIONS —
SOUTH AFRICA, 1999

From 1 to 8 December 1999, in the last month of a new century and a new millennium, Cape Town, South Africa, witnessed an extraordinary and diverse communion of the world's most revered religious and spiritual representatives and their respective traditions at the Parliament of World Religions. Dada was an honoured guest on the occasion.

His first stop was Johannesburg, where he addressed a massive cosmopolitan gathering on 'Amazing Secrets of Happiness' at the Mayfair Cultural Centre. Lectures, seminars, workshops, symposia, performances, inter-religious celebrations and evening plenaries were held at different venues. Dada was invited to represent Hinduism and Indian traditions at the Parliament. He was one of the visionaries who provided the major presentations of the Parliament at the Good Hope Arena, the central venue of the activities of the Parliament. He spoke at different symposia and also conducted a guided meditation for the delegates.

In his inspired thirty-minute address on the first day of the Parliament, Dada said, 'Man has alienated himself from God and his creation. Man has lost his sense of at-one-ment with nature and with life. All nature is one. All life is one. If a new civilization is to be built and if man is to grow in the peace that passeth, surpasseth understanding, he must make friends with all life. He must bear witness to the great ideals of friendship, fellowship, unity and peace. Unless man becomes a protector of every creature that breathes the breath of life, and a guardian of his environment, the earth will recoil and strike back at the greatest destroyer of nature and life, namely man.

'The time has come when we must all pledge that we will make friends with all life. For at the heart of creation is love – nothing but love. The time has come when we must cultivate reverence for all life, regard all life as sacred or perish! There is no other choice!'

On the morning of 3 December, Dada spoke on 'How to Meet the Challenges of Life', to a large audience at the Good Hope Arena. In his heartwarming style, Dada urged his listeners, 'The right way to take on the challenges of life is to meet them with courage, hope and love – the courage born of the realization that man is never alone, God is always with him; the hope that the best is yet to come; and the love that turns every winter into spring.'

On the afternoon of 3 December, Dada was one of the key speakers at the Symposium for 'Building World Movement for Non-violence' at the University of Cape Town. Here, Dada touched upon a theme very dear to his heart.

'We have talked of non-violence for many years and centuries together. But how many of us are prepared to walk the way of non-violence? Non-violence, in other words, is non-killing. How many of us are prepared to walk the way of non-killing? How many of us are ready to bear witness to the great ideal of non-violence in our life, in our diet, in our dress and daily living?' he asked, getting right to the heart of the matter.

On the following day, Dada was the keynote speaker on the Earth Charter, a global initiative working to draft a common statement of ethical and practical considerations for the care of the earth and the human family. At the Symposium, 'Prominent Religious Leaders Respond to the Earth Charter' held at the University of Cape Town, Dada said, 'Any Earth Charter to be acceptable must take note of the fact that human beings are not the only inhabitants of the earth. There are also countless other creatures including birds, animals, fish, fowl. There are trees, flowers, rivers, rocks, and streams. The earth is the Mother of us all. Man has forgotten the truth that he is only a part of nature. He thinks he is the master, the sovereign of nature and can do what he pleases with other creatures and the environment. The Earth Charter must take into account the fact that every living thing has certain rights. And that man, because he is an elder brother, has duties towards his younger brothers, creatures that breathe the breath of life.'

AT THE MILLENNIUM WORLD PEACE SUMMIT, 2000

Following two years of careful planning and strenuous effort, the Millennium World Peace Summit was inaugurated on 28 August 2000. The UN's routine assembly of diplomats and politicians gave way to men and women of faith, spiritual leaders, resplendent in their ceremonial attire gathered at the august main hall.

The UN had deemed fit to hold the inter-faith meet well before the world's political leaders would gather for their summit at the same forum. Perhaps this was a positive sign for the new millennium: That faith should take precedence over politics and that the world's great religions had valuable insights to offer to the world's leaders.

The Vice President of the UN General Assembly, Senator Bonifico of Nigeria, welcomed the delegates to the UN saying, 'Your presence is a powerful testimony of the desire and commitment to see peace prevail in all corners of the world.'

Following these opening remarks, leaders of various faiths and traditions came up one after another to offer prayers and cumulative blessings for world peace. The hall reverberated with chants. Among those that shared the prayers were Israel's Chief Rabbi, Meir Lau, His Eminence Cardinal Francis Arinze, President of the Pontifical Council on Inter-Religious Dialogue at the Vatican, Sri Mata Amritanandamayi Devi, His Excellency Abdullah Al-Obaid, Secretary-General of the World Muslim League and a delegation of Tibetan monks representing His Holiness the Dalai Lama. The litany continued for more than three hours. Midway through the chanting came the magical moment of Dada's memorable benediction, 'My hope is in education more than politics,' said Dada. 'My hope is in an education which is inspired and directed by men and women of illumination.' He called on his audience to include children in their plans to foster peace. 'Let us pay attention to children,' he pleaded. 'They will be the builders of a brave, new world!' Dada's words echoed through the crowded hall.

On 9 September 2000, at Staten Island, New York, has been etched in history for over 30,000 members of the Indian community in America came together to greet the Indian Prime Minister, Atal Bihari Vajpayee and pay their respects to 108 religious and spiritual leaders hailing from India, who had congregated to attend the Millennium World Peace Summit. The reception was held in a public park overlooking the magnificent Atlantic Ocean. It was hosted by several prominent Indian organizations based in the US, including the VHP of America, the Federation of Indians in America, the Overseas Friends of the BJP, the Association of Physicians of Indian Origin, and the Indian–American Forum for Political Education.

The chanting of Vedic prayers and traditional music performances by a second-generation Indian–American group were part of the programme, which culminated with an address by the then Prime Minister of India, Atal Bihari Vajpayee.

The guests of honour at the reception were none other than Swami Dayananda Saraswati, Sri Sri Ravi Shankar and Dada himself. The head of the UN delegation, Swami Chidananda Saraswati invoked peace with the chanting of mantras, praying to God to bless the Indian community.

Addressing the Indian community, Dada exhorted each one of them to become ambassadors of India's ageless, deathless culture. 'Living in America, you must do as the Americans do,' he told them. 'But do not forget your roots. You must bear witness to the great Indian ideals, to the teachings of the Bhagavad Gita, the Mahabharata and the Ramayana.' He urged parents to pay greater attention to their children, even suggesting that they open a school where their children could learn about their homeland, its faith and its culture.

He concluded his soul-stirring address by urging them, 'Tell your children about our tradition so that they can declare with pride, 'I am an Indian, I am a Hindu!''

AT THE FIRST ASIAN VEGETARIAN CONGRESS, DONA SYLVIA — GOA, 2001

Mr Jasu Shah, President, Asian Vegetarian Union, welcomed Dada warmly. Former President of India, Sri R. Venkatraman, a strong votary of vegetarianism himself, presided as the chief guest on the occasion.

Dada spoke enthusiastically on the subject that is very dear to his heart. He said that though India had adopted Ashoka's Dharmachakra as its symbol, Indians did not bear witness to Emperor Ashoka's deep sense of compassion towards animals. He told the members of the Congress that a monumental task lay ahead of them since they were to bring to light the dismal conditions under which animals are slaughtered. Dada, who has always believed that youngsters are the torchbearers of the future, pointed out that the youth are receptive, sensitive and ardent animal lovers. So, it was essential that these attributes of the youth be harnessed to uphold the cause of vegetarianism.

WITH THE EDITOR OF *HINDUISM TODAY* — HAWAII, 2002

Dada was on a private visit to Hawaii, to take a breather and take in the spectacular sunrise and sunset of Hawaii in an idyllic setting. But the news of Dada's stay in Hawaii spread. Swami Sivaya Subramuniya, editor and publisher of the prestigious magazine

Hinduism Today, invited Dada and warmly welcomed him to his ashram in Hawaii. Here, Dada donned the role of a messenger by imparting the teachings of the sacred Gita.

A few days later, on 5 September 2002, New Yorkers filled to capacity the theatre district's landmark venue, the Town Hall, to hear Dada speak on 'A Healthy and Harmonious Life'. In honour of Dada's lifelong contributions to the cause of world peace and spiritual growth, *Hinduism Today* presented to him, the 2002 'Hindu of the Year Award'. A cheque for $ 75,000 was also presented to the Sadhu Vaswani Mission by the India Development and Relief Fund for providing assistance to victims of violence in Gujarat.

AT THE WORLD COUNCIL OF RELIGIOUS LEADERS, BANGKOK, 2002

Dada was one of the pre-eminent religious figures to participate in a new initiative launched by the Millennium World Peace Summit (MWPS) in Bangkok. The objective of the conclave was to launch The World Council of Religious Leaders, intent on reducing religious conflicts. The three-day conference began on 12 June 2002, with the Crown Prince of Thailand, Maha Vajiralongkorn inaugurating the proceedings. The Council of Representatives of the world's major faiths held prayer ceremonies in the huge auditorium of the Buddha Munthan Park.

In his thought-provoking speech, Dada urged the gathering to live religion, and not merely speak of it. Religion has not failed us, he affirmed; rather we have failed religion, he reiterated.

Living religion in daily life may sound like a herculean task, but Dada assured the audience that nothing is impossible. He broke it down into manageable aspects to make the idea simpler to grasp. He began by telling the listeners to be true to their duties by performing them diligently and faithfully. But he also asked them to transcend their duty and do a little more. Life indeed takes on a magical turn when we go beyond ourselves and make little differences in the lives of others, Dada elucidated. It is only awakened hearts that can usher in a new era of peace, Dada observed. Therefore, let love enter our hearts; it is only love that can save our sinking civilization, he emphasized.

YOU ARE OUR OWN!

Queens Borough President, Helen Marshall, presented Dada with a plaque honouring him and proclaimed 5 September 2002, as 'Dada J. P. Vaswani Day' in the Borough of Queens. The youngsters, who were crushed by the tragedy that led to the downfall of the twin towers of World Trade Center, found a haven of hope in Dada's answers.

The Mayor of Miami presented him with a proclamation in which 25 November 2002, was slated to be observed as 'Dada J. P. Vaswani Day' in the city of Fort Lauderdale, Florida. It acknowledged Dada's multi-faceted personality as a writer, academician, spiritual leader and philosopher. He also presented Dada with a key to the city of Miami saying to him, 'The doors of Miami are open to you – our hearts will be open too, waiting to welcome you again. Come back soon! America needs people like you to come and reinforce strength, courage and spirituality within it!' He had indeed realized the power within Dada to uplift America's spirits.

At St Thomas, Governor Charles Turnbull was the chief guest at the Wyndham Sugar Bay Hotel, where Dada communicated the message of appreciating others, admitting when you are wrong, helping others as well as thanking others. Though simple, Dada's speech went straight to the hearts of the gathering. Profoundly moved by Dada's talk, Governor Charles Turnbull presented Dada with a golden key, just like the Mayor of Miami! He also handed over a proclamation to Dada declaring 25 November as 'Sadhu Vaswani Day' in St Thomas.

ASIAN YOUTH FOR PEACE ASSOCIATION CONCLAVE, BANGALORE, 2003

The Asian Youth for Peace Association invited Dada to deliver the keynote address at the opening of their week-long programme on 9 August 2003 at Bangalore. Young people, ranging between the ages of eighteen and twenty-five, had gathered together from various parts of Asia to make a unified attempt towards world peace. Some of the participating countries were Nepal, Cambodia, Indonesia, Philippines, Taiwan, Singapore and Laos.

The young gathering gave Dada a standing ovation upon his entry to the venue. Dada addressed them in his sweet, resonant voice and told them that although he was 85 years old, he felt like one of them, for age, he said, was a state of mind not dependent on physical ageing.

Dada, like a master musician, played the seven musical notes needed to move towards a world of peace. These were: (1) Love (2) Friendship (3) Equality, (4) Tolerance to all religions (5) No discrimination among countries (6) No exploitation of one nation by the other and (7) Compassion to all, including birds and animals – to all of creation.

As Dada headed amidst the youngsters towards the exit, he waved out the little souvenir cap that he had received from them. The continuous rhythmic applause that followed was symbolic of the waves of joy that Dada had been sending out to them.

HUMANITARIAN OF THE YEAR

On Friday, 10 September 2004, Dada was at the auditorium of the Sri Swami Narayan Temple in Secaucus, for a ruh-rihan satsang organized by the Sindhi Association of New Jersey (SANJ). The programme began with the offering of a cheque of $2,000 to the Secaucus Animal Shelter on behalf of the Sadhu Vaswani

centre, to help in their efforts to save the stray and lost animals of
Secaucus. The town of Secaucus recognized and honoured Dada
and presented him with a plaque. The Deputy Mayor of Secaucus
addressed Dada and all present and expressed his appreciation for
the Sadhu Vaswani Centre's admirable work.

'The Humanitarian of the Year' award was presented to Dada
by the Mayor of the Town of Southwest Ranches, Florida, amidst
thunderous applause at a crowded meeting held at the South Florida
Hindu Temple, on 14 September 2004.

INDO–PAK REVERENCE CONFERENCE, PUNE, 2005

The Indo–Pak Reverence Conference (15–21 January 2005)
unfolded a new chapter in the ongoing Indo–Pak peace initiatives.
Pune, with its mix of industry, education and culture, played the
perfect host to the 130-strong Pakistani delegation, in the city for
the seven-day conference.

After an exchange of Puneri pagdis for Pashtun ones from
Peshawar, an emotionally charged speech on love, humanity and
the need to blur borders by Dada J. P. Vaswani changed the mood.

There was an instant emotional connection established with the
visiting delegates from Pakistan. 'My friends, this earth belongs
neither to you nor to me,' Dada told the visitors. 'We are here on
earth as pilgrims, our stay on this earth is just for a brief while.
The earth belongs to God. The earth belongs to Allah. Call him
by whatever name you will, he is our president and under him let
us establish a World Federation in which every nation can live as
a brother or a sister to every other nation. Let us begin with India
and Pakistan, let us begin with India and Pakistan! Let our two
countries be joined together in a federation so that they continue to
be sovereign independent nations, continue to have their freedom
and identity – but also simultaneously, show the world that they

can live together as friends, as brothers. India needs Pakistan – and Pakistan needs India, for we cannot live at loggerheads any longer. Over fifty-seven years have passed, while we have lived apart, in mistrust and separation; it is time we got together in amity and brotherhood. Fifty-seven long years have passed, and during this period I do not know how many billions of rupees must have been spent by our countries over what we call trying to maintain our own independent identities. Once, we were together in our struggle for freedom; now, if we joined together in our freedom, we shall continue to cherish our independence but at the same time we will learn how to live together and work together.'

Dada's friendship poem had a powerful impact on the audience:

Tear down the walls,
Tear down the walls, for we all are one,
We cannot live apart.
God is One, the earth is one and One is the eternal heart.
We may discover nature's secrets, we may plumb the depths
of the sea,
We cannot atone for all the walls which separate you from me.
Tear down the walls in the name of Allah, who is Rehman,
who is Rahim,
The Master's call has gone forth, work together as in a team,
Ye all are one! Ye all are one! Ye all are one! Ye all are one!

The conference ended with a warm invitation from the visitors for Dada to visit the land of his birth – Sind. The invitation was readily accepted and Dada's historic trip to Pakistan came about very soon, when Dada and a small band of devotees took a trip to the land of their birth, Sind, between 14 and 21 March 2005.

Dada arrived in Karachi on Monday, 14 March, 2005, to an ecstatic welcome from the local administration and from thousands of Sindhi Hindus who had travelled long distances to meet and greet Dada. Their loving presence and their fervent pleas to Dada to visit their homes detained Dada for over three hours at the airport.

It was with great excitement that Dada and his group set out from Karachi on the 15 March for Keenjhar and Jhirkan. After all, these were the hallowed grounds that had inspired Sadhu Vaswani, over a century ago, to embark upon the creation of his immortal devotional compositions under the pen name, Nuri.

The rough and turbulent waters of the Keenjhar Lake did not deter Dada and his group, who decided to take a boat ride to the samadhi of Nuri located on a hillock, on a small island in the middle of the lake. The lashing waves and the heavy sprays of water drenched them, and many of them were afraid, but not Dada. He fearlessly stepped off the boat on touching land and briskly walked up a steep hillock to the actual location of the samadhi. There were no protective walls around the samadhi, humble as the queen whose mortal remains it enclosed. As they sat on a small parapet to catch their breath, members of the group felt that the boisterous winds would blow them off the hill into the rolling and murky waters below. Dada, lost in a world of his own, meditated a while and from the depths of his heart flowed a beautiful song. It was a moment for and with the gods.

Dada and the others then went to Jhirkan village, for it was here that Sadhu Vaswani had beheld the sacred vision of Nuri. From Jhirkan they proceeded to Hyderabad, Sind, where a warm Sindhi welcome greeted Dada.

In Hyderabad, they visited the very first St Mira's School, originally set up by Gurudev Sadhu Vaswani; it is now a government school for girls. Imagine the nostalgia with which they entered the original sanctuary hall where Sadhu Vaswani's motto for the school – Simplicity, Service, Purity and Prayer – was still inscribed on the wall. Dada unveiled Sadhu Vaswani's portrait and delivered an emotional speech, with the powerful message, 'Be strong, be simple, and spend your strength in the service of the surrounding world.'

Next they visited the building which was the original venue of the Sakhi Satsang, where Sadhu Vaswani had stayed on the second floor. Thereafter, they visited the house where Dada Jashan was born and where now, one Mr Abdul Ahmed lived. As Dada came out of the house, he was greeted by the people of the neighbourhood, eighty per cent of whom were Muslims. They surprised everyone with their fervent devotion. They touched Dada's feet and sought his blessings.

In the evening, a ruh-rihan in Sindhi was organized by the Sindhi Graduates Association at the Mumtaz Mirza Sindh Museum Auditorium. The function was presided over by the vice chancellor of Sindh University, Mr Muzahar Allakh. In his speech, he said to Dada, '*Bhali Kare Aaya*. Sind is also your country.' All the people assembled there were enchanted by Dada's sweet smile and urged Dada to visit Sind again. Dada presented Mr Muzahar with a copy of the Nuri Granth in Sindhi.

Back in Karachi, a grand function was held at the Marriott Hotel, where Mr Muhammad Mian Soomro, the Chairman of the Senate of Pakistan was the chief guest. He welcomed Dada with great warmth and respect and wished that Dada could visit Karachi again and again and share his wisdom with the people. He added, 'We live in a world of turmoil and there is dire need of the message of love which beloved Dada has brought with himself and we are grateful to him.'

On 19 and 20 March 2005, Dada held satsangs in the evening, providing welcome sustenance to thirsty souls aspiring for the grace of the guru.

On 21 March, the last day of this trip, a unique event was scheduled – Dada's visit to D. J. Sind college, both Sadhu Vaswani's and his alma mater, where he had received a fellowship and worked as a professor for some time. Dada was warmly welcomed. Professor Ravi Shankar Harani, the principal of the college, spoke about Dada emotionally. He lauded Dada's academic achievements. The president of the function, Dr Hameeda Khusro, the Minister for Education spoke highly about Dada. She requested Dada to return to Sind at his earliest so that thousands of Sindhis could benefit from his teachings. Sadhu Vaswani had brought about a great social change in Sind, she pointed out. Sind could never forget him. Amidst thunderous applause, she announced that Hyderabad–Sind would soon have a Mira College.

After Dada's opening remarks, a question-answer session commenced. One student asked, 'You were a brilliant student, you could have gone for ICS and become a collector. Why did you choose the other path?' Dada smiled and replied, 'With an ICS degree I would have been only a collector, but now I am a distributor. Wherever I go I spread the message of my master and distribute his wisdom and love.' Dada was felicitated by the college authorities. A few senior professors also paid their tributes to Dada.

In the evening, Dada held a Sindhi ruh-rihan at Swami Narayan Temple. Brothers and sisters gathered there in large numbers. Dada expressed the wish to visit some needy families as he felt that his mission to Pakistan would be incomplete without the service of the poor. Accordingly, he was taken to visit the houses of a few people, to whom he distributed gifts in cash and kind.

During this trip to the land of his birth, Dada travelled on the highways; he conducted satsangs and delivered public lectures; he visited a temple and a well-known college. He visited the homes of devotees and conducted satsangs every day. Well-wishers and authorities pleaded with Dada to accept police security, but Dada declined the offer resolutely yet graciously. Indeed, Karachi had in those days, been under threat of violence and insurgency. But such was the master's grace that Dada's visit went by peacefully.

ASIAN HERITAGE COMMITTEE HONOURS DADA

In 2006, the Asian Heritage Committee felicitated Dada with a special award, recognizing him as a 'Living Master Transforming

Humanity'. With his characteristic humility, Dada received the award on behalf of his master with the response, 'I am not a living Master but a living disciple of the Master.'

During this programme held at the Lincoln Center in New York, Dada gave a short discourse in English on 'Do Your Duty and a Little More'.

VEGETARIAN CONGRESS, GOA, 2006

The Vegetarian Society invited Dada to deliver the keynote address at the 37th International Vegetarian Congress held in 2006, with over a hundred delegates from twelve countries in attendance.

At the start of his rousing speech, Dada emphasized the need for activists and volunteers who have a fire in their hearts for the cause of vegetarianism. Volunteers would become the voice of birds and animals – dumb, defenceless creatures – and would work not only for animal welfare but for animal rights. All animal lovers must unite and form a charter of animal rights, he added. In this connection, Dada referred to the SAK association and explained how it encouraged vegetarianism through the meatless day campaign in which people all over the world not only promise to abstain from all food of violence but also go out of their way to help animals. Reverence for all life, he observed, is the only solution for the survival of our sinking civilization.

'I COULD NOT HAVE BEEN BORN WITHOUT YOU!'

When Sadhu Vaswani College of Nursing, located in the Sadhu Vaswani Mission Medical Complex, Pune, India, in conjunction with the Society of Midwives (India), Pune Chapter, held a national conference in 2006, Dada J. P. Vaswani gave this inspiring message about the importance of access to midwives, especially in a country like India:

The birth of every baby ... is a joyful and welcoming experience. Unfortunately, due to the presence of either poverty or ignorance, this marvellous moment is converted to one of tragedy because of the inaccessibility of medical institutions or skilled help ... In India, over the ages, the presence of midwives is an integral part of childbirth. In rural India, even today, the presence of a skilled midwife is paramount, at every delivery, to ensure the health and safety of both mother and child. It is commendable that the Society of Midwives (India), along with their base in tradition, have evolved and grown with modern techniques and skills, to provide safety and succour to both mother and new-born child, ensuring that each birth continues to be a joyful expression of the divine. Later, when Dada met all the delegates in an exclusive session, his first words to them were: 'I would not have been born without you.' There was laughter and applause.

DOUBLE HONOURS FOR DADA

In 2007, Dada was honoured with the Interfaith Peace Award for his noble and selfless service to the cause of universal peace. The award was presented to him in New York by the president of Interfaith Center, Rev. James Parks Morton.

Mr Morton referred to Dada as the Swami Vivekananda of this century who, at this time, gave the West a deep insight into the sanctity and the rich treasures of Hinduism. With deep admiration and respect for Dada, he explained how Dada had come back in this age to revive the universal truths of Hinduism – a rare personality who, with love and peace, rich and profound spiritual wisdom would help the fundamental truths of Hinduism to be put into practice by the multitudes all over the world.

At the same function, the chairman of Bharatiya Vidya Bhavan, Dr Navin Mehta, conferred on Dada a lifetime achievement award in recognition of his outstanding and unparalleled services to the promotion of religious harmony and his commitment to promoting compassion, understanding and global friendship. Dada gave an inspirational, soul-uplifting talk in English and conducted a meditation session at the gathering.

MIT WORLD PEACE CENTRE

World Peace Centre is the seat for the UNESCO chair for human rights, democracy, peace and tolerance.

Dada spoke of the two saints, Saint Dnyaneshwar and Saint Tukaram as true awakeners of humanity, who awakened people from the slumber of the senses. Dada outlined five tips for a peaceful life:

1. Grow in simplicity, be desireless and accept the will of God.
2. If you want to be wiser, be an early riser. One can gather spiritual energy in the wee hours of the morning when there is a descent of holy vibrations from above.
3. Stop complaining and start thanking.
4. Listen twice as much as you speak. We have two ears and one mouth, for God meant man to listen more and talk less.
5. Develop a state of equanimity. Have a smile on your face always.

MAHAVIR AWARD FOR DADA

Young Indian Vegetarians, Sri Satya Service Organisation, UK, and members of the Swaminarayan Temple Trust came together to confer upon Dada the prestigious Mahavir Award.

He was reverently and warmly welcomed before he approached the podium. After paying homage to his master, Sadhu Vaswani, Dada proclaimed that religions are worth no more than straw if they do not teach us to love and serve suffering ones, along with care for animals and birds. Citing Albert Schweitzer, the Nobel Peace Prize winner, Dada emphasized the need for compassion and reverence for all life. All forms of human tyranny must stop, he urged to the cheers of the Young Indian Vegetarians and the followers of Lord Mahavira present in large numbers.

Dada was then honoured with a citation and the Mahavir Award followed by a standing ovation by the appreciative audience.

SPECIAL MEET WITH DEFENCE PERSONNEL

In 2009, a multitude of defence personnel came to hear the inspiring words of Dada J. P. Vaswani in a one of its kind events at the Mission for defence officers. As Dada took to the stage, he warmly thanked the officers for their gracious presence at the event and recounted to them the message of Sadhu Vaswani: 'Love and peace in your hearts, but keep the powder dry,' adding that while officers' hearts should always be filled with love and peace, they should be prepared when duty comes calling. In his talk 'Change Your Attitude, Change Your Life', he told the audience that if they wished to change their lives and be truly happy, then all they had to do was to tune their attitude.

Following the talk was an interactive question-answer session. Some of the questions put to Dada by the officers were:

Q: As a Kshatriya by profession, I understand my duty. As a human being, what should be my mission in life?

A: Do your duty, and a little more.

Q: Do we have to wait until the next reincarnation of God, for us to experience peace on this earth?

A: Peace is your birthright. You can have it this very moment. But peace belongs to those who build their lives in the will of God. If this be the mantra of one's life, then one will never be disturbed. You can be the master of limitless power and wealth, but without mental peace, you can never be happy.

Q: How do we combat the negative forces in the environment around us, which constantly discourage us from developing a positive attitude?

A: Prayer will help you. Prayer is the greatest, but most unused power, power greater even than atomic power. Go to God with this faith. We have ignored him for a long time.

Dada concluded the session with his message for the officers: 'Turn back to God. There is a ring of darkness around us, but it is of our own creation, our own shadow, because we have turned our backs to the light – the light that is God. Make a U-turn, face the light, and then there will be no more darkness.'

WORLD PARLIAMENT OF RELIGIONS

The Parliament of Religions which convened in Melbourne, Australia, in 2009, was like a confluence of several holy rivers all flowing into the same ocean: the representatives of world religions from all over the globe were present, all with a commonality of purpose, generating a massive flow of positive, universal energy. Dada's message to the group of Buddhist monks from Tasmania was Buddha's teaching, 'Hatred ceaseth not by hatred, hatred ceaseth by love. Therefore, love ye one another!'

At the plenary session of the parliament on the five pillars of spiritual life, he emphasized how spirituality is a cohesive force which binds people together.

Today, science and technology have been unable to provide us inner joy and peace of mind. Only true spirituality can enable us to attain peace within and be at peace with the rest of the world. For this, the daily practice of a period of silence is essential; our day, he said, should be full of little turnings towards God, in whichever way possible.

Dada's scholarly compilation of the essence of world faiths, entitled *Many Paths: One Goal* was released at the conference and received with universal appreciation by the eminent delegates.

CONVOCATION OF HINDU LEADERS

At the sideline of the parliament, Dada addressed a convocation of Hindu leaders from all over the world on the surest way to peace. He focused on the most important message of Hinduism, which is the oneness of all creation and the sanctity of life. Life, he said, sleeps in the mineral and the stone; dreams in plants and vegetation; it stirs in animals and fauna; it is awake in human beings. But it is one life which permeates all creation; hence Hinduism reveres all forms of life from stone to man.

Dada urged all Hindu parents to inculcate in their children qualities of character that made our country great in days of yore. He said that truthfulness, courage, faith, compassion and forbearance will always be relevant to human civilization; and these qualities, when they are inculcated in our children, will benefit the whole of humanity.

LIFETIME ACHIEVEMENT AWARD

In the first World Parliament of Spirituality, held at Hyderabad in 2012, Dada was conferred with a lifetime achievement award at the hands of the chairperson of the forum, Dr D. R. Karthikeyan. This parliament was a historic event, where world spiritual leaders and thousands of seekers from more than a hundred nations of the world came together to usher in a new era of peace and harmony on earth.

In his address, Dada said, 'Spirituality is the new religion of this age. And the "s" of spirituality is smile and serve all the while! Spirituality does not just mean going to the church or the temple or reading voluminous scriptures or going on pilgrimages. Spirituality is an illumined personal experience of God. The true spirit of religion, which is also the secret of spirituality, is "love". True love is to reckon oneself as nothing and the Beloved as all.'

Dada also addressed the parliament on the topic, 'What is spirituality?' He said, 'In simple words, spirituality is knowledge of God, not an intellectual knowledge but an illumined personal experience of the supreme.' He went on to explain that spirituality teaches us to look within for answers. Dada told the audience, 'Spirituality is a gift of God it is a reality given freely and spontaneously. All we can do is to keep the door of our heart open, and entreat God to enter therein. 'When wilt Thou enter the home of my heart?' should be our constant prayer.'

Dada narrated the story of Rabbi Kotzak, who repeatedly asked people, 'Where dwelleth God?' They laughed and told him that God was omnipresent, that he was everywhere. The Rabbi then gave his answer and said: 'God dwells wherever man lets him in!'

Dada's moving speech closed with the powerful imploration: 'May I, with folded hands, ask every one of you, whose good fortune it is to be present at this first World Parliament of Spirituality: Let Him in! Let Him in! Let Him in!'

YOUTH PARLIAMENT

With a spring in his step, an enchanting smile on his face and an enthusiastic gleam in his eyes, Dada faced the 5,000-strong student body present at the MIT grounds, Pune, for the Fourth Indian Student Parliament, organized by the MAAER's MIT School of Government (The Maharashtra Academy of Engineering, Education, and Research, Maharashtra Insitute of Technology), Pune.

Dada spoke on politics, a topic of prime importance for students, so they can participate actively towards a bright future of the country. His speech was fiery and enlivened the hearts of the youngsters. Dada said, 'Though they tell me I am ninety-five, I still feel a youth at heart,' winning over the hearts of the young ones eagerly absorbing all his words.

Continuing his speech, he proclaimed, 'There is hope for India to rise supreme, once again, to her initial glory.' True education is not only that of the brain, but of awakened hearts, he pointed out. Moving on to the subject at hand, he emphasized that we, being the servants of Bharat Mata, service should be our politics. He advised:

1. Be an Indian. Forget differences of caste and creed.
2. Be a builder filled with simplicity and dedication.
3. Always speak the truth.
4. Never yield to anger.
5. Always give respect to women.
6. Focus on reconstruction of villages.
7. Learn to share.

India will be truly free, when its people will learn to serve their motherland selflessly. They have to be workers and labourers, *sipahi*s (soldiers) ready to give their all to the welfare of the country and its people. Only when India is rejuvenated and recharged with the spirit of the educated, principled, and committed youth can the nation be truly free from poverty and backwardness, corruption and nepotism, hunger and violence.

Every answer elicited cheers and loud applause, as though the youngsters were on the same wavelength as Dada!

PRIYADARSHINI ACADEMY GLOBAL AWARD

On receiving the Priyadarshini Academy Global Award in 2014, in his speech, Dada recalled with gratitude how his master had taught him to see God in everyone. Then, in his innate humility, he remarked that he did not deserve this award and that he was only accepting it on behalf of everyone at the Mission. Stating that each one made an invaluable contribution to humanity and thus deserved to receive the award, Dada recognized and accepted the oneness in everyone. What we need today is peace, he added, but there is no peace because we have forgotten the truth that we belong to each other. If only we would be aware of this, there would be no hatred, there would be no war. Then Dada asked all to bless him with more opportunities, occasions, options, possibilities, time, chances, and openings, so that he can go on serving more and more. For, it is service alone which is the main purpose of life, Dada continued. While man puts in so much effort developing the material life, man is essentially the spirit divine – and that is the aspect which needs to be developed. To this end Dada offered five practical tips:

1. We should do unto others as we would have them do unto us.
2. We must always be true to our duty. Instead of constantly harping on our rights, we must do our duty conscientiously, honestly, righteously and faithfully.
3. We must learn to be compassionate and kind.
4. We must cultivate the spirit of acceptance and understand that all that happens to us happens at the will of God.
5. We should develop a strong bond, a permanent relationship, an unbreakable link with God. He is the source of everything. With his hand entwined in ours, there is nothing that we cannot achieve.

D LITT AWARD

Dada was honoured with the D Litt (Doctor of Literature) award by the President of India, Pranab Mukherjee, at the 11th convocation ceremony of the Symbiosis International University (SIU), held at their campus in Lavale in 2014.

In his speech, Dada said that true education is that which not only trains the mind and body, but helps in cultivating the soul. 'Cultivate the soul,' he urged the mammoth audience present at the convocation. 'We have thrown God out of our schools and colleges. Turn back to God!'

The President, Pranab Mukherjee, in his speech, concurred with Dada, saying, 'Educating the mind without educating the heart is not education at all.'

The university awarded the honorary degree to Dada 'in recognition of his immense contribution to the field of social sciences and for transforming the lives of people across ages by being a role model for them,' the citation read.

LIGHT UP ROTARY!

Dada had always been a great favourite with Rotarians all over India, having delivered memorable addresses and inspirational talks to them at their conferences and special gatherings. And so, it was no surprise that the Rotary International chose to invite Dada to their international conference to be held at Chennai. The theme was 'Light up Rotary'.

In December 2013, Dada addressed a large audience of a thousand Rotarians who had gathered from all over India and the world, many of them the crème-de-la-crème of society, the educated and elite, from different walks of life. Their eminence and prestige lit up the packed hall, which eagerly awaited the words of wisdom from Dada.

Touching upon the topic of the day, Dada stressed on the importance of light bearers to carry forth the flame of sympathy, compassion and care. To keep this flame burning bright and in order to spread its light, he placed before the receptive audience seven helpful suggestions:

1. Thoughts, ideas and activities should be positive in order to illumine one's own life, as well as that of others.
2. Words that are spoken should be sweet, gentle and true.
3. Prayer should become a habit.
4. Lives should be lit up with the spirit of gratitude.
5. Everyone should cultivate the will to forgive.

6. We should let into our lives the sunshine of laughter.

7. We should light up our life with service.

The Rotarians were so touched and awed by Dada's impressive delivery that they gave a standing ovation to Dada and the claps simply did not seem to end. Once again, Dada had conquered the hearts and minds of the Rotarians with his wit and wisdom!

DADA UNVEILS MAHATMA GANDHI STATUE AT SECAUCUS

Dada, the pilgrim of love, honoured Mahatma Gandhi, the apostle of peace on Saturday, 31 May 2014, with the formal unveiling of a statue of the great leader at the Sadhu Vaswani Meditation Garden in Secaucus, New Jersey. As the Keynote Speaker, he was joined by several other national and local community leaders and politicians, including Mayor Michael Gonnelli, Congresswoman Tulsi Gabbard, and Wayne Pacelle, CEO of the Humane Society of the United States.

Dada observed, 'Mahatma Gandhi was born in India but he belonged to humanity.' He spoke on Gandhi's great message of ahimsa, or non-violence, with his own special focus on urging the audience to work towards animal rights. 'Forget all differences of caste, creed or colour; renounce all sense of separateness, come together, join hands together in the one creative, the one constructive task of building a new world order, a new civilization, a new humanity,' he told the audience.

Congresswoman Tulsi Gabbard struck an instantaneous rapport with Dada. She echoed Dada's message on service, quoting Mahatma Gandhi's famous words, 'The best way to find yourself is to lose yourself in the service of others.' Ms Gabbard is the first Hindu in history to serve on the US Congress and the first to take her oath of office on the Bhagavad Gita.

US SENATOR TULSI GABBARD VISITS DADA

In 2014, on Christmas, US senator Ms Tulsi Gabbard met Dada in Pune. She attended a session at the spiritual camp, arranged by the Sadhu Vaswani Mission. Dada felicitated her and said, 'Man has had his chance. Man has blundered. Man has built up a civilization of wars and violence, of hatred and strife. This civilization is already crumbling underneath its own weight. A new civilization is to be born and of this new civilization, the woman soul will be the builder. And Tulsi Gabbard is one such woman soul. She is one of the great builders for whom the world is waiting.'

Tulsi Gabbard in her address said, 'I am coming to you today all the way from Hawaii in the spirit of Aloha: deep respect and an open heart.' She said that her motivation and inspiration has been the Bhagavad Gita, which teaches us to live for others. 'Lord Krishna's teachings to us are timeless, they are relevant and they are for every single one of us. His teachings truly have the power to solve the world's problems.'

Later, she led the kirtan session with great enthusiasm, singing and chanting Lord Krishna's Holy Name, singing on in tune to her musical instrument – the ukulele.

NATIONAL ROUND TABLE CONFERENCE, PUNE, 2015

The meeting of the National Round Table Conference on Religion and Holy Scriptures of World Religions, was held at MAEER'S MIT, Pune, in 2015. The gathering attracted speakers and leaders of various faiths, such that the whole meet was charged with a unique and powerful energy.

Among other speakers was Dada. His talk was carved out of the depths of wisdom and truth and embellished with his wit and humour, touching the core of every heart present there. Religion is not a matter of rites and rituals or creeds and ceremonies, Dada said. It is a life of sympathy and service, sacrifice, new awakening, self-effacement and self-realization. Dada emphasized upon the thought that India's ancient wisdom holds the ideal that 'all creation is one family'. Our hearts are given to us to love and not to hate. Irrespective of who we are, the divine spark exists within each one of us.

'Religion is love, the highest force is love,' Dada concluded. 'Love is in truth the profoundest philosophy of life, for love is the expansion of self. The Lord of Love is the inspirer of all religions.'

As all the religions and their respective teachers agreed, the call for the day was for oneness, peace, love and unity among mankind. The meeting was a platform for the eradication of dissension, strife, divisiveness and differences from the face of the earth.

DADA MEETS WITH SOCIETY OF CIVIL SERVANTS

A special meeting held at the auditorium of the Sadhu Vaswani Mission in 2015 saw the civil servants of Pune come together, with their wonderful blend of insight, intelligence and wide experience of service to civil society.

The interaction began with Dada's question to his audience: 'Why is it that you want a particular thing? The answer to this will be a common one – all of us are in quest of happiness. Unfortunately, in this quest we are all moving along wrong routes. Therefore, we are not always happy.'

The ice-breaker question from the audience was:

Q: Dada, have you always been so wise and knowledgeable or were you ever like us too?

A: I am just like you even today. Life is a school and experience is our teacher. Each one has their own set of lessons to learn. We should not run away from difficult experiences. Once we learn even from a formidable experience, it stops being difficult and unmanageable.

Q: Are spiritual centres able to give long-term succour and peace, or is their effectiveness diminishing?

A: In answer, I will discuss the theory of the four *yugas*: Satya Yuga or the Golden Age, in which the true spirit was charged in each of these qualities – truth, purity, prayer, simplicity, and service. In the next, Treta Yuga, or the Silver Age, there was seventy-five per cent of truth in the above qualities. In the third, Dwapara Yuga, or the Copper Age, there was fifty per cent truth. In the final, Kali Yuga, or the Iron Age – the current one – there is only twenty-five per cent. But, often, I do not even find that. [*Audience burst into laughter*]

We must live our lives according to the principles we believe in. Unfortunately, our will is weakened.

Q: Do you have any special message for Indian bureaucracy in the Kali Yuga?

A: Be kind, understanding, truthful and honest. There is no religion higher than truth – the highest truth being compassion. [This was followed by applause]

Q: How can we handle stress in the work environment?

A: The best way is (*a*) by letting go. The measure in which I am a spectator and not an actor, the stress goes away; and (*b*) by realizing that in every incident or accident there is the meaning of God's mercy. We are so terrified by the packaging of the experience, we do not look into its inner meaning.

Q: Why do good people suffer?

A: Maybe they are not good enough. Just as gold through the crucible is purified, so also suffering is the purifying fire. Whatever happens to you, do not forget it is your own coming back to you. It is the universal law – action and reaction are equal and opposite to each other.

At the end of the meet, all the participants gladly queued up to have a personal handshake with Dada.

THE HUMANE SOCIETY

In 2015, Dada addressed the members of the Humane Society of Washington D. C. at their headquarters. It is America's largest animal-protection organization, and its president, Mr Wayne, was deeply touched that Dada had taken the trouble to visit them despite the hurdles of health and age.

Welcoming Dada, Mr Wayne observed how Dada verily lived all that he preached. 'I see in Dada a picture of compassion,' he said.

Dada spoke passionately, advocating the cause of animals' rights to life. He said that no nation could pronounce itself free until all its animals had been set free. He added that in the US, the trend had already begun to shift in favour of protecting animals. India too should become a flag bearer in leading the march of kindness and mercy towards animals.

The fervour with which Dada spoke brought tears to the eyes of many. He was commended by one and all for his passion and for living his compassion.

CONFERENCE OF INDIAN DIASPORA

In 2015, Dada was also invited to address the delegates at the Conference of Indian Diaspora at Airlie Resort, Virginia. It was a forum which brought together Indian–American leaders for a three-day summit of candid conversations, strategic discussions and cultural experiences in order to advance the causes of community harmony. Dada spoke to them on the five pillars of a meaningful life.

'We are aware of the three basic dimensions in our lives – length, breadth, and height', Dada began. He further added:

1. Length involves doing your duty towards your immediate family members.
2. Breadth comprises assisting our extended families, and all people we come in contact with in our daily lives.
3. Height involves raising ourselves higher, with our thoughts focusing on the one above. But there is something beyond these which most of us are unaware of.
4. The fourth dimension consists of seeing the vision of the one in all.
5. The fifth dimension is indescribable; it can only be realized. We are all vibrating at particular frequencies. This frequency must be increased if we want to be capable of leading a meaningful life.

Dada proceeded to enumerate four practical means through which one could precipitate this vibration:

1. Whatever you do, ensure that it is right and true.
2. Trust in the divine and realize that the right thing happens at the right time.
3. Take care of every moment.
4. Be a giver.

This enlightening talk was followed by several one-on-one meetings of the participants with Dada, all assured of getting their doubts and queries answered by him. The surgeon general, Vivek Murthy, was among one of them. He asked Dada's advice on the right kind of life to live. Dada shared with him the knowledge of two basic laws:

1. Take care of your food. Watch what you put in your mouth, for often that is the cause of all the troubles that arise.
2. Do not react to all that occurs, for it is the cause of the imbalance that arises within us. Instead one should always respond, as that gives rise to equanimity and balance.

WRITERS MEET DADA

A few writers came to interview Dada during his retreat in Washington D. C. Among them was Jennifer Greene, who got completely bowled over by Dada's humility. When she spoke highly of him, Dada reiterated that he was nothing. When she referred to him as a messenger of God, he responded that he was merely a listener of God's message. Jennifer found Dada to be a dispenser and radiator of love with beauty. Dada refuted this, saying that he was only a reflector of God's love, who wants each and every human being to be such.

On another day, Carl Stanton, an author cum photographer, interviewed Dada for one-and-a-half hours. He emerged completely influenced and touched by this experience. Dada told him that we all want God's grace, but, he clarified, the process of getting has its root in giving. Dada elucidated this with a story.

There was a man who was thrown into the pits of poverty overnight. Totally disheartened, he approached a holy man and asked for the reason for his sudden misfortune. The holy man asked him about his current possessions. He said he owned only two shirts. The holy one asked him to give away one of his shirts. This person gladly parted with his shirt, lovingly giving it to someone in need. It was after this, that the process of receiving started in his life. When we give, we live. When we don't give, we are no better than dead souls, Dada stated firmly.

With a grin Carl said, 'Dada, today I want to give you something. My forte is photography. Right now your face is beautiful and the light is perfect. I would love to capture it on my camera and not lose this ideal moment.' He then proceeded to click some remarkable pictures of Dada.

ROUND TABLE ON EDUCATION

In July 2015, during a retreat in the picturesque shores of the Arabian Sea in Goa, Raju Bharat, eminent hotelier and devotee of

Dada, organized a round table meet on education where leading academicians met and interacted with Dada. The management and principals of prestigious colleges and institutes were present at this exclusive interaction. In his talk to them, Dada spoke about how man is made of body, mind and soul. The educational system founded by Gurudev Sadhu Vaswani laid great emphasis on cultivation of the soul. We have divorced God from our schools, colleges and homes and now we regret to see the result.

'The solution to many problems is to bring God back into our schools and homes. At least one period in the daily schedule of the college or school should be solely dedicated to building up the character of the students and for cultivation of the soul,' he said. It was unanimously endorsed by one and all and they agreed that there was a need to change the prevalent educational system and inculcate value education and character building in their courses.

The meet moved Raju Bharat to start a school on the lines of the Mira Movement in Goa, and Dada blessed his efforts whole-heartedly.

CHAMPION OF FORGIVENESS AWARD, 7 OCTOBER 2016

In 2016, Dada J. P. Vaswani, along with Desmond Tutu and Nelson Mandela (posthumously), was honoured with the Champion of Forgiveness Award by Worldwide Forgiveness Alliance, in association with major organizations including the Shift Network and Unify. These associations recognized Dada as a new-generation forgiveness leader for his influential work in promoting global forgiveness.

Warm appreciation was expressed for Dada's forgiveness campaign, the Moment of Calm, which forges ahead in alliance with major organizations to bring about world peace through the power of forgiveness. 'Hearts at peace will create world peace,' as Dada says.

CONFERENCE ON WORLD PEACE AND HARMONY THROUGH INTERFAITH DIALOGUE, 28 APRIL 2017

Religious leaders from different faiths came together at the meet on 'World Peace and Harmony through Interfaith Dialogue'. It marked the foundation day of Ahimsa Vishwa Bharti, an organization founded by Jain Acharya Dr Lokesh Muni.

The special guests included Sri Sri Ravishankar of Art of Living, spiritual leader Rameshbhai Oza, Chief Jathedar of Akal Takht Golden Temple Giani Gurbachan Singh, Dr Imam Umer Ilyasi, Buddhist monk Drukpa Thuksey Rinpoche, and Dr Binny Sareen of Brahma Kumaris, the organizers of the event. Among non-religious leaders who attended the meet were state and union ministers.

The spiritual leaders spoke on the various ideals and practices that can ensure world peace. In his address, Dada emphasized that there can be no peace in the world without peace in the hearts of the people. 'Peace or Perish; there is no other choice,' his ending words echoed in the hall.

SPIRITUAL LEADERS CALL ON DADA

Dr Imam Umer Ahmed Ilyasi Seeks Dada's Blessings

The chief imam of the All India Imam Organization, with his family, called upon Dada in January 2016 to receive his blessings. Earlier, the imam had met Dada in New Delhi and had been thrilled with Dada's positivism, universal vision and his message of unity. '*Ham sab ek hain*' he reiterated, echoing Dada's words.

'We need leaders like you, Dada,' he said fervently, 'to keep India's unity and the harmony between communities alive!'

The chief imam was accompanied by a delegation, and expressed the wish that a conference be organized in Pune, where he and other imams would gather with their followers to honour Dada and spread his message of brotherhood and harmony.

Radhanath Swami Visits Dada

Radhanath Swami, the well-known writer, a *vaishnava* sanyasi and ISKCON teacher of the devotional path of *bhakti-yoga*, visited the Mission headquarter in Pune to pay his respects to Dada in January 2016. Their fascinating exchange of dialogues on the nature of the atman and Krishna-consciousness was an intellectual feast for everyone present. Swamiji said he felt blessed by the monsoon of love showered upon him with every glance Dada cast on him. Dada replied that with his profound Krishna-consciousness, he was already in the midst of the Pacific Ocean and needed no monsoon showers in that vast setting of *bhakti*!

Quoting Sri Chaitanya Mahaprabhu's words, Radhanath Swami said he felt the essence of Krishna bhakti in Dada's presence. He humbly requested Dada to continue spreading the love of Krishna, which Dada personified in his life.

Swami Krishnananda

Swami Krishnananda, a senior monk from the Ranchi headquarters of Yogoda Satsanga Society of India (YSS) visited the Sadhu Vaswani Mission to seek the blessings of Dada J. P. Vaswani in January 2017. He was accompanied by the Pune group of followers of Sri Sri Yogananda Paramhansa. They were inspired by the experience of their visit, which included the Darshan Museum and Tranquil Tuesdays – a combined session of ecstatic kirtan and guided meditation; 'We were fortunate to be a part of the session. It was a wonderful experience, best Diwali gift and beginning of a great year,' said Sudha Vaddadi, a member of the group. Their invitation to Dada to address them on a function for their centenary next year came at an interesting time, when Dada's own centenary would shine upon the horizon in 2018.

Pujya Anandmurti Gurumaa

Coming to the city of Pune for her Amrit Varsha Talks, Pujya Anandmurti Gurumaa visited the Sadhu Vaswani Mission in November 2016. Meeting Dada J. P. Vaswani for the first time, Pujya Gurumaa was wonderstruck with his smiles. A contagious session of smiles and laughter ensued between the two leaders. As they parted, she smiled saying he would still be there in spirit and in her words at the Sant Samagam organized by her ashram. Pujya Gurumaa is an avid supporter of Sadhu Vaswani Mission's International Meatless Day. She was deeply impressed when she saw the Darshan Museum based on the life and teachings of the founder and paid homage at his sacred samadhi.

Pujya Gurudevshri Rakeshbhai Jhaveri

Pujya Gurudevshri Rakeshbhai Jhaveri met Dada J. P. Vaswani on his visit to Pune in November 2016. Welcoming him to Sadhu Vaswani Mission, Dada referred to him as 'Bapa' – as his followers lovingly call him. The spiritual leader and founder of Shrimad Rajchandra Mission, Dharampur, was on a dharam yatra to Pune. Both felicitated each other in the presence of the evening sangat, with ensuing sounds of kirtan adding a beautiful setting to the presence of two great ones.

Pujya Acharya Dr Lokesh Muni Ji

The city of Pune was blessed with the visit of Pujya Acharya Dr Lokesh Muni ji in January 2017. It was a moving scene as he paid homage at the sacred samadhi of Sadhu Vaswani, close on the heels of the 51st Mahayagna (varsi) of the saint. Pujya Acharya ji also met Dada J. P. Vaswani, where he shared the joy of Dadaji's soon-approaching centenary.

Jetsunma Tenzin Palmo

Jetsunma Tenzin Palmo, the founder of Dongyu Gatsal Ling Nunnery, met Dada J. P. Vaswani on her visit to the city of Pune on 4 February 2017.

An advocate for equality of women and girl's education, Jetsunma is a *bhikkhu* from the Drukpa Lineage of the Kagyu school of Tibetan Buddhism. 'There is a rare flower that blooms once in a century. And you are that flower,' she greeted Dada.

They shared their common vision for character-based education – the dire need to develop the heart and not just the intellect, to develop ethics, human values – an education that gives values beyond just passing exams, getting good jobs and earning more money.

Learning of Dada's age and achievements, Jetsunma remarked, 'It is very inspiring to see somebody who has sacrificed his whole life in service to others and until the last breath – whenever that may be – will still be in service to God and to others, not at all thinking of his own well-being or anything – this is extraordinary.'

She also saw the Darshan museum and later paid homage at the master's sacred samadhi.

She had a ready smile and hugs too for the many devotees that sought her blessings.

'I am delighted for all the devotees that your guru has the compassion to keep going for as long as possible and to help you all,' she said.

Sri Sri Ravi Shankar

'You are the hope for the future of many aspiring hearts,' Dada said warmly, welcoming Sri Sri Ravishankar to the Mission. The spiritual leader responded quickly, 'Dada, you along with your master, have laid the path on which we are walking now.'

'It is time for you to fly now!' smiled Dada, 'for the goal we seek is still far away!'

Sri Sri Ravishankar accepted prasad from Dada's hands. The gift of Dada's books, he remarked, was 'an intellectual feast'.

COUNSELLING THE CONSULS

Dada met Dr Norbert Rèvai-Bere, consul general of Hungary, consul officials of Egypt and the Netherlands, and local dignitaries in May 2017, in Mumbai.

They were delighted upon meeting Dada and gaining insight from his wit and humour. A few of them confessed that the questions lurking in their mind were answered through Dada's talk, without having to utter them aloud to him. One of them shared her experience. She had recently lost a family member and was still reeling in grief, as she arrived to attend the meeting. And speaking directly to her heart, Dada spoke of love – love without attachment.

The interaction with Dada touched upon many other topics. There are two paths in life, Dada said. You can either move on the path of *preya* or on the path of *shreya*. *Preya* means the pleasant. It is a path of pleasure, it is smooth, it is slippery; you do not have to put any effort to walk on this path of pleasure. But it is a path that will lead to your doom. However, there is the other path. The other path is the path of *shreya*. *Shreya* means the good. It is the path that will lead you to your highest good. But it is a difficult path, it is a stony path, it is a thorny path, it is a rugged path, it is a path paved with flames. But if you move on this path it will lead you to your highest good. These are the two choices that are given to you, at every step, in every round of life.

A RARE ENCOUNTER, OCTOBER 2017

Two brilliant stars of the spiritual firmament came face to face and the entire surroundings were suffused in brilliance. Such was the impact when Dada J. P. Vaswani met Pope Francis at the Vatican on 11 October 2017. This was in fact Dada's second visit to the Vatican. Earlier on 19 July 1997 he had met with Pope John Paul II and delivered a discourse on 'Unity of Religions' to the Pope's Council for Inter-Religious Dialogue.

Dada was welcomed by Prince Hugo, one of the chief aides of the Pope. Dada was ushered to where the Pope was already addressing the thousands gathered at St Peter's Square in Vatican City.

After his address, the Pope approached Dada and greeted him warmly and affectionately. He bowed before Dada and asked for his blessings. Dada too simultaneously sought the Pope's blessings. The Pope reiterated his request a few times: 'Pray for me, bless me!' Finally, Dada took both the hands of the Pope and placed them upon his own head. It was such a treat to watch this warm camaraderie laced with deep humility.

Pope Francis was amazed that Dada had authored over 150 books and showed keenness in the work accomplished by Dada in the field of education. Dada, for his part, requested the church to pay special attention to the home and the school as it is there that children get their basic grounding and grooming. He reiterated that it is the children who are the builders of a brave, new world. The Pope agreed upon the importance of education, expressing that focusing upon it was the need of the hour.

Dada gifted the Pope with a shawl and a few of his books. In return, the Pope presented a silver memento to Dada. Dada then invited the Pope to come and visit him in Pune.

SPECIAL VISITORS

Gaur Gopal Das, spiritual leader and motivational speaker from ISKCON met Dada in January 2018. He recalled his student days in Pune when he would often pass by the Mission and be thrilled to see and meet Dada. Quoting Chaitanya Mahaprabhu, he observed that it was the greatest honour to meet a great saint like him. Dada smiled and said, 'There can be no great saint; when a man becomes a saint, he becomes the humblest of human beings.' The ISKCON leader described Dada as a lighthouse of spiritual wisdom. Taking a photograph with Dada, Gaur Gopal Das remarked, 'This is special, because I am with the youngest person who will be hundred very soon!'

Amish Tripathi, bestselling author of the Shiva Trilogy and the Ramachandra series, was among the celebrities who called on Dada in October 2016, when the latter was in Mumbai. He told Dada that as a devotee of the lord, he had been upset and disturbed by the kind of harsh and disrespectful language people used to question Lord Rama, and that was the starting point of his series on Ramachandra. The two of them discussed characters from the Ramayana, and Dada observed that it was easy for us to read about Rama and Sita, perhaps even easier to criticize them and find faults with them, but impossible to lead the kind of lives they led. Author Amish, as he is fondly called, found Dada's presence so positive and peaceful, that he said the age of the terrorist bombs that we are passing through today, was transformed into the age of love and devotion thanks to people like Dada. He requested Dada's permission to click a 'selfie' with him, and Dada said to him smiling, 'Take whatever you want. Nothing belongs to me.'

The writer said he felt blessed to have met Dada.

Karenna Gore, American author, journalist, and attorney, and the daughter of former US vice president, Al Gore, met Dada in New York. As the director of the Center for Earth Ethics at Union Theological Seminary, one of the bastions of progressive scholarship in the US, she had a lot of issues to discuss with Dada, especially on education. Dada said to her, 'The world has yet to understand that politics cannot change the life of a nation. What can change the life of a nation is education.'

With her was Jonathan Granoff, the American lawyer, screenwriter and lecturer, widely known for his work as president of the Global Security Institute. He spoke of the power of words and Dada told him, 'Every word we utter is recorded in the testimony of the universe. That is why in Hindi it is *akshar*... Akshar is that which cannot be thrown out of existence. It is eternal.'

Jonathan asked Dada whether we will ever know the purpose of creation. Dada smiled and said to him, 'The purpose that the One knows, we cannot know ... just as our pets do not know what we are doing, or why we are doing it ... We don't have the capacity to know that.' Dada added with a smile, 'We think we are everything. But we are nothing.'

'So many of us regard love as a noun, but it is a verb,' was Dada's parting message to the visitors.

Cory Booker, senator for New Jersey and former mayor of Newark, came to visit Dada and pay his respects, in May 2017, when Dada was in New Jersey. As a committed vegetarian since his youth, and a vegan since 2014, Senator Booker was delighted to hear about Dada's advocacy for a *sattvic* diet and spent quite some time discussing Dada's views on vegetarianism.

Dada said to him that he must always be a pillar of strength for the people, as their representative in government. Senator Booker sought Dada's views on the ways to cultivate will power and develop a positive attitude. He was fascinated to hear about Dada's early life and his decision to devote his life to Gurudev Sadhu Vaswani. He said to Dada very earnestly, 'I have been trying to find my duty. I think I know what it is, but I also worry about making sure that I am worthy to be a good, effective human being and a good public servant.'

Dada spoke to him of the Gita's concept of dharma, and urged him to fulfil his duty, working as an instrument of God for the welfare of the people. The senator was profoundly touched by Dada's words: 'Forsaking myself, make me an instrument of thy help and healing in this world of suffering and pain.'

Dada met His Holiness Dharmabhushan Swami Brahmeshanandacharya Maharaj of Tapobhoomi in December 2017. Goa's renowned spiritual hub, Tapobhoomi, located at Kundaim in Ponda Taluka has reached great heights due to the incessant efforts of the present Pithadeeshwar of the renowned Padmanabh Shishya Sampraday H. H. Dharmabhushan Swami Brahmeshanandacharya Maharaj. The revered Swamiji has been instrumental in reviving Goa's lost historical identity as Devbhumi and not just a hub for tourism oriented fun and frolic.

Anita Moorjani, the *New York Times* bestselling author of the book *Dying to be Me*, motivational speaker, and intercultural consultant for multinational corporations, came to visit Dada in January 2018. There was an interesting link with the Mission that her family had, Anita's mother, Neelu, had been a student of the Mira School in Hyderabad–Sind, and had looked upon Sadhu Vaswani as a mentor. Neelu had come to re-establish her link with the saint and his Mission, and to receive Dada's blessings.

Anita's bestselling book had been written from a personal experience. In 2006, after suffering cancer for almost four years, her organs started shutting down and she slipped into a deep coma. She was rushed to the hospital where she was in coma for nearly 30 hours and felt she had crossed into the afterlife, during what is often referred to as a near death experience (NDE). She discussed afterlife with Dada, and was delighted to receive Dada's book *Life after Death* for insights.

The emotionally charged meeting ended with the family requesting Dada for a thought to carry with them. Dada said to them, 'There is only one advice that we all need, which Sadhu Vaswani gave to us. He said, clasp God to your heart and let your hands be busy serving people ... Keep God in the heart within, serve those that are in need.'

THE HARBINGER OF LOVE AND PEACE

Wherever Dada went, he introduced himself to the gathering as a wanderer, a vagrant of the lord, in quest of fellow pilgrims thirsty for the simple values of life.

Describing himself as a servant of Sadhu Vaswani, Dada would refer to his master as a sage and seer who freely mingled as a man among men, solving their problems. Sadhu Vaswani believed that there was no religion higher than the religion of unity and love, service and sacrifice. Everything we have is a loan given to us, to share with those whose need is greater than ours. This refers not only to material things, but also to our knowledge, experience, position, prestige and our life itself.

At ninety-nine, Dada has not once suggested cancellation of his engagements or commitments, for personal reasons like pain, illness, exhaustion or just the need to rest. If at all trips are postponed and engagements rescheduled, it is on the insistence of Dada's team of devoted doctors.

As for Dada, he moves onward, forward, on his pilgrim path, ever impelled by his infinite, timeless, selfless love.

All glory to this pilgrimage of love! May the blessed pilgrim move on and on, transforming lives with love!

EIGHT

His Life is His Message

'Love is not something that can be taught by someone or learned from somewhere; but in the presence of the Perfect Master we can feel it, and in due course, develop it.'

– Mata Amritanandamayi Ma

DADA: THE MAN AND HIS MESSAGE

By education and training Dada was a scientist; it would be true to say he was still scientific by temperament with his analytical, practical approach to issues and problems. In fact, he regarded spirituality as a science of the spirit – *atma vidya*. He was a philosopher as he was fascinated by concepts, ideals, values and universal precepts; true to the original meaning of the word philosopher, he was indeed a lover of wisdom. His family background, his roots and, to a considerable extent, the genetic link to his father and his uncle ensured that he was, and always will be, a humanitarian. Deeply reflective by nature and a voracious reader, his rigorous academic career had made him an eminent scholar. And the crowning glory of this modern day saint, his early apprenticeship and invaluable association with his master, Sadhu Vaswani, had turned him into the best of teachers and mentors. Far less accomplished people tend to be swayed by the weight of their own worth and value, but not Dada. He remained the very soul of simplicity and humility. Over and above all this was his spiritual power, the mantle that he had inherited from his uncle and mentor.

Our poor words can by no means do justice to the wonderful personality that Dada was – indeed, a man in a million, or a 'smile-millionaire' as admirers referred to him. Thousands of devotees all over the world regarded him as their guru; but he regarded himself as a seeker, a student; 'The day I have not learnt something new is indeed a wasted day,' he maintained.

Sindhi, English or Hindi, Dada spoke the language of the heart. Dada had the incredible power to captivate and mesmerize his listeners wherever he spoke, at the Town Hall, New York, with crowds overflowing, or at a ruh-rihan satsang, with his fluent language, logic and reasoning, profound ideas, practical wisdom and unique wit and sense of humour. Dada was equally at home in gatherings of students and young professionals, rotarians and civil servants, doctors and businessmen who found his magnetism, humility and aura irresistible.

Described as a '21st-century mystic who walks in the footsteps of the great masters who come to this earth to teach and transform', Dada's words reached and touched people from all walks of life, all over the world. He is the author of over 150 books; and as a writer, there is rarely any subject of human interest which he has left untouched; from karma to liberation, from simplicity to prosperity, from compassion to management, from friendship to parenting, from marriage to education, Dada's inimitable wisdom and humour has illumined every topic he dealt with.

The gift of writing came to Dada very early in life. Even as a college student, Dada edited no less than three monthly journals – *Excelsior*, *India Digest* and the *East and West Series*, all of them widely circulated and appreciated by his readers. Dada's writing is lucid, inspired and free-flowing, much like his oratory. It is simple in style, profound in thought and in precise language. A unique feature of his books is that they are not the kind you read once and put away. Instead they are read and re-read to draw inspiration and spiritual strength. They are an inexhaustible source of wisdom and faith for countless readers.

People were eager to hear Dada speak wherever he went – it could be an informal gathering of professionals, teachers or doctors or a meeting with writers or executives. At times he would be delivering keynote addresses or presiding over an international conference – whatever the forum, wherever the venue, Dada's words of wisdom were deeply treasured by his audiences.

Dada's discourses are organically linked with his books, which are in effect, compilations of his public lectures, talks, ruh-rihans – the books grew naturally out of the talks. This chapter presents what can be regarded as a bouquet of Dada's special insights and wisdom, the distilled essence of his message which is fundamentally the message of his master, the message of the rishis of ancient India.

SHORTCUT TO GOD

Dada's public lecture in English during his 86th birthday in 2004 celebrations coincided with friendship's day. Dada wished everyone with a beautiful and bright friendship's day message, 'Before you can get a true friend, be a true friend, 'he said to the receptive audience', 'the friend of all friends is God – cherish your link of love with him.'

God 'is'. We may be unable to see, hear, touch or understand God. For comprehending the Divine in its entirety is like a child trying to empty the ocean by handful of water into his little bowl. God and his ways cannot be grasped through the mind alone.

Today, our emphasis is on the mind, and the heart is ignored. Most people go through an existential crisis. Philosophers like Jean-Paul Sartre say that life has no meaning. If that is so, then why live at all?

On the other hand, great souls of ancient times – Lao Tzu, Gautam Buddha, Mahavir, Guru Nanak, Kabir – all speak of unending bliss and ecstasy in the divine. But to attain that state, we have to make God a reality in our lives. 'Closer is he than breathing, nearer than hands and feet,' says the poet Tennyson. God is not a distant being dwelling on a far-off star. The mercy of God is so intimate that like a parent or a friend we can share our innermost secrets with him, sans any reservations or fear.

The malady of modern man arises mostly due to his way of life in this excited, agitated age of science overpowered by comforts and conveniences. But science makes man egoistic, for he feels that he can do whatever he wants on his own. Thus, civilization has become sick with passion for power, lust for fame and greed for gold.

Mental, moral, spiritual and physical well-being can be restored to us only when we look at God as the source and sustainer of life. We can know God and have contact with him by talking to him with love and intimacy, feeling him constantly by our side. Hence it is the simple village folk who experience him more closely than the apparently intellectual city dwellers who live by their minds.

To awaken our hearts, we must make the effort of cultivating longing and love for God; this, in turn, will lead us to love our fellow men and creatures. For, as Sadhu Vaswani asked, 'How can we claim to love God and not love his creation?' This will pave the way for universal brotherhood among people and nations; and we will learn to greet other communities and races with love in our hearts, instead of wars and aggression.

The ways to God are many but it will take several births for us to reach him. However, there is a shortcut available – it is the way of love and longing, pining for the Beloved. We should love God to distraction, to intoxication. To many, God is like a shopkeeper with endless wares which we ask for incessantly. But in silence when you ask only for him, then he will come unto you and reveal himself.

Dada offered ten shortcuts to get close to God:

1. Conquer the ego. A true lover lives a hidden life in the hidden God. Exhibitionism is egoism. One should be humble and sincere.

2. Every day devote a little time to dwell with God, to talk to him and think of him. However busy you may be, spare some time for God; prioritize your activities; wake up early in the morning to create your time with God.

3. Do not meet anger with anger; therefore, do not react, but respond to every situation.

4. Begin your day with a reading or a thought from the scriptures. Reflect on this thought throughout the day.

5. Never miss your daily appointment with God. Let your day be full of little turnings to God.

6. Whatever you eat, whatever austerity or charity you perform, do it as an offering to the lord.

7. Offer all your work to God. There are a hundred ways of doing the same thing – some right, some wrong. But the best is that which is done as an offering.

8. Rejoice in everything that happens, knowing that there is a meaning of mercy in all incidents and accidents of life. This faith will bring acceptance and closeness to God.

9. Hand yourself over to God completely with all your faults and failings, knowing that he will make you 'new'.

10. Help the less fortunate lift their load on the rough road of life. For no man is an island.

'The shortcut to God is the way of loving God,' Dada reiterated. 'It is the way of yearning for God, it is the way of creating thirst for God, it is the way of creating a vacuum in our hearts and sure as the sun rises in the east, the vacuum will be filled by God. He whom the Vedas have called *be-anta* – he himself will come and reveal himself to you and your visit to this physical plane will be amply fulfiled.'

DADA WRITES ON THE HINDU FAITH

'I love to think of my Hindu way of life as a faith without beginning or end,' Dada would say. 'This religion has been existing from the very remote past. Therefore, if it is necessary to call it *Sanatana Dharma* – the Eternal Religion.'

He asserted emphatically that he did not like to use the word Hinduism; as the Hindu faith, he believes, is not an 'ism' – it is not a creed or a dogma. He recalls the words of his revered master, 'Creeds are broken reeds, and dogmas divide.' The Hindu faith is a way of life. 'We should therefore speak of the Hindu outlook, or the Hindu spirit, or the Hindu faith,' he observed.

Dada wrote and spoke about the Hindu faith on several platforms, including world conventions on Hinduism such as Vishwa Hindu Parishad and Global Vision 2000, as well as at the World Parliament of Religions.

In its essence, Hinduism is essentially monotheistic, Dada would tell us, but it is misunderstood by many people as polytheistic. Our sages declare in the Upanishads: *Ekam sat viprah bahuda vadanti* – 'The truth is one, it is spoken under various names.' He quoted the lines:

Aakasaat patitam toyam yadha gachchati sagaram
Sarva deva namaskaram Keshavam pratigachchati

[Just as rain water which falls from the sky, irrespective of where it falls, it ultimately reaches the ocean; so too, the worship offered to all deities reaches the supreme reality that is Keshava.]

The evolved Hindu, who has truly understood his religion, does not worship multiple gods, said Dada. Rather, he believes in various aspects of the One behind the many. As the *Ishopanishad* tells us so beautifully, *Isha Vasyam Idam Sarvam* [All that is, is a vesture of the Lord].

The main note of Hinduism is one of respect and goodwill for other creeds. Hinduism does not believe in proselytization or conversion. The Hindus never went out to conquer or convert. They have always been worshippers of truth and ultimate victory belongs to the truth.

Hinduism has been rightly regarded as the mother of all religions. Therefore, all religions have thrived in India. No religion has ever been persecuted here. Thanks to the predominant influence of Hinduism, India has always stood for religious harmony and understanding.

According to Dada, the fundamental truths of Hinduism may be summed up as follows:

1. The law of the seed or the great law of karma: As you sow, so shall you reap.
2. The law of the wheel, or the truth of reincarnation.
3. The law of *niddhyasana* or the necessity for assimilation of the great truths of the Vedas.
4. The law of reverence, or the law of *shraddha*. The essence of the Vedas – what we call Vedanta – is one of the fundamental principles of Hindusim. It teaches us that there is but one life in all. Therefore, all life is sacred, and all life must be revered and protected.
5. The law of yajna, or the law of sacrifice. For every Hindu, true yajna is this: to make of your entire life, an offering to the lord; to sacrifice your ego-self (not animals or silks and gold or silver); sacrifice your desire, and whatever you do, do it for the love of God.

Dada was aware that the ravages of time and history have had their impact on the Hindu faith and culture. There have been periods when prophets of pessimism have proclaimed that the Hindu faith has declined – that it has been dealt a death-blow. But the periods of such decline have invariably also led to new beginnings and new development for the faith. He asserts that this will also be an era of self-purification and enrichment for us.

GOD *IS*: SO WHY WORRY?

When Dada asserted the truth that 'God is,' one would need no further reassurance on the point; and when he would follow it up with 'so why worry?' it seemed only too easy to break the futile habit of worry. Celebrating the 125th birth anniversary of Sadhu Vaswani, in Novemeber 2004, Dada's much-awaited public discourse in English touched a chord in the eager listeners. Dada began by sharing the findings of a survey conducted on one 1000 people, who were chronic worriers. He said the survey revealed the following findings:

1. Forty per cent of worries concern matters that never happen eventually.
2. Thirty per cent are about events that have already occurred and cannot be changed.
3. Twelve per cent relate to illness, mostly imagined.
4. Ten per cent relate to friends, relatives and kids who are probably quite capable of taking care of themselves.
5. Only eight per cent have some cause or basis for worry.

'For that miniscule eight per cent, why worry ninety-two times as much?' Dada asked, and proceeded to give his listeners what he called 'Ten Fingers of a Carefree Life':

1. Realize the total uselessness of worry.
2. Having realized this, develop the will to not worry.
3. Metaphorically, in your visualization, throw your worries, immediately, into the dustbin.
4. Live one day at a time; each day brings its own strength and wisdom to face any problem.
5. Begin the day with a small, simple prayer which places all your burdens on the lord.
6. Count your blessings. Have a positive attitude: do not focus on the dark side of life which can lead you into a state of depression.
7. Develop a healthy sense of humour. Do not take life too seriously.
8. Keep yourself busy all the time.
9. Set apart one day in the week in which to worry. Put your worries daily in a worry box. By the time you get to them, the source of worry may already have resolved itself.
10. Develop faith in the goodness and caring power of God.

Leave your worries behind you in the sacred precincts of the Mission, Dada said to his listeners: 'I shall have them swept away after you leave.'

Even the most chronic 'worriers' returned home as 'warriors' on this day.

DADA SPEAKS ON THE GITA

From 1981 onwards, Dada spoke and wrote on the Gita on formal and informal occasions. In the year 2004, his talks were compiled together in an insightful and brilliant book which distilled the essence of the Gita, entitled *The Seven Commandments of the Bhagavad Gita*. According to Dada these commandments are:

1. Thou shalt not identify thyself with the body.
2. Thou shalt always do thy duty.
3. Thou shalt do thy duty and a little more.
4. Thou shalt keep thy daily appointment with God.
5. Whatever thou doest, thou shalt do it for the love of God.
6. Thou shalt rejoice in everything the will of God brings to thee.
7. Thou shalt always seek the lowest place.

In 2011, once again graciously acceding to the request of his many admirers and readers, Dada wrote the book *Bhagavad Gita in a Nutshell*, which teaches not to restrict oneself to memorizing the Gita or reciting its slokas every day – but to live the Gita in daily life, to translate the message of the Gita in deeds of daily living! As Dada himself put it: 'I would like each and every one of you to read the Gita; reflect on it; interpret it in the light of your own life; and translate all that you have learnt into deeds of daily living. The Gita is first and foremost a dynamic scripture, a scripture of action and life.'

Dada's numerous enlightening discourses and his beautiful reflections on the Gita, which Sadhu Vaswani described as the universal scripture and the Bible of humanity, enable one to realize that the Gita is not only for philosophers and scholars, but a book of life for ordinary mortals.

PEACE OR PERISH: THERE IS NO OTHER CHOICE!

In April 2006, the auditorium at the Ivy League grounds of Princeton University was glittering, bedecked with stars. The memorable occasion was the launch of Dada's book *Peace or Perish: There is No Other Choice*. Great intellectual and scientific minds of Princeton University were present as well.

Dada's aura of peace and tranquillity enveloped all through his calm demeanour and an ever-smiling face, with love, warmth and compassion pouring from his glance. Merely by looking at him, many were assured of obtaining the key to unlock the door of everlasting peace and happiness.

From his symphony of science and the spirit, Dada enchanted all with the music he created in his memorable talk, 'The Seven Notes on the Musical Scale of World Peace':

1. Love: The true peacemaker must handle all life situations and address all people and creatures with sincere love.
2. Respect: The true peacemaker will respect all people's views and paths, as well as revere all life, including not only other humans, but animals as well.
3. Tolerance: People of all religions must realize that the same one truth flows in all religions, and all paths lead to the same goal. Do not work to convert other people to your opinion or faith, but rather encourage them to follow the path that suits them best and to follow it truly, sincerely and to the utmost.
4. Cease all exploitation and work to establish true justice for all: our leaders must not fall prey to being a party to exploitation or corruption.
5. End racial discrimination: do not discriminate between fellow beings, especially based on race or skin colour.
6. Love all countries as your own: let us live as citizens of the world, seeing all countries and people as equal.
7. Compassion: Finally, and most importantly, the most vital characteristic of a peacemaker is that he is compassionate towards everyone. For without compassion, there can be no peace.

To establish true and lasting peace, we must all become active peacemakers.

Following its brilliant launch at Princeton University, Dada's timely book on peace was successfully available at several global centres as well as all over India.

KILL FEAR BEFORE FEAR KILLS YOU

In July 2006, as Western Maharashtra and Konkan went on flood alert due to the incessant rains, rain gods relented on the afternoon of 30 July allowing an eager Pune public to attend Dada's English talk 'Kill Fear before Fear Kills You'.

The title had already aroused debate: Dada mentioned that a gentleman had written to him objecting to the word 'kill' in the title. 'How could a word associated with violence be used in the title of your talk,' he had asked Dada.

Dada pointed out that Gautam Buddha had once said to his disciples, 'People should not kill innocent animals; instead, let each man kill the animal within himself.' Therefore, Dada said, let us allow the word kill to be used in this context.

Fear, Dada said, paralyzes our mental faculties. It is the cause of several ailments including hypertension, acidity, ulcer and stress. Unless we conquer fear, we cannot really live meaningful lives.

Dada had seven practical suggestions to pass on to people in this connection:

1. Nothing is as bad as fear itself. Realize that being afraid is the worst thing that can happen to someone.
2. Cultivate the will to be free of fear, through perseverance and determination.
3. Never forget that fear is a kind of atheism; faith in God and fear can never dwell side by side.
4. Always remember that with God, all things are possible.
5. Learn to relax in God's presence so that you can receive his power.
6. Do not be afraid of what may happen tomorrow.
7. If you want to kill fear, go out of your way to bring help and comfort to others.

Dada's address had the audience spellbound, for 'fear psychosis' is beginning to haunt many of us today.

PRAYER WORKS WONDERS

The day of 19 November was abuzz with activity as the Sadhu Vaswani Mission was commemorating the 127th birthday of its founder, architect and saint. The Mission grounds thronged with people to listen to Dada talk about how prayer works wonders.

Dada began with the thought that the greatest underdeveloped resource and the greatest unused power in the world is the power of prayer. 'Prayer,' he said, 'can be more powerful than atomic fusion, but when constructive, it can save the world from the brink of destruction, to which we seem to be heading now.' He dispelled myths surrounding prayers by indicating that there is nothing rigid or dogmatic about prayer. 'Prayer is not concerned with grammar or vocabulary; it is our heartfelt communion with God. It is not rocket science; there are no hardbound theories or formulae involved. It is direct conversation with God, who is closer to us than our own breath and nearer to us than our hands and feet. No knowledge of scriptures is required, for prayer is a movement of the heart towards a loving parent – God.'

One does not need to be highly educated or gifted to pray, Dada observed. Prayer is not concerned with arithmetic – how many; geometry – how long; music – how melodious; logic – how argumentative; or the method – how orderly. The only thing that counts is our sincerity and longing for God.

Dada enumerated three ways in which prayer can be offered. The first is vocal or uttered prayer in which one talks to God aloud. The second is mental prayer – a prayer uttered in the silence of the heart. The third kind of prayer is the utmost form of experiencing God, through spiritual communion. This gives one visions and mystical experiences, awakening the soul to cosmic awareness, momentarily enabling the seeker to taste *sat-chit-ananda*.

Dada enabled the listeners to see prayer in a new light when he articulated the thought that no prayer is ever wasted; God may not always answer a prayer in the way we expect him to because he knows what is best for his children. Sometimes, he says, 'Yes, here is the answer to your prayer.' Sometimes, he says, 'Here is something better!' At times, he says, 'Wait, the time is not yet ripe.' And occasionally, he says, 'No! I cannot grant your wish, as it is not in your interest.'

Dada then guided everyone along the steps ascending which they could attain true closeness with the Divine all through the power of prayer.

- The first step is having faith in God, as the all-powerful.
- Once unshakeable faith is invested in God, the second step is remembering all that he has done for us in a life filled with small miracles.
- The next step is saying our prayers with sincerity and devotion, while hoping for the prayers to be answered.
- The fourth step is that of humility, admitting that we are frail, feeble and fragile and only his strength flowing within us helps us to face all vicissitudes of life and emerge victorious.
- The last, or the fifth step is praise of God and gratitude for all the prayers not granted, for achievements not accomplished. For God, in his wisdom, knows how to respond to our prayers.

Constantly thanking God, building a ladder of praise and reaching the pinnacle of peace is the wonderful consequence of climbing these steps.

IN ALL RELIGIONS THE LIGHT IS THINE

The brotherhood of all races, the unity of all religions and the universality of teachings of all great ones from the East and West has been the theme of several of Dada's brilliant discourses and best-selling inspirational books. It is a topic on which Dada would like all of us to become knowledgeable, as he believes that true insight, understanding and clarity on this subject can lead to greater peace and harmony among people of different faiths.

In 2006, Dada published his book *Many Paths: One Goal*. The launch of the book coincided with the World Parliament of Religions held in Melbourne and the book was received with universal approbation. The scholarly work emphasizes Dada's cardinal belief that each system of faith, each religion, is a pathway hewn out by a community of believers to bring them closer to God and salvation. The paths may be many, but the goal is one for all seekers. Most of us are not found to be wanting in loyalty or reverence to our own faith; the challenge, however, is to cultivate a healthy respect for others' faiths and beliefs.

Dada presents each faith as a jewel embedded in the crown of human civilization. Each of them is a unique, precious and distinct artefact; but at their core is the common belief that is eternal and unchanging: Faith in the One Supreme Being and the unity of all His creation.

Running through all faiths is the golden thread that binds them all together: The Ultimate Law which every faith holds absolutely – that we should do nothing that may cause pain to another. This commonality of ideals, values and precepts is brought out in what we may regard as the second book on this theme, *Many Scriptures, One Wisdom*.

The question may arise: Do we really have time to go back to the scriptures today? And not just to the scriptures of the faiths to which we belong, but to all scriptures of all faiths? Dada feels that the grave mistake we have all made in our generation is turning away from the sacred texts. We must return to these sacred texts, so that our lives may become meaningful, worthwhile and beneficial for us and others. The sacred scriptures are not mere books; they are springs of eternal wisdom, treasures of universal truths which cannot be deconstructed by post-modern perception. They contain the power of the word, the *logos*, the *shabda* that was the very source of true life. It is to these great texts that we must return if we wish to have peace and joy in our lives.

Dada always rejected the titles of teacher or scholar and chose to refer to himself as a pilgrim on the path of life. As a friend and fellow pilgrim, as one who places the highest worth on brotherhood, mutual understanding, love , tolerance and respect for all, he selected sacred texts from world faiths which influenced his life and shared his insights on these scriptures in this sagacious and appreciative work.

Completing the trilogy of books on this theme is the bestselling anthology, *Immortal Stories from the World Scriptures*. Answering the inevitable question of why turn to the stories when we have the scriptural texts, Dada, himself a raconteur of excellence, explains that every story is a speaking picture which helps one relate to the universal predicaments and the common human values that the characters and situations in the stories depict for us. The stories from the scriptures and from lives of the great ones articulate values and precepts that are vital to one's well-being and moral growth. They offer memorable characters caught in unique experiences which one relates to, because of their human interest. One can enter into the experience of the story, even as the original teachers and students featured in the stories did. The stories are meant to promote reflection, absorption, assimilation and as a sequel, enlightened action and awakened awareness.

Characteristically, Dada attributes the phenomenal success of this great trilogy on world faiths to the teachings of his master, Gurudev Sadhu Vaswani, who taught him to see the One behind the many.

IN ALL THE SAINTS THE PICTURE IS THINE

God made all men equal, and his divine spark animates every being he created. All men are equal, and yet there are a chosen few whom we call men of God. Why are they special? What makes these men and women the chosen ones? What makes us venerate them as saints, mahatmas and spiritual leaders?

The answer is simple: They become the chosen ones because they choose the Lord above all else. They made bhakti – devotion – the foundation of their life. To whichever faith or religion they belong, they choose to do good to all. They choose truth, goodness, compassion, simplicity, service and sacrifice, and thus attain an exalted status among human beings.

Dada observed the sacred days of the *jayanti* (birthday) and *punyatithi* (death anniversary) of the great souls of the East and West by delivering special discourses in the satsang. On popular demand, his Hindi discourses on the saints were specially recorded for Sony Television and Sanskar Channel. These discourses were also published in several volumes devoted to the lives of saints.

In these volumes, Dada introduces to us many of these saintly souls, each one of them a guide and saviour of humanity. A universalist and great spiritual leader whose religion of love and unity transcended all narrow creeds, Dada helped us touch the very heart of the mystery, the great spiritual shakti that these saints represent.

Dada wrote of saints from all faiths: The great Acharyas, the Alwars, the Buddha, Mahavira, the Sikh gurus and the saints of the Bhakti Movement are presented in his books. Equally, we find moving accounts of Biblical figures, such as Moses, Abraham and John the Baptist; saints of the Church, such as Francis of Assisi, Ignatius of Loyola, Augustine, Monica and Mother Teresa are also featured; the great Sufi saints also have a place in the effulgent galaxy that Dada created for his readers.

Ten Companions of God is Dada's moving tribute to the great Sikh gurus, who were always a tremendous source of inspiration to his family from his early days, especially to his uncle and mentor, Sadhu Vaswani. The book is much more than a biographical account of the great masters; nor is it a collection of their works and teachings. Dada talks about their contribution to the community, the special values they emphasized and so beautifully translated into their thoughts, words and deeds.

Dada's beautiful book *Japji: An Interpretation* came out of a series of talks he delivered in the satsang. In this book are brought together the commentaries on this wonderful scriptural text that Dada heard at the feet of his master, as well as his own reflections and thoughts on the immortal hymn composed by Guru Nanak.

THE PERFECT RELATIONSHIP

In an age where youngsters shy away from the word commitment, Dada J. P. Vaswani proceeded to elucidate a relationship that was binding and lasting not only during the life one was born, but for the lifetimes that followed. Dada described the perfect relationship that exists between the guru and disciple – not bound by iron links or golden chains, but by a tender, silken thread woven out of love and devotion, which makes the bond eternal.

The occasion also saw the launch of Dada's book with the same title, *The Perfect Relationship*, where he was called first as a perfect disciple to his master and now a perfect guru to all – and thus the perfect candidate to present this perfect relationship.

Dada described many types of relationships, which are all temporary and ephemeral, lasting at best until death. The only relationship that transcends death is the one between a guru and his disciple. The guru is the great cleanser and purifier. The snares of desire and cumulative bad karma entrap oneself, but the guru can extricate and lead one to divine light.

What are the marks of a true guru? Dada enumerated ten aspects:

1. A true guru desires nothing for himself.
2. He transcends the ego.

3. He lives in the light and the light lives in him.
4. He never refers to himself as a master or guru.
5. He never chooses his disciples. He allows the disciples to find him.
6. He instills in the disciple the imperishable truth.
7. He does not use his wisdom or knowledge to earn a livelihood for himself.
8. He teaches through precept and the example of his own life.
9. He is a master who has disciplined his senses.
10. He is tolerant, friendly, peaceful and sublime.

What about the disciple? Dada outlined four distinguishing traits of the perfect disciple:

1. Humility
2. Absolute obedience to the guru
3. Wholehearted service to the guru
4. Unconditional surrender, which is the ultimate form of guru bhakti

He underlined two essential disciplines to evolve as a disciple: *simran* and seva.

The audience was filled with gratitude towards Dada for embodying and presenting through his being, the qualities of the perfect disciple and guru.

ARE YOU IRRITATED, ANNOYED, UNHAPPY? YOU CAN COME OUT OF IT!

In July 2007, as eager devotees welcomed Dada enthusiastically, he entered with folded hands to greet over 3,000 people who had gathered at the satsang hall of the Mission to listen to his English talk.

Dada's address that evening dealt with a question that vexes many: 'Are you irritated, annoyed, unhappy? You can come out of it.' Dada offered consolation to all victims of constant irritation, by stressing four basic rules for a happy life:

1. Seek to please God; do not try to please men
2. Take serious things lightly and light things seriously
3. Laugh as much as you can
4. Cultivate the spirit of acceptance

This was followed by eight easy-to-follow precepts to conquer irritation:

1. Be aware that God is always watching you and giving you strength
2. Always be relaxed in body and mind
3. Do not neglect your daily appointment with God
4. Always see the bright side of things, be an optimist
5. Count your blessings: Be grateful to God for all that he has given you
6. Keep busy: Engage yourself in creative activity
7. Smile, smile all the while: Develop a healthy sense of humour
8. Follow the technique of Tong Leng: breathe in all your annoyances and irritations. Breathe out relief and peace

Finally, one must be conscious of the fact that God is the controller of destinies of individuals and nations, so nothing goes against his plans, even if we think otherwise; hence, we must thank God for everything that happens. This builds a ladder of consciousness which enables one to reach the pinnacle of peace.

The crowd repeated the powerful words after Dada – 'Thank you God' and 'Praise the Lord'. The anger or anxiety built up within them dissipated as gratitude and humility took over.

TEACHERS ARE SCULPTORS

An exclusive interface with Dada J. P. Vaswani had drawn over 3,000 teachers from Pune and around India to the Sadhu Vaswani Mission campus in January 2008. Filled with awe, and unblinking gaze and unwavering attention, they imbibed Dada's thought-provoking words on the topic, 'Teachers are Sculptors'.

Giving the example of the Mira Movement – the system of education envisaged by Sadhu Vaswani – Dada pointed how education should teach students the right way to live, rather than pumping facts and figures into their brains. Elucidating on the role and importance of teachers, he added that being the beacons of light, teachers should, as friends, sculpt and mould the lives of young students so that they become ideal members of society and the nation.

Echoing his thoughts, the guests of honour and the dignitaries present encouraged educational institutions to commence with their own *shramdaan* projects, benefitting not only students and teachers but also the society at large.

ATTITUDE THAT ATTRACTS SUCCESS

On the occasion of his 90th birthday, Dada gave a discourse on how attitude is a powerful force in the life of an individual. Citing the wisdom of the rishis of ancient India, which holds true even today, he explained that attitude is more important than facts. How one reacts to facts and events is what counts, rather than facts themselves.

He went on to offer a few practical suggestions to cultivate the right attitude:

1. The most important thing is to have a positive attitude, for expectations have a magnetic power.

2. Develop right thinking, for thoughts are building blocks of life, forming our destiny.
3. Stop complaining, start thanking. Stop criticizing, start appreciating.
4. Learn to be in touch with your subconscious self, for it is the repository of tremendous powers.
5. The most essential thing is to contact the source of all success: God.
6. Develop a healthy sense of humour, for laughter is an all-round tonic.
7. Finally, never, never, never give up.

MANAGEMENT — MOMENT BY MOMENT

The pulsating energy that emanated from hundreds of students from premier management institutes of Pune was channelized by fifteen minutes of guided meditation by Dada; their distracted minds were now energized and well-focused.

The B-school stars had congregated at the Sadhu Vaswani Mission to listen to Dada's talk, 'Management — Moment by Moment'. His words brought to them a new vision and approach to management which could not be found in textbooks or elucidated in the best of classrooms.

Dada proceeded to outline the five principles to facilitate ideal management:

1. Your attitude should be a positive, constructive and friendly one. Attitude is transformed into power. You do not become what you want, you become what you believe.
2. Do your duty. It is not the work you do, but the way you do it that counts. Every act should be performed in the best manner that you are capable of. Remember, every action you perform in the course of your duty is an offering to God.

3. Do your duty and a little more. Therefore, go out and help others. The one who learns the art of sharing is the richest in the world. The difference between the ordinary and extraordinary is just that extra mile which you walk willingly.
4. Always see the good in others; you draw to yourself that which you think.
5. Develop a healthy sense of humour. Laughter is a physical, mental and spiritual tonic.

The inspiring talk was followed by an invigorating interactive session with innumerable questions, which Dada answered patiently and to the entire satisfaction of the audience. This scintillating session came to an end amidst thunderous applause.

Every student received a copy of the book *Management – Moment by Moment*, written by Dada. They left taking with them a little but precious part of the Sadhu Vaswani Mission along with them, and with the guidance of bringing in effective management in their lives and careers.

SPREADING 'SINDHISM'

As mentioned in earlier chapters, Dada always made it a point to urge his Sindhi brothers and sisters to preserve and protect their language and culture. He felt that the contemporary generation of young Sindhis has been brought up in an environment of affluence, luxury, economic prosperity and security, which was denied to their great grandfathers. While everyone salutes their spirit of enterprise which has earned them this well-deserved prosperity, the regret is that many of these young Sindhis – scattered as they are, all over India, indeed all over the world – are quite unaware of the rich heritage which belongs to them, as children of one of the world's oldest civilizations.

Dada felt that their Sindhi identity was important owing to the fact that it had survived centuries of trials and crises, culminating in the Partition of India – which deprived them of their homeland and left the community as stateless citizens in the newly independent India. But he rejoiced in the fact that today's Hindu–Sindhi diaspora is a unique example of a community that was driven away from its native land, became refugees in their own country, and rose like a phoenix from the smouldering ashes of Partition, to become one of the most successful and philanthropic people in the world.

Also, through his book *I Am a Sindhi*, Dada wished to tell his non-Sindhi brothers and sisters about his culture, language, literature and civilization – for Dada believed, as his master taught him, that the children of this world are all one, and must know, understand and appreciate each other's culture and history.

WHAT TO DO WHEN DIFFICULTIES STRIKE

As part of the celebrations for the 130th birthday of Sadhu Vaswani, Dada spoke on the topic 'What to Do when Difficulties Strike'. He began by citing the familiar adage: When calamities strike, the comforter is not afar! The pathways of life are strewn with trials and tribulations, but the destroyer of difficulties is ever with us. The problems we face in life are like soiled packages concealing a rich treasure within. All we need is faith in God which will leads us to miraculous solutions to all our problems. Dada placed before the congregation five practical suggestions to cultivate faith:

1. Let go, let go, let God. Let go of petty irritations, frustrations and anger. Hand your problems over to God: Let him in his infinite wisdom and mercy solve your problems.
2. Always expect the best but be prepared for the worst. Be optimistic and positive. An optimist lives longer and healthier.
3. Keep moving, get on with your work, doing the best you can and leave the rest to God.

4. Learn to take risks, but only calculated risks, for nothing ventured is nothing gained.
5. Remember that with God, everything is possible. Make God your partner in all your endeavours.

Dada ended his talk with the hope that we take up at least one of the practical suggestions and bear witness to it in daily living.

The audience was delighted and recharged with his words of wisdom and his highly practical insights.

FORMULA FOR PROSPERITY

Millions aspire to become successful and prosperous in life. Dada began his talk 'Formula for Prosperity' by clarifying that there is nothing wrong in wishing to become prosperous or wealthy. This statement was hugely lauded and appreciated. It came as a surprise too, for everyone thought that a spiritual person looked down on material wealth with disdain. Dada then qualified his earlier statement with the words: 'The problem arises when riches begin to possess, control and overpower us, and run our lives!'

Addressing the audience in Singapore, Dada shared with them his formula, outlining the four crucial aspects of prosperity:

1. Physical well-being, health and fitness
2. Financial well-being, which gives us economic independence
3. Emotional well-being, which brings stability and efficiency
4. Spiritual well-being, through which one understands the true meaning of life and attains peace and joy

Dada also spoke of the universal laws of prosperity:

1. God helps those who help themselves
2. God helps those who help others

3. Honesty is the best policy
4. Make God your partner

He added that prosperity is a function of hard work, God's grace, honesty, philanthropy.

After a guided meditation on prosperity, everyone left with a positive intent of prospering in the right way.

NEW EDUCATION

It is only through the right type of education that all of India's, in fact, all of the world's problems, will be solved, Dada would say. With this firm conviction, his book *New Education Can Make the World New* was launched at the National College Auditorium in Mumbai.

'Education should teach man to live in the right manner,' he said, adding the following necessary requirements for it:

1. Character building
2. Seva
3. Love of Indian ideals
4. Reverence for all life
5. Cultivation of the soul

Dada outlined the features of the right type of education, which should:

1. Be a character-building education
2. Integrate head, hand and heart
3. Inculcate the highest ideals and values
4. Emphasize life rather than livelihood

Quoting Sadhu Vaswani, Dada pointed out that true education is not just a withered parchment, but the living waters of the spirit.

It is the answer to our problems, one that will help us counter the forces of darkness and destruction and awaken the best that is within us. Such an education will both liberate and transform society. Transformation will lead us from chaos to order, from mindlessness to self-realization, from darkness to light, from falsehood to truth, and from death to eternity.

MAKE FRIENDS WITH LIFE

The May–June 'results season' following the board examinations had brought about traumatic experiences and tragedy to many families in Maharashtra. Student suicides in the state had caused grave concern to the people, school authorities and teachers, who felt that students had been sadly let down by the system.

Dada too, received pleas for help from many students and their families. Apart from psychological counselling and communication with helplines that had been specially set up by the state, many people believed that what the students needed most was spiritual reinforcement and the voice of a mentor, a master who could reach out to the youngsters and offer them help and healing. The teachers from the many Mira institutions placed the same request before Dada: to organize a special students' meet and address the critical issues raised in this state of affairs. In response to this appeal from all quarters, Dada addressed the students of Pune and Bombay at special events held at various institutions, including the Mission headquarter.

People often lament that life is a battle which must be fought, it is a challenge, which must be faced. Dada's view of life was different: Life is the greatest gift bestowed on us, a gift which we must treasure and cherish. His message was especially meant for the youth: Make friends with life; make the most of this valuable gift. Frustrations, failures, disappointments and setbacks are all part of the complex weave of life; they embellish life by making us wiser, stronger, more aware and sensitive. They help us evolve and grow in maturity and emotional strength. They also help to highlight the positive aspects of life, which we often tend to lose sight of, or even take for granted.

Suicide is not an option, Dada warned, for it offers no solutions to any problem; it brings an end to life before solutions can be sought and found. With his inimitable wit and wisdom, Dada also urged the youngsters to shake hands with life, offering them practical suggestions on how to cope with the stress, strain and pressure of a student's life:

1. Take care of your thoughts
2. Develop courage
3. Contact the source of all success: contact God
4. Count your blessings
5. Set aside time for creative pursuits
6. Never, never, never give up
7. Believe in yourself: believe and achieve
8. Stay connected: with friends, family and God

A beautiful, inspiring booklet, *Make Friends with Life*, was also published, which was distributed free of cost to thousands of students in the state.

MANTRAS FOR PEACE OF MIND

Dada always spoke about the power of the Name Divine and the simple and beautiful sadhana of Naam Japa. It was his firm belief that one could establish a beautiful and meaningful relationship with God by simply thinking of the Lord, by taking his name into our hearts and our consciousness, by the repetition of a sloka or mantra. For, as Dada put it, what was a mantra but a specially charged set of words and sounds that becomes an expression of one's devotion and faith? As one repeats it, the mantra acquires the power to make this love and devotion firmer and stronger. It becomes, in effect, one's permanent link with the divine.

Japa yoga, or repetition of the Name Divine, is the easiest sadhana that is available to one today, Dada said. Sweeter than nectar, more auspicious than good luck and good omens is the power of the Name, and the power of the Name is focused, concentrated in the great mantras that have come down to us from our ancient scriptures. We know that they were heard in states of elevated consciousness by realized souls and handed down to us for our benefit. Is it not incumbent upon us to claim our birthright as inheritors of these treasures?

Dada also outlined the many benefits of mantra jaap:

1. First and foremost, the rare and precious gift of peace of mind; calmness and tranquility; freedom from needless tension and anxiety.
2. The secure feeling of linking with a power that is higher than us; the mature perspective that we have our place in the vast cosmic order that is controlled like divine clockwork.
3. The power to conquer negative thinking and lower sense desires.
4. The generation of a new spiritual energy that can neutralize past *samskaras* and clear the mind of accumulated *vaasanas* which drag us down through the endless cycle of birth-death-rebirth.
5. Constant chanting, repetition, remembrance of the mantra takes us closer to God – and this feeling cannot be described in words; it has to be experienced.
6. Each mantra, properly chanted with devotion and faith, helps us achieve the fourfold goals of this human life – *dharma*, *artha*, *kama* and *moksha*.

IT IS NOT ENOUGH TO BE WEALTHY

On 23 November 2011, the streets of Pune cantonment were transformed into modes of *parikrama* when the Rath Yatra led by

Dada J. P. Vaswani started its blessed journey. As always, thousands of faithful devotees joined the yatra, following the *rath* with a life-sized statue of Sadhu Vaswani. The roads were lined with spectators of every caste, creed and age, waiting eagerly to pay their respects to Pune's own saint.

In his speech addressed from the rath, Dada had a clear and crisp message for all: 'Do not stop with aspiring to be a *dhanwaan* (a wealthy individual); be an *Atmavaan* (spiritually rich). It is not enough to be wealthy, aspire to become spiritual!' Sadhu Vaswani gave up his lucrative career, his coveted post of a principal to follow the path of the spirit. Even on the spiritual path he attained great heights. The world looked up to him as a saint, a yogi, an intellectual and much more. Yet he remained ever-so humble, choosing to live a life of utter simplicity and self-sacrifice. Dada urged everyone to focus on becoming spiritually wealthy. For this, three steps are essential:

1. Introspect, go within and discover your true self.
2. Give up attachment. Develop a true and close relationship with God. It is only this meaningful and lasting association with God that will sustain you.
3. Forgive freely all those who have wronged you and forget all the wrongs done to you. Do not hold any resentment or nurture hatred against anyone.

THE NEW AGE DIET

In a world where over eighty per cent of the population is given to a non-vegetarian diet, Dada remains a committed advocate of vegetarianism. With dedication, passion and zeal, he actively promotes the sattvic lifestyle of vegetarianism, wherever he goes. Even the most habituated meat-eaters are compelled to stop and take note of his fervent plea for the vegetarian way of life.

In a sense, Dada has been a visionary, promoting the cause of vegetarianism from the early days when a vegetarian diet was considered 'the cult of the crazy'. Dada spoke about a vegetarian lifestyle tirelessly, wherever he went, urging people to promote animal rights and stop all slaughter.

What we need for the new age is a new age diet – or rather a new approach to life and living which is consciously and purposefully different from living to eat! Now that vegans have taken the world by storm, Dada is admired as one of those rare and courageous teachers who has the spiritual fibre to stand up and be counted for a cause he believes in: Namely the right to live of all creatures. We must eat to live and not live to eat, Dada says. Dada's bestselling book, *The New Age Diet – Vegetarianism for You & Me* catalogues the triumphs and challenges of vegetarianism.

ABHYASA AND SADHANA

Following the teachings of the Buddha and his own master, Dada held the firm belief that desire is the root cause of all human suffering. 'There is only one cure for human misery and suffering,' he told: 'Expel desire! Renounce attachment! Stop the wandering of the mind! ... It is difficult, but not impossible to control the mind,' Dada said, quoting Krishna from the Gita. To expel desires, two things are necessary: *Abhyasa* and *Vairagya*. Abhyasa is regular practice; it is learning to repeat a good act or routine over and over again. Vairagya is the spirit of detachment. You realize that all that you see, touch and conceive is passing – it has no value. It is only with the guru's grace that one can attain these two qualities.

There are hundreds of sadhanas or means that one can undertake in pursuit of spiritual growth: Prayer, organized ritual worship, meditation, japa yoga, fasting, penance, tapasya and so on. However, Dada's chosen way of sadhana is a simple, straightforward one, recommended by his master: The three s – sadhana in silence, sangha and service. He encouraged the practice of meditation in his discourses all over the world. Dada called this an inner journey: It is a process of self-awakening through which one connects to God.

As always, Dada has a few practical suggestions for beginners:

1. Sit in silence in an easy and comfortable posture with the spinal cord, the neck and head in a straight line.
2. Practise meditation preferably at the same place and at the same time, every day.
3. Sit facing the east or the north.
4. Go to God as you are – with your sins and imperfections.
5. Think of an object or a symbol, or an incident from the life of a great one.
6. As you sit in silence, wear a soft smile.
7. Let your daily life be one of sacrifice.

SAY NO TO NEGATIVES

If there was one thing that Dada affirmed tirelessly, it was the message of hope and optimism: No matter who you are, no matter what circumstances you are placed in, you must realize that happiness is your birthright. You are entitled to happiness, and there are no conditions to fulfil, no strings attached.

Our mind is often filled with thinking and ideas which are negative. We must cleanse the mind of all the dirt and negativity that we have accumulated over the years. We draw closer to the divine in us, in the measure in which we overcome the negative energies in us. What is divinity, but the complete absence of all negative forces?

How can we conquer these negative tendencies? How may we arrest the negative energies that rob us of true joy and contentment and restore our own positive self-image? How can we live our precious life as well-balanced, mature individuals?

Revealing the secrets about how to conquer these negative tendencies, Dada listed positive thinking, right attitude, conquering the ego, overcoming anger and irritation, cultivating faith, optimism and taking charge of life. His books *Therapy of Thanksgiving* (2005) and *Stop Complaining, Start Thanking* (2011) are little handbooks of positivism and optimistic thinking. In the slim volume entitled *Say No to Negatives* (2013), he describes the various complexes that beset our psyche, such as pride, ego, jealousy, gluttony, lust and envy, and shares with us practical techniques to conquer these 'enemies within' as he describes them. He also shares with us the secret to an integrated personality, a well-balanced personality which is the first and most vital requisite to happiness in life. For this, he offers his wonderful practical suggestions:

1. Begin the day with God
2. Let your mind rest in God
3. Count your blessings
4. Accept the will of God
5. Pray without ceasing

THE MIRACLE OF FORGIVING

In July 2012, Dada delivered an inspiring discourse on forgiveness highlighting its vital characteristics. He said, during our lifetime, we are faced with situations where we have to choose between love and hatred, forgiveness and retaliation. It is always better to opt for forgiveness. Living by the precept of 'an eye for an eye', as Mahatma Gandhi pointed out, would only leave the world half blind.

As outlined in an earlier chapter, Dada describes the four stages through which one passes before choosing forgiveness as the best option:

The first stage is when one feels the hurt and pain caused by another. This suffering is not really experienced by the individual, but by his 'ego'.

The second stage, sees the hurt and pain developing into hatred.

In the third stage, God's grace descends upon us and the wounds caused by the arrows of hatred are healed.

The fourth stage leads us to a higher level where we embrace the person who has hurt us as a friend, developing a relationship of love.

Dada also offered his eminently practical tips and suggestions to cultivate the virtue of forgiveness:

1. When anyone hurts you, immediately offer a prayer to God.
2. If you are hurt and depressed, unburden yourself to a spiritual elder, mentor or guru.
3. Learn to forgive yourself – do not carry the burden of guilt on your heart.
4. Never hold resentment against anyone in the heart within, for this can only harm you.
5. Make forgiveness a habit. Learn to forgive again and again. Once is not enough. Forgive a hundred times. No effort is too great to destroy the evil within us – the evil passions of anger, bitterness, grudge and resentment. How can we cease to practise forgiveness until we have conquered ourselves?
6. Forgive before forgiveness is asked. Do not wait for apologies and recriminations.
7. When you forgive, make sure you forget.
8. Always speak kindly about the person against whom you hold a grudge.
9. Rise above your resentment and actually love the person who has wronged you.

To walk the path of forgiveness one has not only to forgive, but also to ask for forgiveness, as each one of us is filled with flaws and errors.

Very appropriately, Dada ended with the words from the Lord's prayer, 'Father, forgive us our trespasses as we forgive those who trespass against us.'

SLOW DOWN YOUR PACE

It seemed as if most of Pune's harried and stressed citizens had decided to take a break to attend Dada's talk in August 2012, as thousands of them filled the Mission campus to hear him speak on the topic 'Slow Down Your Pace'.

Dada began by saying that modern life is an unbalanced existence. We are always hurrying, scurrying about like squirrels in a cage, getting nowhere. Even when the body is stationary, the mind is racing, thus building within us stress which is manifested in the form of several illnesses. There is also the incurrence of petty irritations, burning precious nervous energy, to no purpose.

He then provided practical suggestions to slow down one's pace:

1. Be careful about your attitude. Always have a positive attitude.
2. Do not anticipate trouble.
3. Cultivate faith in the goodness and caring power of God. Faith should be cultivated with no worry, fear or anxiety.
4. Learn to smile all the time. Laughter has therapeutic value.

When asked if there would be a pile up if one would slow down, Dada suggested one must change their lane. One must work only for the love of God and not worry about delivering the many expectations that trap oneself. Ultimately, and the most important, is that one must work at their own pace and be happy.

SPIRITUALITY IN DAILY LIFE

In 2012, the World Forum of Spirituality conferred on Dada its lifetime achievement award. Dada was someone who practised spirituality in daily life. For him spirituality was true freedom, which led to the highest knowledge that man can aspire for, namely self-knowledge; it is the essence of the life-force within us. Dada believed that spirituality is a matter of experience: it is opening our consciousness to the fact that we are not the body–mind complex, but the immortal spirit that dwells within.

He reinforced this dictum, asserting that once a person realizes the truth of their being, they will be able to overcome the bonds and fetters that hinder them from feeling true freedom within the self. Within oneself lies a centre of tranquillity, serenity, true awareness and self-knowledge. When one reaches out to this centre within, they will experience true freedom: Freedom from the fears, desires, tensions, insecurities and complexes that haunt the subconscious mind as one carries on their everyday living. For the atman, the soul, is shakti – it is infinite, boundless energy and light. When one grows in awareness of this truth, they will no longer be bound to the material world, and will experience all the freedom of birds flying high in the firmament of the spirit.

For his book on this vital subject, Dada chose the title *Spirituality in Daily Life* deliberately and consciously: The book is based on his firm belief that spirituality is not an abstract, complex pursuit that it is often made out to be. It is born out of an awakening to the realization that there is more to life than making money and running the rat race.

AN UNFORGETTABLE WOMEN'S DAY AT SADHU VASWANI MISSION

On Women's Day in 2013, women from all walks of life congregated at the Sadhu Vaswani Mission to join in the launching of Dada's new book, *Women: Where Would the World Be Without You?*, this book was a glowing tribute to the woman shakti. Dada spoke reverently about women who have, throughout the ages, carried the load and cared for men. Now it is time for the female soul to lead the new civilization upward, Dada remarked. Their gentleness, compassion, care, courage and innate spirituality would become the guiding light for society.

It is a vital necessity to provide women with value-based education, integrating the hand, head and heart – a belief that gave rise to several educational institutions through the Mira Movement for girls, focusing on the development of Stree Shakti.

He spoke about how women should push themselves forward, such that empowerment comes from within as well. There are certain duties women must perform in the best way in this cosmic drama, which the Bhagavad Gita refers to as one's own duty – Swadharma. It is important to maintain a balance to resolve the conflict between family and work. Again, one must not feel alone but instead turn back to God for all the solutions.

BE IN THE DRIVER'S SEAT

Taking charge of our own lives is a fundamental human desire. Dada's talk during the 134th birthday celebrations of Sadhu Vaswani drew a huge crowd as people gathered to hear him speak on the topic 'Be in the Driver's Seat'.

Beginning with a citation from Thales, the Greek philosopher, who rightly said that the easiest thing to do is give advice to others, Dada said that when one is driving, there are many backseat drivers offering numerous suggestions. But finally, one must follow one's own head and heart.

In relation to this situation, he provided some valuable practical suggestions, for those who wish to be firmly in the driver's seat:

1. Listen with patience to everyone, for, we never know through whom wisdom will speak to us. But to do the right thing, you must do what the heart tells you to do. Therefore, keep the heart clean and pure.

2. Learn self-control. If there are instant emotional reactions, then you are not in the driver's seat. You are being driven by the person who makes you react.

3. Learn the art of forgetting your frustrations, resentments, disappointments and regrets. Move on, ever forward and Godward.

4. Accept others as they are. The biggest mistake is to wish that others are different and to try and change them. This leads to resentment and resistance. Help them to be themselves.

5. Silently bless everyone you meet, even those who speak against you and are unable to love you.

6. Keep yourself connected with the source. Life and energy will flow through you.

7. Forgive even before forgiveness is asked. The blame game destroys our mind. Bearing grudges harms you.

8. Let love be the mantra of your life.

9. Smile, smile all the while.

10. Be compassionate. Perform random acts of kindness, for everyone, at every time and everywhere.

11. Always speak the truth. There is no religion higher than truth.

One should build one's life in the teachings of the scriptures – those are the guidelines for driving and will enable one to follow the right path. As one listens to the voice of the heart and brain, in order to enjoy it, one must perform all actions as an offering to God.

STAY CONNECTED

In the Youth Meet by the Bridge Builders in 2013, Dada spoke on how it is important to stay connected. He said, 'There is darkness around us, the cause of which is that we are disconnected from God. The cure is to turn back to him.'

Providing some practical suggestions, he said:

1. Begin the day with a thought from a great one or a scripture; repeat it during the day to stay connected to God.
2. Read positive literature before retiring for the night, so that your subconscious stays connected to God.
3. Keep yourself relaxed all the time. Do your work; but do not let your work drive you.
4. To know God, love God.
5. You must choose between the world and God, for you cannot serve two masters.
6. If you wrong someone, make amends immediately to keep the connection alive.
7. Equally, if someone wrongs you, forgive immediately to stay connected.
8. Make all your work an offering to the Lord. There are right and wrong ways of doing the same thing. But there is only one way which is the best: Do all that you do for the love of God.
9. Help as many as you can to lift the load on the rough road of life.

Dada's closing meditation at the event left people with the peaceful feeling of being connected with God.

EMPOWER YOURSELF

One must realize that they are the architect of their own destiny and must, therefore, discover the shakti within. One must take charge of their own life. This was the robust and inspiring message that Dada delivered at a public talk at Logan Hall in Central London, on 14 April 2016.

Dada had a few tips to offer to his audience:

1. Embrace your life at this moment, here and now. Today is the first day of the rest of your life, so make a new beginning right at this moment. Do not waste your time regretting the past. As for the future, it is in God's safe hands: why should you waste your energy interfering in his plans?

2. Shift your focus: Quit focusing on what is missing from your life; focus on your blessings; visualize what you want to achieve, do not dwell on fears and anxieties. 'As a man thinketh, so he becomes,' is the immutable law of human nature. Fill your mind with thoughts of joy, love, peace and harmony – these aspects will be reflected in your life.

3. Acknowledge right now, that you are the hero of your life story; and determine that you will play your part well.

4. Invest in optimism and faith: They are your safest insurance against misery, despair and worry. When you place your faith in God and cultivate a spirit of optimism, believe me, the battle of life is won.

5. Stay connected with cosmic energy. All around us, there are electrons of hope, joy, peace and power floating everywhere; make sure you pick up their frequency.

6. Switch on the sunshine of your smile. Spread happiness everywhere. For it is an immutable law of life that what goes out from you, must come back to you: therefore, send out a smile, spread the sunshine of joy and laughter, and you will find your life flooded with more and more smiles and joy and laughter.

7. Get the balance right: Balance your perspective; balance work and life; balance your relationships; spend time on yourself and your interests; spend less time on your cellphones and more time with yourself, your family and friends.

8. Last and the most important of all: Draw on the greatest power source in the universe: and so, stay connected to God. When he is with you, there can be no lack, no want, nothing missing in your life.

'Let God take over our lives,' Dada concluded, 'for he makes the impossible possible. All the time, while we are attending to our daily work, let our minds and hearts be fixed on God. Let the ship of the body move hither and thither, attend to its multifarious duties, but let the needle of the heart's compass be ever directed towards God. 'For thy sake, o, Lord!' Let this be the mantra of our life – and we will see that true happiness fills our lives.'

The house came down with the thunderous applause that followed this positive message.

BHAKTI IS BLISS

One of the questions that people asked Dada again and again was this: How can one grow closer to God?

Dada's answer to this question was simple: 'Grow in love. Love all life, for all life is sacred. Love animals, birds, trees, flowers, the sick and the distressed, the lonely and broken human beings.' According to Dada, this is true devotion, real bhakti; bhakti begins out of such love. Expand your heart to enfold the world in the embrace of your love, and you will indeed acquire the gift of bhakti, Dada would urge.

Our rishis and sages tell us: 'This world was born out of *ananda* (bliss); it subsists in ananda and it dissolves in ananda.' A bhakta says: 'This world has come out of love; it subsists in love and it dissolves in love.'

'Bhakti is both ananda and love,' Dada says. 'It is the highest and purest form of love that a human being can feel and express, and it is pure bliss, at its best.'

Dada's book *Bhakti is Bliss* was released during the Sadhana Camp of December 2015, based on the same theme.

In the Hindu way of life, the concept of bhakti denotes absolute devotion to the lord; in its highest form, it is a truly sublime feeling, arising out of a pure heart and totally free from the contamination of desire for worldly goods or attainments; the true bhakta or devotee seeks God and God alone, for his only goal is liberation from worldly life and union with his beloved Lord.

Dada is firm in asserting that bhakti is not to be taught or discussed; it is to be caught, it is to be experienced. It is not a science or an art that needs to be learnt; it is an attitude to the divine and a great gift that has been bestowed upon us. It is not a toll-paid expressway meant for the exclusive and the elite; it is the simplest, swiftest and shortest route to God that is open to each one of us.

There is no grammar of bhakti, no mechanical formula that Dada offered; what he did give is the miracle of bhakti, its transformative power, in all its many-hued splendour.

FACE THE WORLD WITH LOVE

The year 2015 saw the release of one of Dada's powerful books, *Face the World with Love*, released in the US.

Is it possible for us to love all the world, all the people in it? For Dada, the answer was most certainly yes. He had a cosmic vision, a vision of oneness and unity that sees the world as one family of God's creation. Just as it is perfectly natural for one to love the members of their family, it is perfectly natural that one should love their fellow beings – human and non-human – if they believe in God and believe that all people are God's children.

Taking as his inspiration the Vedic phrase *vasudhaiva kutumbakam* (the world as one family) Dada spoke eloquently on his firmly held motto: we must love one another or perish! This universal love is the answer to all our vexing problems: When one faces the world with love, where is the scope for dissent, differences and strife?

He offered a few easy-to-follow and easy-to-implement suggestions on how one may grow in the spirit of love and understanding:

1. Follow the golden rule: Do unto others as you would have them do unto you.
2. Do not just fall in love; rise in love with God, and in love with your fellow human beings, as also with brother birds and animals.
3. Speak softly, gently and with loving kindness. Treat everyone with love and respect. Greet God in everyone you meet.
4. Stop judging others, for true love is non-judgmental. Do not see the faults of others.
5. Learn to love unconditionally. Do not enquire whether he or she deserves your love; for this is trade, bargain, not love.
6. Breathe out love to those who ill-treat you and speak harshly to you.
7. Whatever you do, whatever you say, whatever you think, whatever you give – do it for the pure love of God.
8. Learn to forgive others who have harmed you or hurt you in any way. Forgive before they even ask for your forgiveness.
9. Cultivate the virtue of detachment.
10. The law of love is the law of selfless service and compassion. Therefore, go out of your way to help others; and rejoice in everything that the will of God brings to you.

Dada's dearly held belief was this: The greatest gift of human life is that we can love one another.

SWITCH ON THE LIGHT

Dada's much-awaited public lecture in English on the eve of his 98th birthday was on the catchy theme 'Switch on the Light.'

He began by talking about how today people are surrounded by darkness which is ever-growing. How does one emerge from darkness into light? 'Love lifteth the veil', Dada stressed that love should blend with renunciation, which leads to inward light.

Even the Buddha endorsed this view, exhorting mankind with his memorable words: Be ye lamps unto yourselves.

Dada spoke of a triple light:

1. Light of the body: Keep the body pure, strong and healthy. It will radiate light. Learn to still the tumult of the senses.
2. Light of the mind: This is evident in our capacity for reflection and the power of understanding. When we keep the mind pure, our thoughts and words and actions will also be pure and wholesome.
3. Light of the heart: The divine light lives within each one of us; all we need to do is to enter the temple of the heart and behold the vision within.

We should switch on this triple light in daily life, Dada said. There is no particular way to God he added, for he is here and now. There is no essence of God – he is all or nothing. There is no secret to know God, for he is the greatest truth.

Dada graciously provided a few practical suggestions on how we may switch on the light:

1. Seek association with men of God.
2. Do not be dominated by passion and its flames of negativity.
3. Keep away from the worst darkness which is selfishness.
4. Cultivate the virtue of detachment. Those who give, live.
5. Grow in the awareness that this life is but a fleeting moment in eternity.
6. Pray to God for his special grace.
7. Seek the guidance of a spiritual mentor, who is the most powerful source of light and inner wisdom.
8. Fill your heart with love of God and all of his creation.
9. Follow the law of love which is the law of service and sacrifice.
10. Know yourself by spending time in silence.

WHAT THEN?

Tateh kim? This thought-provoking question from Adi Shankara was the theme of the Sadhana Camp held in Pune in December 2016. Dada's inaugural address and subsequent ruh-rihans on the theme were compiled into a best-selling booklet, *What Then?*

What then? Tateh Kim? For many of us who are living life on the fast lane, blindly pursuing the rat race and our worldly goals, this question may seem irrelevant. 'I'm so busy living my life,' we might retort, 'I don't have time to pause and ask myself these speculative questions.'

There is nothing more to life than pursuing ambitions, climbing up the social ladder, making money for oneself and one's loved ones, acquiring status symbols such as cars, houses, fat incomes and that which money can buy. Can this be the overall goal of one's life – thus far and no further?

After acquiring degrees, amassing millions of dollars, gaining approbation and applause of crowds, a wealthy, successful man passes away like any other man. He does not – cannot – carry with him his degrees, his wealth, his prestige and power. What is the purpose of life? What is its goal? Is one living their precious human life meaningfully, consciously, purposefully?

To this end, Dada offered his invaluable practical suggestions:

1. Take charge of your life.
2. Never forget that you are just a traveller here on earth ... and that your time is limited.
3. Remember that pain and pleasure are but two sides of the same coin: mindless pursuit of pleasure will only lead to pain, ultimately.
4. Develop the spirit of detachment, for nothing, no one belongs to you!
5. Self-effort is the best effort; therefore, act now to achieve the goal of this earthly life.

6. Remember: this too shall pass away. Nothing is permanent in this life.

Not only did Dada raise tough questions, he also provided enlightening answers. He showed us that there is more to life than what is existing at the mundane level of material pleasures and possessions. And the practical philosopher that he was, he was down-to-earth in his approach and suggestions. In short, he helped his followers discover what is next on their life's agenda, himself showing them the way.

THE POWER OF SILENCE

At Sadhu Vaswani's 50th Mahayagna, it was the Bridge Builder's special event on the theme of silence. While sharing a few thoughts on silence, Dada spoke about how a time comes in the life of every aspirant when he is filled with the rapture of silence. In several scriptures God is referred to as the spirit of silence. In a Sufi account of Jesus, it is told that Jesus had once said that devotion or bhakti is made up of ten parts – nine of which are attained in silence and the tenth in solitude.

If one wishes to grow in the spirit of bhakti, they must learn to love silence. With every word, shakti – energy – is spent, which could be used instead to develop spiritual power. Therefore, speak as little as possible and before speaking ask oneself the question: Is what I am about to speak better than silence?

Reminiscing about his Guru, Dada explained the three laws of the Alpa Marga – the little way – that his master preached:

1. Speak little
2. Eat little
3. Sleep little

In addition, Dada said, silence is better when blended with the repetition of the Name Divine within the heart. This prevents the mind from wandering.

DADA ANSWERS ...

'Q & A Sessions' with Dada were popular among the youth, and enjoyed by everyone. Dada, was a master of repartee and handled all questions thrown at him with a great sense of humour and aplomb. Of course, serious questions and personal doubts were also placed before him and he responded with empathy and compassion, as only he could.

At the end of his public discourses, at Sadhana camps and youth programmes, Dada would pass the microphone to his audiences and allows their questions to take centre stage. We offer you a sample of lighter and more serious moments from a few of these sessions:

Q: You are at the head of such a prominent and leading institution. How do you pace yourself even at ninety-four?

A: I refuse to believe I am ninety-four. Youth is a state of mind which should be fresh, open to receive new ideas. A childlike faith in God will bring miracles in your life. It is not I, but God and the guru who do everything.

Q: We are in the inner lane, the fast lane on the highway of life. If we slow down our pace there will be a pile up. How can we slow down?

A: Change your lane.

Q: There are so many expectations from us. How can we deliver on expectations?

A: Work only for the love of God.

One of the most unforgettable Q & A sessions with Dada came at the centenary event at the Dome in Mumbai, when Karan Johar addressed his Rapid Fire questions to Dada.

KJ: What does freedom mean to you?

Dada: Freedom does not mean doing what you want to do, or what you wish to do. It means doing what you should do.

KJ: What is the one thing that is essential to living a balanced life? And what is the one thing we must absolutely do away with, to lead a balanced life?

Dada: Faith.

KJ: Faith. And what should we do away with?

Dada: Ego.

KJ: And Dada, how would you describe love in your own words?

Dada: I would not describe love... I will come and show you. Love in words is not worth it. (*Dada embraces Karan Johar in a tight hug*)

KJ: No, it's true. There is no way you can describe it. You can feel it, sense it and spread it the way you like it.

KJ: Which is the song, Dada, that you love and can listen to all the time?

Dada: *Ek tu hi tu, ek tu hi tu, ek tu hi tu*!

Overwhelmed, Karan Johar asked Dada for one practical tip that the huge audience could take back with them for the day. Pat came Dada's answer: bring back God into your life!

Karan Johar, who had hosted a hundred chat shows with over two hundred celebrities could only conclude with the words, 'To me, this session was not just a conversation, it was almost an enlightenment. Thank you, Dada.'

MAKE THE RIGHT CHOICE

In his talk during the week of his 99th birthday celebrations, Dada spoke on the topic 'Make the Right Choice'.

At every step, every turn on the pathway of life, one is forced to choose – choose a job, car, spouse and much more. Thus, man has the freedom and can become new based on the choices he makes. When making a choice, one should quieten the mind, open the heart and practice the presence of God, ask for what is good for oneself, and not just for what one wants. The law of attraction makes the universe into a huge copying machine, simply drawing one closer to what one desires.

Elucidating on the concept of preya and shreya, Dada added that two of the noblest disciplines of spiritual life are humility and acceptance.

WHAT IS DADA'S MESSAGE?

Dada's humanitarian spirit transcended caste, creed, colour and religion. His life reflected the essence of the Gita as well as the Sermon on the Mount. He was one of those remarkable men whose life was their message; a remarkable teacher who taught by example, an embodiment of love and compassion. His reassuring presence blazed forth the comforting message of the Gita: 'All is well, all was well, all will ever be well both now and a hundred years hence!'

NINE

What Dada Means to Us

'In character, in manner, in style, in all things, the supreme excellence is simplicity.'

– Henry Wadsworth Longfellow

DO YOU KNOW DADA?

Many of Dada's devotees say, 'I have known Dada since I was ten years old,' or 'I have been associated with the Mission for over forty years. I know Dada very well indeed.'

Could this be true? Yes, but only in a limited sense. Of course, it is wonderful to have known Dada for any length of time; and a privilege and blessing to have been associated or connected with the Mission for any number of days, months or years. One is reminded of the scholar who remarked, 'The association with or knowledge of the guru is not just a physical phenomenon. Name and form, in fact, do not matter much as far as knowing the guru is concerned.'

Indeed, one can recall Dada often telling audiences with a smile, 'This kurta or shawl that I wear is not J. P. Vaswani.'

The truth is you know the guru only when you are transformed by your association with him.

Award-winning biographer and acclaimed documentary film-maker Ruzbeh Bharucha would vouch for the truth of the statement that one can know the guru only if the guru wants the person to know him. Ruzbeh, as everyone in the Mission calls him, intended to write a book on Dada and make a film on him. But he was nonplussed when Dada refused to talk even a little about himself. This is how he records his misgivings:

> He keeps quoting his master. I wonder how I am going to write a book on Dada if he keeps saying, 'It is all my master's grace … Sadhu Vaswani will decide … Sadhu Vaswani knows best' … I mean, how am I going to fill three hundred pages … I told Dada, 'Dada, I truly love your love and devotion towards your master. I hope I feel the same for Baba Sai, but I can't write a book if you leave everything squarely at the feet of your master…'

Maharishi Valmiki tells Sri Rama, 'He alone can know you to whom you make yourself known; and the moment he knows you, he becomes one with you. It is only by your grace that your devotees come to know you.'

It is grace that leads one to Dada; it is grace that will help one know him and feel his influence transform oneself. Love, faith, surrender and obedience are the steps that will enable one to know Dada truly.

And yet it can be claimed: Dada is all things to all people. Not that he claims any such thing. He likes to describe himself as a zero, as the underserving one, as a fellow pilgrim on the path. But the point is, one can get to know him in the measure that one imbibes his teachings, takes them to heart and lives them in the deeds of daily life.

'Even my mother doesn't understand me as well as Dada does,' said a distraught teenage girl, who found hope and comfort from Dada's discourses and question-answer sessions.

'Dada is my friend, philosopher and guide,' said a young businessman. 'All that I am, I owe to him.'

'For me, Dada is *mata, pita, bandhu, sakha*,' said a mother. 'I am able to cope with a difficult and complex family life because Dada is there for me.'

So who is Dada? All of these things and more. To put it simply, he is all things to all people. If one was seeking wisdom and insight, he was the true teacher who offered it to them. If one was seeking hope and faith in the surrounding darkness of despair, he was the harbinger of light. If one was seeking wellness and healing in severe affliction, Dada gave spiritual solace. He was the true disciple to his master.

It is said that only a true guru knows his guru. This certainly applied to Dada. And yet he tells us in all humility, writing of his master:

> To be able to write of him I must have magic in my words and music in my heart – the music which makes life a hymn of dedication and love. And I must have within me a fire, a flame burning ceaselessly, until it reduces all I have and all I am to naught!

Would one not be foolish to attempt what Dada himself could not do?

> I have neither the magic of words nor the music of the heart, and the spiritual flame has not yet been kindled within me. I but aspire to be an echo of the echo of his voice…

In this section, we shall attempt to capture the sheer goodness, godliness, love, wisdom and compassion that was Dada.

THE PERFECT DISCIPLE

If there was one quality that took precedence over all others in Dada, it must be his guru bhakti! For Dada, devotion and surrender began and ended with his beloved Gurudev.

Dada would say that in this Kali Yuga, God, in his kindness and compassion had anticipated the drawbacks and shortcomings of humanity and therefore he has given us the simplest sadhana that we can all adopt painlessly to attain liberation, which is guru bhakti. It is not only the easiest – but also the highest sadhana that is open to all of us. There are certain ways in which every disciple undertakes this sadhana: 1) Service to the guru 2) Faith and devotion to the guru and his teachings 3) Surrender to the guru 4) Obedience to the guru. Dada himself embodied all these qualities.

Dada made a very interesting distinction between disciple and devotee. A disciple, according to Dada, is one who has surrendered his mind, heart and life totally to the guru and retains, thereby, no identity of his own. In return, he gets the protection of the guru. Disciples, therefore, are very rare. A devotee, on the other hand, is one who reveres, loves and admires the guru and pays heed to his teachings, but does not surrender totally to the guru. Therefore devotees give other kinds of offerings to the guru. Since they cannot give of themselves completely, they offer whatever they can by way of wealth or time and personal effort for voluntary work, so that the guru's work may spread and so that more people may benefit from it. It is their way of expressing gratitude for the many blessings received from the guru.

As his master's successor, Dada chose a life of surrender and dedication; he chose to live by his master's will, chose his master's message as his life's vision and chose to make himself an instrument in the master's service.

And then, hailed as a master and mentor by thousands, he chose to call himself a disciple of all rather than a guru; attribute everything to his guru's grace; live and move by his guru's name, and to surrender his life completely to the guru's will.

As the nom de plume for his poetry and prayers, his entire life was *anjali* – an offering – to his guru, a pure expression of devotion in word, deed, and thought. In Sadhu Vaswani's lifetime, Dada served him day and night while absorbing his wisdom and virtues. After his guru transcended the material world, Dada's every moment had been devoted to conveying his message and furthering his mission.

In a loving, moving reference to his dear disciple, on his 41st birthday, Sadhu Vaswani had said:

> He is a live spark of inspiration. How blessed are we to have one such as him in our midst! And on this auspicious day, I breathe out an aspiration that my dear Jashan may go from heart to heart, home to home, nation to nation, carrying with himself the message of the rishis and sages of India!

Again, in utmost humility and self-effacement, Dada would not accept any recognition or honours for himself but attribute all that was praiseworthy to his guru. Apart from three book-length biographies, hundreds of articles and poignant poems about the master, Dada never ever began a speech, either at a satsang or on any international stage, without a soul-stirring eulogy to the guru!

THE FORM OF THE GURU

This difficult question was once placed before Dada: 'Even though we always carry your image in the heart within us, wherever we go, why is it that nothing can match the joy of actually seeing you in person? Is it that the form is more powerful than the formless?'

Dada had come out of his room to meet people, when a devotee, with tears in his eyes, addressed this query to Dada: 'Do you miss Sadhu Vaswani's physical presence?' Dada himself had faced this question several times. And his answer was clear and firm: 'I believe he is with me. I believe, even from the physical point of view, that he, and it is only he, who is doing everything for me. I believe I am just an instrument carrying out his work and his mission. I may not be doing it very well, but I am trying to, with the best of my ability and with all of his grace.'

Now, facing a similar question, Dada smiled. He explained that the world was, after all, physical, and we feel and experience a great deal on the physical plane. The physical presence of a saintly soul has such powerful vibrations that all of us are actually able to feel them. Dada added characteristically, 'I do not refer to myself.' But the joy we all felt had its own story to tell.

'In ancient times too,' Dada continued, 'our sages urged that we should meditate on a form and a mantra, rather than on *shunya* or nothingness.' And Dada narrated the thrilling story of the little boy Dhruva, to whom Maharishi Narada described the effulgent, radiant form of the four-armed Mahavishnu, his eyes brilliant as the sun, the sacred *shanka* and *chakra* in his hands, the mace and the sword at his sides, his divine presence inspiring awe and ecstasy at the same time. When the form was clearly etched in Dhruva's mental vision, Maharishi Narada taught him the sacred mantra, *Om Namo Bhagavate Vasudevaya* and thus young Dhruva was initiated into meditation.

Having explained to us the joy of beholding the truly beloved form, Dada said that the converse was also held by a few holy ones; that is, the sense of separation, the yearning that one feels for the divine is also equally ecstatic, for it is the greatest feeling that we can experience here on earth, where actual union with God is not possible for us.

The exquisite longing in separation and the inexplicable joy of being in the divine presence: had not all of us felt it for Dada?

ALWAYS THERE FOR HIS SIBLINGS

As the eldest son of his parents, Dada has always fulfilled his responsibility to his siblings, even though he chose to follow the path of the spirit.

In 1958, Ram, Dada's younger brother and the second son of his parents, got married in Mumbai. Gurudev Sadhu Vaswani was ailing at that time, and Dada was loath to leave his side even for a minute. However, Sadhu Vaswani insisted that Dada Jashan, as the eldest son of the family, be there at the wedding to give his brother away. So Dada drove to Mumbai, participated in the marriage ceremony, and left immediately for Pune.

Truth to tell, Dada Jashan had seen his own guru perform all his filial duties. Sadhu Vaswani had obeyed his mother and remained in his career during her lifetime, even though his heart had been elsewhere. While she lay dying, he had personally nursed her, bringing her comfort and solace. Before dying, she had placed the hand of her unmarried daughter, Papur, in his hand, entrusting her to his care. In 1965, when Papur passed away, Sadhu Vaswani personally performed her last rites, even though his health was frail. Duty to the family and obedience to the parents were values that both master and disciple have held sacred.

Dada was extremely fond of his mother, known as Bhabhi to one and all. Being the dutiful son that he was, Dada would first bow before her to seek blessings and then enter the satsang.

Once when Dada was on a yatra to Delhi, Bhabhi expressed a desire to see him while she was on her sickbed. On receiving the message, Dada cancelled all his scheduled public programmes at once and flew back to be by his mother's side. How Bhabhi's eyes shone with love and joy when she saw her loving son! In the following fifteen days, Dada served his ailing mother day in and day out, responding to every twitch of pain that she complained of. Sensing that her end was near, Bhabhi beckoned her younger son Hiro to her side. She took his hand and placed it in his elder brother's. 'Take care of him when I am gone,' she whispered to Dada.

On 14 April 1977, with Dada by her bedside, Krishnadevi breathed her last. Soon thereafter, Hiro took ill and was confined to bed for over fourteen years. How tenderly Dada took care of Hiro! He made it a point to spend some time with him almost every day despite his pressing engagements.

There came a stage when he even lost his speech and the ability to eat. Despite this extremely painful situation, his mind remained clear and unaffected. Those who took care of him, as also devotees who visited him regularly, were amazed to note how he remained cheerful and optimistic right through those long years of physical helplessness. Dada, whenever he was in town, visited him almost every day, and would spend time with him, regardless of how busy his own schedule was. Hiro passed away suddenly while Dada was in Dubai in July 1993.

The same evening, Dada was to deliver a discourse at the Astoria Hotel on how to face the challenges of life. It was as though fate was playing an ironic game with him and challenging him to face his own personal battle. The devotees wondered if the programme should be cancelled; but Dada said he would not want to disappoint a large gathering. Calmly he went through with his commitment, delivering his discourse at the appointed time. Soon after the event, Dada drove directly to the airport to catch a flight to Bombay. He arrived in Pune and performed his brother's last rites. It is such a devout being whom the Gita calls a *stitha prajnya*.

Years later, in June 2007, Dada's elder sister, Dadi Hari P. Vaswani, known as Ma Hari Devi to her devout and loving followers, moved on to the other shore. She had been ailing for some time and had been admitted to the Inlaks & Budhrani Hospital, where Dada visited her frequently. On the last day, when the doctors declared that the end was very near, Dada asked the sangat in the room to sing kirtans softly. Dadi Hari then opened her eyes and looked at Dada who was tenderly stroking her forehead, and quietly passed away.

When her mortal remains were brought in front of the sacred samadhi, after recitations from scriptures, Dada offered a prayer. There were unending lines of people who wanted to pay their last respects to her and offer flowers and *chaddar* to the teacher and mentor whom they loved and revered. Dada, along with a large number of devotees, went on to the Vainkunth Dham Samashan Bhumi where her mortal frame was consigned to the fire.

In May on Shanti Yagna Day, Dada in his upadesh spoke of both Sister Shanti and Dadi Hari: fortunate souls who had come into very close contact with their guru, Sadhu Vaswani, at a very young age. Both had deep love for the eternal, both were committed to simran and seva and lived a pure, guileless life. While Sister Shanti, he said, aspired to live a hidden life in a hidden God, Dadi Hari, who was a poetess and orator in her own right, went ahead to spread the master's message far and wide.

PRECIOUS MOMENTS WITH DADA

A saint like Dada reveals himself in the small deeds of daily life too. It is as if a curtain has parted – if only for a brief moment – allowing us to have a glimpse of something precious and rare.

An admirer asked Dada, 'What is the thing that you love to do the most?'

Dada answered, 'Whatever I am doing right now, that is the work God has decided for me for this particular moment. And what God decides is what I love to do the most.'

Another person wanted to know why Dada had to undergo so much physical suffering. Dada replied in a manner that moved many hearts, 'Suffering? Do you call it that? It is a blessing! And blessings are always a surprise accompanied by joy and wonder. Joy and wonder make you young!'

A visitor was aghast to see Dada's writing table cluttered with small items – a bar of chocolate, a tiny pencil, a little slip of paper with a message from a devotee, a flower, among others. So he asked Dada, 'How can you work at such a crowded and messy table?' With a smile on his lips Dada answered, 'I learn more from these small gifts of love than from all the books in a library.'

In a serious mood, someone asked him, 'Dada, what is life's heaviest burden?'

Pat came the reply, 'To have nothing to carry.'

To a mother complaining about her child's persistently naughty behaviour, Dada's practical answer was, 'Love her and hug her every three hours.'

In answer to another devotee whose question was, 'What is the urgent need of the world today?' Dada asked with a twinkle in his eye, 'In how many words would you like the answer?'

The person said, 'Six words only.'

Dada's quick rejoinder was, 'Good mothers, good mothers, good mothers.'

An anxious teenager about to enter the portals of senior college asked Dada, 'I have just cleared my twelfth exam. I wish to become successful in life. What advice would you give me?'

Dada's succinct response was, 'First, do not take decisions when you are angry. Second, be like the echo which does not talk unless spoken to.'

An agitated youth came to Dada one day and asked, 'How is it, Dada, that you are always so relaxed? Can you tell me the art of true living?'

With a twinkle in his eye, Dada answered, 'The art of true living is to put all your worries down in the bottom of your heart. Then put the lid on and smile. The simple act of smiling again and again, will change the structure of your life.'

Dada was sitting among a few brothers and sisters who had gathered together to plan an event at the Mission. He noticed a girl going hurriedly over a list of activities that she had to carry out.

Seeing her frantic hurry, Dada gently said to her, 'Be a painter, not a potter. The potter rushes about as he prepares pot after pot. The painter takes time to perfect every picture that he paints.'

I AM NOT ALONE, GOD IS WITH ME

Dada was to fly from Penang to Singapore, and a private aircraft was to carry him and a few devotees. It was that time of the year when heavy showers lashed peninsular Malaysia. Dada was thus advised to leave Penang by mid-morning before the noon showers began. But given that people kept pouring in to meet and consult with Dada, it was almost 2:30 p.m. by the time he reached the aircraft. He was asked to postpone his trip to the following day, but Dada just smiled and prepared to board the plane. In order to maintain the balance of the tiny aircraft, a devotee was asked to sit in the front with the pilot. As the devotee seemed nervous about it, Dada hopped on to the passenger seat in front and with a look of amusement upon his face, remarked with childlike glee that he would now enjoy a skyline view of the world down below.

The plane had barely flown a short distance when the skies began to grow ominously dark. Flashes of lightning and rolling thunder heralded the rain, which began to hit hard and fast in thick sheets, obscuring all vision. The two devotees were petrified and soon fear was writ large on the face of the pilot. In a trembling voice, he said, 'You had all better begin to say your prayers.' The two devotees seated at the back, began a continuous chant. Dada maintained his equilibrium, and calm and peaceful as ever, he suggested that the pilot focus on flying the plane.

Things turned worse when the plane lost contact with the Control Tower! In this disorienting situation, Dada tried to engage the nervous pilot in conversation, 'Brother, tell me, what is your name?' Automatically the pilot replied, 'Bhagwan.' Dada clasped his hands in joy, saying, 'As "Bhagwan" (God) is flying our plane, we need not worry!'

Dada's words were prophetic! Soon enough, the force of rain had abated, and clouds parted momentarily, making it possible for

Bhagwan, the pilot, to keep the flight smooth and land safely on the ground.

400 MEMBERS IN OUR FAMILY

Dada always held that God is truth; and it is only the way of truth that can lead us to God. There is a lovely episode from his youth to illustrate how Dada had always been a votary of truth.

It was back in 1942 when Dada was just twenty-four years old. The restrictions and rigours of war were beginning to hit Sind Province, and people's rations were being regulated strictly.

It was Sadhu Vaswani's practice to feed the birds daily at Krishta Kunj. A sufficient quantity of grains for this purpose was procured in the monthly budget. But this year, the ration shop manager had demurred. He refused to allow the purchase of extra grains for the birds. Dada Jashan went in person to explain that Sadhu Vaswani's service to brother birds could not be jeopardized and requested that he provide the extra rations. The manager accepted Dada's explanation and billed him for the grains.

A few days later, a team of inspectors from the civil supplies office arrived at Krishta Kunj. They waved the latest ration bill at Dada and asked him sharply, 'That's a large quantity of grains! Tell us please, how many people eat here on a day-to-day basis?'

Dada replied without a moment's hesitation, 'Around four hundred, daily.'

'What?' said one of the officers, when he had recovered sufficiently to react. 'Are you suggesting four hundred people eat in this small cottage which cannot accommodate even one hundred people standing?'

'Please come with me,' Dada said, and led the team of inspectors to the bird sanctuary on the terrace where scores of birds were pecking at the grains; bowls of water had been laid out for them, and his feathered friends were at their daily meal, chirping away to glory.

'Our master regards these birds as members of his family,' Dada explained politely to the inspectors. 'He will never consent to eat until these winged angels are fed first.'

The inspectors were both touched and awed by Dada's response. They asked to be taken to Sadhu Vaswani's presence so that they could offer their *pranaams* to the saint. They assured Dada that the ration for the birds would be supplied regularly.

TEACHING BY PRECEPT

A young mother once brought her child to Dada. She said to him, 'My daughter is extremely fond of you and regards you as her role model. That is why I have brought her to you. She has the unfortunate habit of being extremely rude to the servants. All of us at home have tried to correct her, but to no avail. She talks very rudely to the servants and feels that she is the boss so she can treat them any way she likes.'

Dada heard her out patiently, but did not say anything to the girl immediately. On her next visit to Dada, he first put her at ease and casually broached the topic of her behaviour. 'Neetu, Neetu,' he began lovingly, 'tell me, whom do you love the most? Mama, Papa, your dog Cheetah, or your friends in school, who?'

Neetu, child that she was, thought deeply and then said, 'My mother.'

'Are you sure?'

'Yes, I am sure.'

'Would you like it, if I spoke rudely to her and ordered her out of the house?'

Neetu had tears in her eyes as she looked at Dada and said, 'I would feel very sad if someone spoke to my mother like that.' She put her arms round her mother and kissed her.

'Remember, God too is our divine mother and we are all her children. The raindrops you see on a sunny day are like so many tears God sheds for her children who are ill-treated. Ramu the servant too feels very sad when you speak harshly to him. Will you promise me, Neetu, that you will not speak rudely to him anymore?'

The kindness in his tone and the love in his eyes softened the heart of the little girl. Her whole outlook changed. From then on she began to speak to the servants politely and gently.

Meetha bolan, neeh chaalan (speak sweetly, behave gently) is a maxim that Dada held very close to his heart.

WHAT ARE EYELIDS FOR?

A young girl who lived in the Sadhu Vaswani Ashram for a while, committed an act of folly which was socially and morally incorrect one day. She did not know how to rectify the error, so she did the next best thing she could. She went to Dada and confessed her offence to him.

In the meantime, the superintendent at the ashram had been told of her behaviour and felt that a mere reprimand would not suffice. They felt that she should be asked to leave the ashram.

When Dada heard about their decision, he was concerned. Dada did not believe that in the long run, punishment was the only mode of correction. Often, forgiveness and understanding towards the erring person could be more effective.

Dada sent for the superintendent to discuss the girl's misdemeanour. The lady justified her decision to send the girl out, saying, 'God has given us eyes, so we can be watchful and observant. When we see someone doing wrong, it is our duty to discipline the individual, and set the proper example.'

Understanding the girl's predicament, Dada said, 'It is true that nature has given you eyes, but then, you have been given eyelids too. Sometimes it is more beneficial to shut the eyes. And this is one of those times.'

Hence, the girl was taken back into the ashram, and chastised for her wrong-doing. She was truly contrite and repented deeply; above all, she was extremely grateful to be given a second chance.

A HELPER OF THE HELPERS

Dada has often shared with the sangat a beautiful story from the early life of Gurudev Sadhu Vaswani, when he was the principal of Mahindra College, Patiala. He was given a spacious bungalow on the campus as his official residence. There was a gardener, a cook and a servant to attend to his needs. On Sunday, the weekly holiday, Principal Vaswani would take time out to cook food with his own hands and serve his team of helpers. When they protested that they were being paid to work for him, he would tell them lovingly, 'You take care of me six days of the week. It is only fitting that I should serve you on the seventh day.' Dada, too, would often take a leaf out of his master's book to help his helpers.

Once, Dada had to stay in Mumbai for three weeks to make recordings for his TV talks. On a free day, Dada insisted that he and his devotees would take charge of the kitchen, to cook food and serve it to all the domestic helpers. The hostess was flabbergasted and the domestic helpers too, were taken aback. Their shock was understandable, for no one had ever done such a thing before, let alone think about it. But Dada was insistent. He assured his hosts that there would be no unpleasant consequences to his act, which was one of love and gratitude. Such a gesture was required from all guests and visitors who enjoyed the hospitality of the house and the service of the helpers. 'If it is by karma that we are at the receiving end of their service and they are the ones in our employ, who can tell whether we won't become their servants in some future birth?' he said to the hosts. 'Therefore, let us sow good karma.' And so,

Dada's devotees who accompanied him prepared *paani puri, dahi vada, chole bhature* and other delicacies.

Dada had always been particular that the food offered as prasad to guests and visitors should be cooked personally and not just ordered from outside, as is the norm in many households today; for the offering of prasad implies the offering of one's own loving effort and time. When the food was ready, Dada personally served the helpers, assisted by his devotees. The family members were also served the prasad and Dada requested the hosts to give the helpers a day off, while his group attended to all the household chores for the day.

Whenever Dada travels, he takes a special effort to thank the domestic helpers of his various hosts around the world. He also offers them gifts, fruits and chocolates as prasad. Once, he was slicing an apple when a Spanish maid came in to clear the waste basket. Dada made her sit down and offered her a few slices of apple; he also gave her some apples to take home to her children. She was overwhelmed by his tender care and kindness.

HIS FAVOURITE BOOKS

Everyone who wished to know Dada really well always asked him: Who is your favourite author? Which is your favourite book?

Dada's personal library of several thousand books covers virtually every subject. When he wanted to share a reference with his friends or devotees, he actually pointed to the particular shelf or section where a specific book could be located. He read constantly from the lives or teachings of different saints. This, he said, had a purifying influence on the mind and, consequently, on one's dream consciousness. Avid readers, even among lesser mortals, find it difficult to name one particular author or book as their chosen favourite. How could we expect Dada to pick and choose among the hundreds of books that he had read?

However, Dada did have books he returned to, again and again. The books that he found especially helpful are *The Imitation of Christ* (1914) by Thomas à Kempis, *The Gospel of Sri Ramakrishna* (1942) by Swami Nikhilananda and Sadhu Vaswani's *Gita: Meditations* and *Thus Have I Learnt* (2003). One of the very first books which made a profound effect on his mind and heart was *The Prophet* (1923) by Khalil Gibran.

The Gita was his constant companion. It takes time, perhaps a lifetime to understand and assimilate it, he said. Going into the depths of slokas, he would select a few and concentrate on them. For him, it was a life guide.

PUTTING OTHERS FIRST

Once, it started to rain heavily at night. The unexpected summer showers were accompanied by lightning and thunder. Dada, who was awake late into the night, requested his devotees to tell all the security guards at the Mission to stay indoors and not venture into the rains. The guards on duty that night, who received these special instructions were overwhelmed by Dada's care and concern for them.

The doctors treating Dada at US medical centres would often find his room overflowing with gifts and flowers and fruits and other offerings. But in no time they would all disappear, as Dada gave them away to nurses, attendants and other patients! 'You've given everything away!' commented a doctor, who happened to return to Dada's room after a few hours. Dada's reply was simple: 'My master, Sadhu Vaswani, taught us this lesson: To live is to give! Those who do not give are no better than dead souls.'

Many devotees have reported of miraculous cures and rapid healing of ailments and afflictions – and this, at a time when Dada himself had been unwell or undergoing severe pain. They firmly believed that Dada had taken on their pain and suffering upon himself, and allowed them the grace of healing. Dada would never admit to such a miracle or indeed allow even the least credit to be given to him; but as he himself has said, God's true lovers 'stay awake so others can sleep; they starve so others can be pain-free. Thus is expressed their love for God.'

CREATING SATYA YUGA IN KALI YUGA

Some eminent jurists were in Pune and were on their way to inaugurate the new district court at Icchalkananji and expressed the desire to meet Dada – and Dada readily agreed to receive them, along with their wives, families and members of the judicial delegation.

Dada observed that unless the judiciary had integrity and honesty, the society and nation could not hope to be safeguarded. He expressed his happiness that the Indian judicial system was safe in the hands of men of integrity. For, as he observed, 'When corruption enters the judiciary, it will truly be the beginning of the end.'

They assured Dada that there might be isolated instances of deviation, but essentially there was no corruption in the judicial system.

'How can we ensure that justice, equity and honesty triumph in the environment of Kali Yuga?' the chief justice asked Dada.

Dada's answer was simple and direct. 'Each one of us must build an island of satya (truth) around himself.' He said. 'When these islands come together, we can create another Satya Yuga even in the environment of Kali Yuga.'

It was indeed confidence inspiring to behold the deeply spiritual side of these eminent men who played such a major role in shaping the destiny of India. The deep reverence and devotion with which they met Dada and received his blessings, spoke volumes for their sense of commitment and responsibility.

Dada saw them off personally – and all the people who had gathered at the Mission campus to catch a glimpse of the VIP guests were moved to see that the Chief Justice held on to Dada's hands with deep respect, reluctant to let go.

SUCH HUMILITY IS OF THE ANGELS

When they were asked to name their one favourite trait in Dada, people from all walks of life, big and small, saints and sages, holy and wise men, chose Dada's humility as his most sterling quality.

'Spirituality begins and ends with humility,' said Dada. According to him, 'Humility is not an attitude or a manner of etiquette; true humility is a way of life, an aspect of one's temperament. Humility cannot be taught. It must be imbibed, inculcated through self-awareness.'

Dada would reach out to touch the feet of anyone who would bow to touch his feet and take his blessings! As an admirer remarked, 'He seeks blessings of all those who come to seek his blessings and his humility embraces you, fills you with warmth and the realization that God hasn't given up on mankind.'

'Dada's humility is all-pervasive,' said Ruzbeh Bharucha. 'It is childlike, and has a beautiful and subtle *khushboo* or aroma.' Krishna Das, singer, described Dada's humility in the most beautiful manner, when he said, 'You know, true and genuine humility doesn't attract any attention to itself. This is Dada.'

People asked Krishna Das, what Dada meant to him, and he replied in his deep, soft voice, 'Asking me that is like asking a stone to describe the sun ... When a saint like Dada blesses you, he reminds you of your own potential and duty to the world outside, and also your potential and duty to yourself.'

'I shall be your dasa ...'

The Grammy award-winning singer, Krishna Das, is an ardent admirer of Dada Jashan. Dada first met him in the U.S. and they took to each other instantly. The acclaimed singer has sung his bhajans at several of Dada's programmes in the U.S. They share a special bond, the singer and the saint. The love of Krishna unites them by the bonds of bhakti.

Once, Krishna Das came to spend some time with Dada at the residence of his hosts in New York. Dada told him about his namesake, a devotee of Sri Krishna originally called Ras Khan, who had lived during the sixteenth century. He was a Pathan Sardar and his birthplace was Kabul, Afghanistan. The son of a landowner, he had lived a life of luxury in his youth. He had travelled to Brindavan with his Sufi mentor; here he had a vision of Lord Krishna, and he remained in Brindavan for the rest of his life, singing songs of devotion to the Lord of Mathura. 'They called him Krishna Das,' Dada said. 'His songs are still sung in some of the temples in India.'

The twenty-first century Krishna Das was listening to the story, riveted by Dada's grace and love. Suddenly Dada asked him, 'Do you know the meaning of the word Krishna?'

'You must tell me Dada,' said Krishna Das in all humility and sincerity.

'Well, the name means one who draws, one who attracts like a magnet. Krishna kept on drawing people to him.' And flashing his brilliant smile, Dada asked the singer, 'Now, you must tell us how to become a true *dasa*.'

Dada continued, in a reminiscing mood, 'My master told me, "Don't become a dasa of Krishna. But go and become a dasa of a dasa of Krishna." Now I have a dasa sitting in front of me. So I shall be your dasa.'

'Do you play the flute?' Dada asked him. 'No, Dada, my instrument is the harmonium,' replied Krishna Das.

'Krishna chose the flute. You are Krishna's flute. Through you he is singing his song ...' Dada told him. The singer's eyes were brimming with tears.

Krishna Das says of Dada, 'When I meet Dada, I know what it means to be loved and to love ... When you have doubts, a saint like Dada washes those doubts away. He gives you more strength to be who you are, to share what you have. And the love you receive from Dada is just so incredible that you become convinced that you don't deserve that kind of love, you are not worthy of it. Except in his eyes, of course we are worthy. It's in our own eyes that we have those doubts and his love just washes those doubts away...'

THANK YOU GOD FOR THE FOOD WE EAT

From his childhood, Dada was always taught to say a prayer before every meal, and Dada continued to practise this wonderful habit. Many of his devotees and followers also took to this habit religiously. Whether they are eating a simple meal alone, or dining with guests at special luncheons or dinners, you can see them close their eyes and fold their hands in a silent prayer before they begin their meal.

Life lessons were shared by Dada through his unique spirituality. Dada once explained, 'When you eat something, and share it with those that are around you, that is *bandagi*, that is bonding and prayer. Prayer is not going to the temple and chanting hymns. Prayer is when you share the best that is in you with others ... When you go to a corner and eat alone that is *gandagi* (being petty). And when you go on eating in front of others, without offering them anything at all, that is *sharmindagi* (being shameful or disgraceful). So, the one lesson that we have to learn is that of sharing. True life is sharing – to share, to bear, and to dare.'

During the early stages of Dada's recovery after the complicated heart-surgery procedure, he had spent a whole day without anything to eat or drink. When the doctor offered him a glass of water, he was amazed to see Dada pause for a minute, with his eyes closed, offering a silent prayer before he drank the clear cool water that had come to him after a long while. 'That incredible inner peace and gratefulness for that simple event … showed me what it was to be in a close relationship with God,' said the doctor.

STAY WITH US PERMANENTLY

Once, Dada was visting San Francisco, and the children of the house where Dada was staying had become extremely attached to Dada. Whenever they saw Dada's bedroom door open, they would creep into his room and quietly sit in a corner, just absorbing Dada's presence. Once, one of them had on a T-shirt on which were the words 'I have a wish'. With a grin Dada asked him, 'What is your wish?' The child said, 'My wish is that you should stay with us as long as you can.' Dada asked, 'Would you like me to stay with you permanently?' Excited the child said, 'That would be a dream come true!'

Dada laughed and then said, 'Physically I may not be able to stay with you. But I can surely reside in your hearts permanently. For that you will need to make your heart clean and pure so I can live in it.'

When the day arrived to bid farewell to Dada, all the family members gathered around him with tear-filled eyes. Dada's final message to them was: Make God the rock of your lives.

TEN

How to Embrace Pain

'Time does not heal everything; but acceptance will heal everything.'
– Unknown

HIS PAIN, OUR DISTRESS

Despite the constant demands upon his time and energy, the never ending stream of aspirants, VIP visitors, spiritual leaders and institutional heads who were eager to meet him, and the incessant travelling from one city to another, Dada never ran out of energy. It was amazing to watch him fulfil all his manifold appointments and commitments and still retain his million dollar smile at the end of a hectic day!

Among the many qualities that Dada imbibed from his guru, one of the most admirable was the capacity to endure pain and suffering with a smile. Dada had been diagnosed with an ischemic heart condition in 1971, when he was just fifty-three years old. Repeated attacks of angina over the years had taken a toll on Dada's health and strength. However, he had always been one who overlooked his own comfort and well-being to carry forward his mission of providing succour to the broken-hearted. He continued to travel and address public meetings.

In March 1995, when the pain in his chest became persistent, Dada's doctors advised him to undergo angiography. On 14 March, the angiography was performed by the distinguished French Cardiologist, Dr. Jean Fajadet at the Clinique Pasteur, Toulouse, France. The results showed a serious blockage for which the doctors recommended a bypass surgery. Until then, Dada was to be put on medication and rest.

However, Dada did not want to go back on the commitments made to his devotees for the year ahead. This included a scheduled address at the House of Commons in London, on 8 June that year; and an address to the participants of the Interfaith Symposium of World Spiritual Leaders at New York to be held in connection with the 50th Anniversary of the UN on 21 October 1995; the newly set up Morbai Naraindas Budhrani Cancer Institute was to be inaugurated at the hands of H. H. Dalai Lama in November of the same year. Dada told his doctors that he would like to postpone the surgery for a while.

On the night of 24 October 1997, when Dada was in Bangalore, he had a heart attack. He felt severe discomfort along with breathlessness. As acute chest pain made it impossible for him to lie down, he sat up the whole night, gasping for breath, but chose not to disturb anyone! Devout disciples were just a call away; just one ring of his bell would have brought them rushing to his bedside. But Dada passed a sleepless night of pain rather than calling for help!

It was only in the morning that he opened the door, just to say that he felt 'a little uneasy', and could the doctor be contacted? The doctor took him in his own car and admitted him to the ICCU of the Wockhardt Hospital. Dada remained in the ICCU for forty-eight hours, being moved thereafter to a special room where he stayed for a week.

Throughout his stay in the hospital, Dada remained cheerful as ever. To the doctors and nurses who treated him with loving devotion, he narrated stories and anecdotes. Smiling at the complex cardiac equipment which was meant to monitor him round-the-clock, Dada remarked, 'Man does not live by the beats of his heart, but by the grace of God!'

In the following days during 1997–98, the angina attacks persisted and Dada's health became a cause of concern to his doctors as well as his devotees. His heart condition was fragile, to say the least, and his movements had to be restricted. The doctors requested him not to leave his room because any form of exertion could prove to be life-threatening.

Despite the doctors' protests and the pleas of the devotees, Dada delivered the keynote address at the World Convention on Reverence for All Life, 22 November 1997. But the strain began to show very visibly now. The doctors finally recommended that he be taken to the Washington Medical Center for an angioplasty.

On 15 February 1998, Dada flew to Washington D.C. From the airport, he was escorted directly to the hospital in an ambulance, where a suite of rooms had been booked for him and his group.

The doctors and nurses at the renowned medical centre knew that a holy man, a great saint from India was amidst them. Throughout Dada's hospitalization, they extended their wholehearted cooperation and services to make his stay comfortable. Further, they showed every possible consideration to the anxious devotees accompanying him.

The doctors performed one more angiography, and arrived at the decision that a by-pass surgery would be the only solution to the problem. Following the diagnosis, Dada withdrew into a period of silence of spiritual communion with his master. After a lengthy period of reflection and contemplation, he finally gave his consent for the surgery.

Devotees all over the world held round-the-clock sessions of prayer and recital of holy mantras. Extensive service programmes, feeding and clothing of the poor were undertaken by the Sadhu Vaswani centres worldwide.

On the unforgettable day of 18 February 1998, a team of doctors, led by Dr Paul Corso, performed a quadruple bypass surgery on Dada. It lasted over four hours.

What transpired on the operating table during those four critical hours is too painful for us to contemplate even today. But Dada had his own mystical experience to relate to them. He felt he had arrived at the heaven world. At its gates, he met his beloved master, Sadhu Vaswani, who said to him, 'My child, there is still a lot of work you must do on the earth-plane. You need to go back.' Dada summed up the experience as only he can, 'I was not by-passed, I was sky-passed!'

However, on that very night at about 8:30 p.m., the doctors who were constantly monitoring Dada's condition in the recovery room, noticed that there was a bleeding from one of the grafts. Dada was immediately rushed back to the operating theatre, where they had to reopen the incision on his chest and seal the wound in the graft. Within twenty-four hours, two major surgeries had been performed on Dada! It was undoubtedly the blessing, protecting, healing grace of the master and the tremendous spiritual strength of an ailing Dada that enabled him to withstand the trauma and pain of it all! Above all, God, in his infinite compassion and goodness, had willed that Dada be restored to us. The emergency passed; and Dada recovered from the crisis gradually.

However, only four days after the surgery, Dada developed a problem of arrhythmia and had to be transferred to the ICCU Suddenly and without warning, Dada's condition took a precarious turn for the worse. The doctors were left with no choice but to put him on an external pacemaker. He responded well to it, and so it was decided that despite his unstable condition, a third surgery be performed so that a permanent, dual pacemaker could be implanted in his heart.

Dr Susan O'Donoghue, Director of the Department of Arrhythmia, successfully performed the surgery on 24 February. The ordeal of pain and anguish was at last over.

Dada was discharged from the hospital on the fifth day of March. All the hospital staff who had attended to him came to bid him farewell and wish him a speedy recovery. Dada flew to Chicago for a much-needed period of convalescence where Dr Chablani and Dr Lalmalani were by his side day and night.

Men of God undergo hardships so that others can live in peace and comfort. Dada is no exception. Just before his major surgery, when Dada was in a semi-conscious state due to anaesthesia, Dr Gopal Lalmalani, the doctor in attendance, happened to overhear Dada softly murmuring the following prayer:

'God, make everyone happy, peaceful and free from all diseases and sorrow'.

Imagine Dada's body being wracked by pain, yet his prayers to God were for the well-being of others. Dada was the most 'giving' person in life, and even in the state of semi-consciousness, he was emanating loving vibrations, filled with peace, goodwill, health and harmony, for everyone.

Whether in the ICCU at the Washington Medical Center, or convalescing in Chicago, his brilliant smile never left Dada's face! How was it possible for him to wear that beautiful smile all the time?

'The divine, blissful smile does not depend on outer conditions,' Dada said to us. 'It is there within us… We do not have to acquire it; we have but to regain it. We lose it when we identify ourselves with our bodies, our senses.'

In this spirit, Dada carried on with his commitments and meetings, never letting his personal discomfort interfere with the Mission's activities. When one thinks of the amount of trouble Dada took only for the sake of others, when one considers the constant travel, short stays at various places and the sheer physical strain that Dada had to undergo, one feels that he was like a river that flows for others. He lived to relieve their suffering and pain and bring them closer to God. And so it was, that people exclaimed again and again, 'Dada! You are really born to love and serve. You are Love incarnate!'

So it was, almost every day during December 2005. Dada spent the whole day recording his Hindi talks for Sony TV in Mumbai. He visited the Colaba centre of the Sadhu Vaswani Mission in the evening looking fresh as a daisy.

It was common at many such events to see the devotees rushing towards Dada at the end of the session, with their hands outstretched to touch Dada's hands. And that is exactly what happened after he delivered his message on 16 December. The sangat rushed towards the stage, calling out eagerly to Dada. And Dada, as always, bent forward, leaning out to touch as many proffered hands as he possibly could. This resulted in a tremendous strain which gripped Dada's back and shoulders. However, he took no notice of it till it became unbearable, a few days later. By 24 December, when he was back in Pune, the pain had developed into a severe spasm and he was advised bed rest. He now began to suffer excruciating pain in the back, but even this could not wipe away the smile on his face. For the next several weeks, he was confined to bed, bearing the pain stoically.

Overriding the instruction of the doctors, Dada decided not to disappoint the Pune sangat on New Year's Eve, for he knew that they had missed him sorely, and were eagerly waiting to see him and hear a few words from him. He also kept up his commitments at the satsang during the Mahayagna programmes that followed, to pay homage to his master, Sadhu Vaswani on the 40th anniversary of his samadhi.

Dada expressed his gratitude to God and to all those who had led him on the path of recovery, specially the doctors, both allopathic and ayurvedic. With a mischievous grin, Dada added that since his recovery was not complete, he would be unable to talk for the stipulated period. But for Dada-enthusiasts, just his presence sufficed to fill them with bliss. They revelled in being enveloped by the warmth of Dada's love while he generously showered his blessings upon them.

Since Dada's arrival in Pune on 22 December, the holy vibrations of non-stop japas and *path*s of *Hanuman Chalisa, Dukh Bhanjani, Ramayana, Gayatri Mantra, Nuri Granth, Guru Granth Sahib, Sukhmani Sahib* and *Jap Sahib* echoed in the city, with the conviction that prayer can work miracles.

THE IDEAL PATIENT

Who is the Patient?

Dada was in Chicago for his annual check-up and yet another surgical procedure. In the wee hours of the morning on 27 March, 2008, while the windy city was still shrouded in sleep, Dada left for the Medical Center in Chicago. His usual radiant smile belied the fact that he was on his way to another surgery. He entered the room reserved for him, where a few devotees awaited him.

The nurse, who came over to complete the formalities, stepped into the room and was astonished to see so many faces. Puzzled, she asked, 'Who is the patient?' A devotee raised his finger to point in Dada's direction. The nurse peered into his face and asked, 'Are you sure?'

In the operation theatre, the procedure was explained to Dada. He would remain conscious and alert throughout while the local anaesthesia administered to him would alleviate any pain. An unperturbed Dada said, 'I have surrendered myself into the safe hands of the doctors and the Lord, who will guide them. I don't need to know more.'

The surgery was smoothly performed; alert and smiling, Dada was absorbed in the chant *Om Namo Bhagwate Vasudevaya* playing in the background. He finally let the devotees in on his little secret when he told them that he had felt the presence of Sri Krishna around him all along!

Dada diligently followed the doctor's advice for the next ten days. By God's grace and prayers from all around the globe flowing in, Dada was soon on the road to recovery.

Dada had always been the ideal patient. He followed the doctors' advice and he recuperated well. The doctors gave permission for Dada to walk a little, and he actually managed to come down the stairs carefully. But great care was to be taken for the next seven to ten days, till Dada recovered completely. Everyone's thoughts and prayers continued to boost him on this road to recovery.

On 5 April, Saturday, a satsang, along with an English talk by Dada, had been organized. Taking into consideration the state of Dada's health and energy levels after the surgery, the doctors were slightly nervous. To be on the safe side, a DVD of Dada's talk was kept handy to play in the satsang, so as not to give him any strain.

But Dada was not one to miss his appointment with the satsang. When he entered the hall that evening, everyone stood up to give him a rousing welcome. Representatives from five religious institutions were present – Chinmaya Mission, BAPS of Swami Narayan, Swadhyaya Parivar, Sikh Religious Society and Nirankari Mission. Also present were members of Alliance of Sindhi Associations of America.

When it was Dada's turn to address the audience, which was waiting with bated breath, Dada refused the mic that was brought to his seat; he carefully traversed the distance to the stage and refused to sit on the chair placed there for him. He told the doctors that he wished to stand and speak, but assured them that he would use the chair at the first sign of exhaustion.

He appeared so weak and fragile. But the moment he started his discourse in a strong and resonant voice, he seemed to glow with a divine luminosity. The audience, who had been silent with apprehension earlier, could not contain their joy and appreciation for Dada. Resounding applause followed his words throughout the impressive discourse.

Dada said that the presence of peace may appear fragile, yet it was attainable in this turbulent world through the choices we make in our personal lives. Peace initially has to be cultivated within each individual, then in his relationship with his family and friends, and finally in his interaction with society; this can lead to universal peace. The seed of peace sown within us can alone grow into the mammoth tree of international peace.

On returning home, many expressed their amazement at Dada's ability to overcome any debilitating weakness. To this Dada replied that at that time he was not in this world, as he sensed his body being taken over, inhabited by someone else, who was talking through him. Even here, Dada refused to take any credit for his will-power and forbearance.

NOT SWAYED BY PAIN

When he was in Bangalore, on 1 September, 2008, Dada had a fall, which left a hair-line crack on his rib. The doctors were adamant that Dada postpone his scheduled trip to the Far East, as the flights and the halts would cause him severe pain.

Dada, steadfast in the belief that he was stepping out for God's work, never once questioned the merciful one. Calmly, he stepped forth on his yatra on 21 September, halting at New Delhi as per schedule. Dada even gave an English discourse the next day.

Ignoring any physical pain, Dada merrily kept his date with students of the Delhi Sadhu Vaswani International School on 26 September. He mingled freely with the youngsters, becoming one with them. A skit by the students portrayed Dada's love, which has transformed lives.

Paying no heed to dire warnings that his health was sending out, Dada proceeded to Kolkata on the 28, where he held a ruh-rihan.

He also honoured his commitment to deliver a lecture in English on the 30.

DADA IN NEW YORK

It was the Sindhi New Year day, Cheti Chand, when Dada arrived in New York to a warm welcome. Devotees in festive clothes chanted the name of Jhulelaal in fervour, transforming the dull and drab atmosphere of the airport with their festive spirit.

Strictly speaking, it was still rest and recuperation time for Dada. But while he was in New York, he went to the satsang every day, and gave brief discourses on the lives of saints. For the devotees of New York, Dada's visit to their hometown proved to be truly inspiring and uplifting. Dada took special efforts to meet people and talk to them. Everyone was aware of the trouble and effort he was taking to make them happy. They realized the discomfort and inconvenience he was putting himself through on their behalf. It made them appreciate how much they had to learn from Dada just by watching his daily life unfold and the way he had made his whole life an offering and sacrifice for the benefit of others.

Dada now began his daily walks in earnest and was thrilled to observe the gradual but steady, relentless changes in nature, while New York bid farewell to winter and proceeded to embrace spring. The first appearance of a few green leaves, with some flowers shyly presenting their colours, was enough to warm the heart. Dada said the reality of our lives was being reflected by nature, and through its processes we should learn some valuable lessons. Our hearts are hardened and bare due to the winter of selfishness. We should let them thaw and this can be gradually achieved through satsang, service and divine blessings, till finally there is one massive shower and we are suffused with the greenery and colour of love, giving, caring and sharing.

Mother Earth has always been our teacher, Dada pointed out; every year, year after year, for aeons, she goes through the hardships of winter and yet through persistence and forbearance is able to supersede these and enter the joy of spring. Similarly, we should learn to put up with life's difficulties stoically and uncomplainingly, with full faith that our Father is looking after us and will send us the joy of spring at the appropriate time.

FLYING VISITS TO MIAMI AND PANAMA

Dada spent a couple of days at Miami, following the doctor's advice that the long flight from New York to Panama might be a strain on him. But in the two days he spent in Miami, he gladdened the hearts of the devotees with his presence, giving a discourse in English at the South Florida Hindu Center on the first day, followed by Ram Navami celebrations. On the second day, there was a Sindhi ruhrihan where he emphasized the recital of the Name Divine as the best sadhana for everyone.

Dada had implicitly followed the doctors' advice in all aspects except for one thing: he did not have the heart to cancel the Panama Sadhana Camp, as he knew how eagerly the devotees looked forward to his presence among them. Devotees everywhere, everyone who was aware of Dada's health – and the effort he was putting in by overlooking his physical discomfort and strain and focusing totally on communicating with them – sent forth a huge and enveloping wave of love, warmth and energy to him, not knowing how else to express their gratitude and appreciation.

DNYANESHWAR WORLD PEACE PRIZE

Dada experienced a physical mishap once again in January 2010. He had a fall and fractured his collar bone, along with a few of his ribs. The pain was excruciating and incapacitating, but throughout the ordeal, the smile of acceptance never once left Dada's lips.

When concerned devotees and doctors asked him about his pain, Dada replied that besides imparting lessons on acceptance and surrender, pain and suffering are a form of training. 'Blessed be the Name of God,' Dada repeated, 'In his will is our highest good.' For Dada, bed rest never meant lying down and dozing off. Despite his immobilized state, he spent most of his time reading and reflecting.

The same month, Dada was invited to the World Peace Centre, Alandi, Pune to receive the Sant Sri Dnyaneshwar World Peace Prize for 2009, for which the committee members had unanimously elected him. Unfortunately, Dada was unable to attend the award ceremony in person. The organizers were sorely disappointed when they learnt of his injury. The sport that Dada was, he agreed to listen to the entire programme through an audio link. When the time came to introduce Dada, before giving them the opportunity to say that he was not physically present, he more than made for his absence by instantly delivering his talk over the phone, connected to the loudspeaker. Dada's voice was crystal clear, belying his physical absence.

Referring to peace, Dada said that humanity is wounded and tortured and sorely needs the soothing and healing balm of peace. To attain peace, we should place our hopes in our children who are the future, and ensure that the right type of education is imparted to them. Peace cannot be attained until we stop all killing. All violence must cease, Dada stated firmly.

Dada spoke with full force and conviction for about twenty minutes and the conclusion of his talk was greeted with a resounding applause.

After the programme, the entire committee proceeded to the Sadhu Vaswani Mission to bestow the award personally on Dada. He was overjoyed to see them, and said that though he could not go to the award function, he was glad that Sant Dnyaneshwara had come in person to bless him. Along with the traditional gold medal and cash award, a gold-plated statue and a beautiful portrait of the saint were presented to Dada, which he accepted with reverence and love. The committee members remarked that Dada was a reflection of Sant Dnyaneshwara himself.

SADHANA CAMP IN PANAMA

It was May 2010. Hundreds of devotees from North and South America had gathered at the Sadhana Camp in Panama, eagerly looking forward to spending a few days in close proximity with their beloved friend and mentor.

The entire day of 7 May passed by in a mood of elevation and bliss. At night, as Dada was on his way to participate in the campfire that had been organized as part of the day's activities, an unexpected event occurred: an unfortunate event that altered not just Dada's yatra schedule, but the life of the devotees for that entire year.

As Dada stepped out of the elevator, he saw some children playing ping-pong (table tennis). Spontaneously responding to their smiles, Dada joined in their game and gleefully played a good volley. Unfortunately, while lobbing one of the shots, Dada stepped backwards, lost his balance, and fell with full force on the hard floor, damaging the right side of his body.

The ever-present group of close followers registered Dada's fall with deep shock. They saw that Dada was in tormenting pain, due to which they could not even try to move him from the floor until the ambulance arrived.

Everyone rushed around him, and hastened to make appropriate arrangements for his care. Dada sensed their stress, their faces indicating fear and worry. In contrast to their anxiety, Dada's radiant smile never left his lips even for a moment. It was the same serene smile with which he had initially greeted them, even though the severity of his pain was obvious and visible to everyone.

The move to the ambulance was not easy. It took its toll. Instead of groaning with pain, Dada only uttered the Ram Naam repeatedly. And there was no wincing with pain, no distortion of his serene countenance in agony. Instead, the same steady smile continued to light up Dada's face.

The ambulance team was wonderstruck by Dada's attitude. Even during his interaction with the doctors and nurses, the degree of his smile may have varied, either very broad, or subtly present, but it never left his face, melting the hearts of all those who were with him.

It was 2010; communications technology had advanced rapidly. Across the globe, as text messages and emails flashed on mobile phones and computer screens, devotees felt their hearts breaking with grief and fear. Could this really be happening to them – to their beloved Dada? What could they do? How were they supposed to face this calamity? How could God inflict such great pain on their beloved master? Why, he had just about recovered from his shoulder injury which he sustained in January of that same year.

He was airlifted and taken to a hospital in Chicago. The doctors who examined him revealed that Dada had fractured the right hip (femur bone), the right shoulder (humerus bone) and the right elbow (olecranon). As treating all this would require major surgery, Dada's delicate condition had to be stabilized first. The doctors also decided that the surgery on the right elbow would be performed after a gap of six days. The slightest movement caused intense pain, but Dada continued to be cheerful, ever smiling and relaxed.

The first surgical operation went off successfully. When he was wheeled out to his room, Dada saw the strained and tense faces of all his devotees. With a gentle smile he constantly recited the words, 'Gratitude to thee, O Lord. Let me bear this for thy sake. I accept this gift from you gladly. *Tere liye, tere liye.*'

Dada's second surgery also went off without a hitch. Our hearts beat heavier and faster, but they were shored up with prayers, and fortified by the awareness of the high level of expertise of the surgeons. The doctors emerged from the operation theatre satisfied with the way the surgery had proceeded.

Prior to the surgery, the doctors had asked Dada if he was comfortable. Dada replied, 'Comfort is made up of two words – 'come' and 'fort'. A 'fort' is a place of refuge. So, if we 'come' and seek 'refuge' at the lotus feet of the lord, we will always be comfortable.' His countenance, at every stage, had only reflected calm and peace. Never did a shadow of doubt, sorrow, frustration or despair ever cross his face. It is unbelievable how such a blow had befallen a body so delicate, tender and frail; the intensity of the pain suffered had been astronomical, far beyond the regular levels of suffering, and yet Dada continued to thank God, the doctors, the nurses and all those who came in contact with him.

After the success of the procedure done on Dada's right elbow on 17 May, everyone was filled with relief and gratitude. But they did not have much time to sit back and feel complacent, for God's ways are mysterious and incomprehensible. He had us on our toes immediately with the information which the doctors passed on to us, that there seemed to be no movement on the left side of Dada's body.

This really alarmed the doctors and had every one of us in shock. Dada's left side would not respond to any touch or movement. After various tests and several discussions, the doctors diagnosed the problem as a mild stroke which had affected the left side of Dada's body. Word went round the globe and prayers and chants for Dada's recovery began immediately.

To say that Dada's condition that day caused a great deal of concern to his doctors as well as to us all, would be an understatement to the nth degree. We, who were with him were devastated by this unexpected blow. To most of us it seemed even worse than the original accident that had occurred just ten days ago: just ten days ago? It seemed years. Since that dreaded hour, there had been very many frightening and fragile moments, when it had been unbearable to watch Dada in acute pain and distress. Even his limited movements would be restricted now.

But it must be stated that it was we who were devastated. Dada's fortitude and spirit remained ever high.

His sweet smile brought tears to the eyes of the devotees in the hospital! How much more pain could he take?

Physiotherapy for Dada had begun immediately the day after surgery. The doctors advocated that physiotherapy was the most important component for healing. Without the instant follow-up of physiotherapy, all the efforts of surgery would be in vain. Surgery is merely corrective, they said; it is physiotherapy that would accomplish mobility and normalcy.

After the stroke that Dada suffered, the physiotherapy became even more strenuous and painful. Between 19 and 26 May, Dada's progress was painfully slow; but his attitude helped the devotees pass through that traumatic week with dry eyes and tears firmly held back. Dada's resilience and patience were unbelievable, and some of it rubbed off on his devotees.

Physiotherapy and occupational therapy continued regularly with Dada. Soon, he was moved to the physiotherapy unit of the hospital for his rehabilitation therapy. Here, his daily programme involved tremendous effort in participating in strenuous daily sessions. Not only was Dada very cooperative at such times, but actually appreciated the efforts of the therapists. With his ever-willing and upbeat attitude, the therapists remarked that the day's therapy was akin to a cheerleading session!

DOES KARMA BIND SAINTS?

Considering the mountainous hurdles that Dada had to overcome so far, he was, by God's grace, doing reasonably well. There was still, of course, a lot of pain and though he was unable to move around much, Dada was not at all inactive or indolent, nor was he depressed or dejected. In fact, fully alert and aware, he poured in all his energy, will power, patience and perseverance in attempting to physically return to normalcy as soon as possible.

In fact, on seeing Dada, the therapists would exclaim that the 'smiling one' had come. It was, indeed, awe-inspiring to see that Dada's smile had not left his face even for a second since his fall.

Since those painful days, several devotees questioned Dada, if karma binds a saint. Responding to this, Dada clarified that karma does not bind a saint, but a saint may willingly pay off the karma of himself and of his devotees. Dada explained that saints often take on their sufferings gladly: one reason for this is that they wish to settle their karmic accounts, and become liberated from the cycle of death and rebirth. The second is that they are profoundly compassionate by nature, and so they take on the pain and suffering of others. For them, bodily suffering has no significance. They do suffer, but once it is in the past, they do not even retain a memory of it. Thus it was that Sri Ramana Maharishi, Sri Ramakrishna and Sadhu Vaswani, underwent a great deal of pain and suffering in their last years.

'Do they actually feel all that pain, or do they simply transcend their suffering?' someone wanted to know.

Dada smiled. 'Pain is real and actual, for everyone,' he said. 'Some of the saints actually suffer far more than the rest of us, because their bodies are very sensitive and their consciousness is profound. Sadhu Vaswani too, suffered on account of the slightest movements and gestures, which perhaps, we would hardly be aware of. Many of us believed that he actually took on the sufferings of others.'

'It is tough and demanding to be a saint, or a holy person, is it not, Dada? And how many of us realize or appreciate the fact that a saint is taking on our suffering? Many of us simply live in ignorance, don't we? Who would want to be holy, if there is so much pain involved?'

Dada smiled and said, 'Saints know the value of pain.'

Dada suggested too, that we should be very careful of what we sow. If there is any thought of ill-will or harm to another, we should immediately replace it with a good thought, and thus get rid of any negativity. In this manner, bad karma will be replaced by good karma.

'Can we ever annihilate all this accumulated weight of karma?' someone asked, after a period of silent reflection.

'Yes,' Dada answered, 'by complete surrender to God – through utter self-annihilation, out of which we may attain self-realization. This is the realization that you are not the body that you wear, but the immortal spirit within. *Aham Brahmasmi* – when we attain this awareness everything is closed. All our karmic accounts are settled.'

Just as the flame of a candle cannot survive without oxygen, so too, man cannot live without satsang, Dada pointed out. Indeed, life in the hospital during those weeks only confirmed what each one of us had always believed: Dada took the satsang with him wherever he went. Simply to be in his presence, was to be showered by grace and blessings and to witness the light.

How much there is that we need to learn from Dada.

One day, a therapist told Dada, 'You look like a young man.' Dada smilingly corrected him, 'I *am* a young man.'

Once, a therapist inquired of Dada if he was tired. Dada replied, 'I never get tired as long as there are three things I can do – pray without sleeping, smile all the while, and serve as many as I can.'

Typically, Dada's sense of humour would surface even during those difficult times, for Dada never allowed himself to feel gloomy and low. When Nurse Jill said that she was sorry about Dada's fall, he replied, 'It is a rise, not a fall. Just as a child rises up after a fall, so too, I have risen.'

One day, the therapist told Dada that his team would help him to get back on his feet in no time. To which Dada said, 'This life is a gift from God to man. We must not try to impose our will on God. We must accept every incident and accident of life as prasad from the spotless hands of God; then we will always be happy.'

Dada's persistence and patient effort with his physiotherapy ensured that his progress was slow, steady and continuous, which was heartening for the doctors and devotees.

Dada's first love had always been the sea. As Chicago is far away from the coast, when the doctors permitted him to go out for the first time, it was decided that the next best thing would be to take Dada to the beautiful shores of Lake Michigan.

It was a bright, beautiful and sunny day, with not a cloud in the electric blue sky. The water of the lake shimmered like pure silk. The waterfront was crowded with people, all out to enjoy this beautiful summer day. Unlike the tumultuous waves of the ocean, the ripples on the lake were gentle and calm. It was such a pleasure to see the sun shining on Dada's face, and the wind playfully ruffling his hair. The balmy breeze was soothing and comforting and Dada continued to enjoy this entire scene through the window of his car. Unlike the rest of the group, Dada's demeanour was one of peace and equanimity. He remarked that whatever the weather outside was like, whether it was sunny or raining, hot or cold, he was always happy and full of bliss, for he believes that whatever God has planned for him is the very best. Dada's doctors expressed great satisfaction with the miraculous progress that Dada had made, in the last few weeks or so. With the grace of God and the ever-present blessings of Gurudev Sadhu Vaswani, Dada was permitted to leave the hospital in July 2010. It was the doctors' collective opinion that Dada's recovery had been nothing short of miraculous.

It was painful and heart-breaking for us to look back on the month that had gone by. What could we call this month? When we asked Dada about this, his answer was unbelievable: he said, 'For me, it has been a Month of Mercy. I feel that God, in his infinite mercy, has chosen me to bear this cross of pain and suffering, in order to lighten the load of others and bring comfort and relief to their distressed lives.'

He left the hospital, scattering behind him countless blessings and positive vibrations that would long linger in their minds and hearts, like the whiff of divinely fragrant flowers.

NEW YORK 2010

The auspicious day of Guru Purnima dawned bright and clear in New York. The golden rays of sunshine seemed to reflect the love and blessings of the guru, its penetrating radiance lighting up every dark nook and cranny, making it a truly blessed day.

Dada woke up in the wee hours of the morning, for he had hardly slept all night. He had been engrossed in silent, internal communion with his guru, conveying his gratitude to the master for his ever-flowing grace and mercy.

The whole of the morning was spent in keeping up with the rigorous regime of the physiotherapy, which Dada carried out with full sincerity. In the evening, Dada proceeded to the Sadhu Vaswani centre, where devotees waited eagerly to get a glimpse of their beloved Guru. An array of emotions played on their faces – some faces were bathed in smiles, others had eyes streaming with tears of joy; some patiently waited with the offering of a coconut in their hands, while others stretched out their hands in an attempt to touch the hem of his garment. Many devotees had come from out of town and others even from overseas. The New York sangat was overflowing with joy to have Dada in their midst on such a special occasion, which in the past had seemed impossible.

Dada spoke with great depth and emotion. He recalled how, two years ago, a sister had asked him when he would celebrate Guru Purnima with them in New York. Dada had no answer for her then; but, as we know, God works in mysterious ways to perform his wonders! Thus, Dada had to undergo this severe fall, and go through so much suffering and pain. In the bargain, untold and unlimited treasures of the Spirit had accrued to him in the past three months, which he could now share with all of them. This suffering also proved to be the source of fulfilling the sister's desire of Guru Purnima being celebrated in New York. Ultimately, it was God's will that was being fulfilled.

Dada spoke about the greatness of the guru, who does not perceive our faults and weaknesses. The true guru is like a friend, with one hand outstretched in order to help us, while the other is behind, supporting the back of the devotee, to prevent him from stumbling and falling.

The New Yorkers later brought out a welcome cake for Dada, and there was a cheery and bright rendition of a song, 'Everybody loves Dada, Dada loves everybody! Jai Gurudev, Jai Jai Gurudev!'

This was Dada's first public appearance after his fall; and the bonus on this special day was that it was accompanied by a talk of over forty-five minutes. It was also the first time that people saw him in his regular attire, making him look exactly like the same Dada of yore. This sight filled everyone with the hope that soon Dada would walk, run and be his normal self again.

For Dada as well as for hundreds of thousands of his devotees whose hearts beat every moment by his name, as well as for thousands of friends and admirers who have always regarded him as one of the world's leading spiritual mentors, 2 August 2010, was definitely a birthday with a difference.

In all these years, it was the Mission headquarters in Pune which played host to the numerous friends and admirers who came from all over India and all over the world to participate in the week-long celebrations. With due apologies, the devotees in Pune had never, ever heeded to their beloved Dada's request that there was no need for elaborate celebrations; each and every one of them felt that it was their birthday, rather than his! If a stranger had walked into the Mission campus on 2 August, he surely would have been bemused to hear hundreds of devotees, volunteers and satsangis blithely calling out 'Happy Birthday!' to each other, wondering how so many people born on that day, had managed to congregate in one place on their date of birth!

In that memorable year, 2010, Dada would be celebrating his birthday in New York. Of course, there were week-long events, special service programmes and prayers at Pune; the Pune sangat knew too, that their Dada would be with them, in spirit, blessing them with the grace of his love. But his physical presence this year would be with the 'brothers and sisters of America' as Swami Vivekananda once referred to them so memorably.

Hundreds of overseas and out of town devotees made travel plans for New York to celebrate the first ever birthday being held there in Rev. Dada's presence.

The birthday events were scheduled to commence on the evening of Friday, 30 July 2010, and continue until Dada's birthday on Monday, 2 August 2010. The events took place in a large ball room at the Crowne Plaza Hotel located in Secaucus, New Jersey. The carefully planned daily schedules included back to back programmes such as invocation, prayers, *Anand Akhand Kirtan*, *Nuri Granth Path*, cultural programmes, professional performances, seva activities, yoga, youth sessions, and *Dada Darshan* with the grand finale being the actual birthday celebration.

The décor of the ballroom was grand with beautiful figurines of Gods adorning the main entrances. It seemed as if the Gods themselves wanted to be present at the celebrations.

The grand four-day celebrations started with the kindling of the sacred havan-fire among chants of the Gayatri Mantra. Devotees from all over the world anxiously awaited Dada's appearance at the venue; indeed, it was a packed hall with anxious hearts beating to have a glimpse of the Gurudev. The singers led a feast of music. Everybody joined in the singing and clapping to the glory of the guru. Their revered Dada had come amidst them from miles away to kindle the ceremonial lamp of this birthday retreat of divine proportions.

Dada's upadesh began on a profoundly moving note, seeking forgiveness for anything he may have done during the year that may have hurt anyone. Dada recalled the first lesson that he learnt from his master, Sadhu Vaswani: always consider the virtues of others, never their faults. If a person has nine vices and just one virtue, one must see the sole virtue and not the faults. Dada urged everyone to inculcate this into their daily lives and be true to the Guru's teachings: for 'it is life that is needed, not words.'

The Sindhi Association of New Jersey (SANJ) and Overseas Sindhu Sabha earlier had declared 2 August as a Sindhi holiday in honour of Dada's contribution to the Sindhi community and encouraged all Sindhis to take the day off and be a part of the saint's birthday.

As soon as Dada came up on the stage, thousands of devotees gave a grand welcome to Dada with flowers, chants and applause while thronging to greet him. As Dada started his birthday message which was webcast live all over the world, the audience listened with rapt attention, absorbing all that he had to say and imbibing his thoughts and values. On this day, Dada once again reaffirmed his message: '*Aai dil na kar fikar, kar shukur, kar shukur!* O my heart, do not despair, but give gratitude to God!' This was followed by the mantra, *Kabool, kabool, kabool!*– accept, accept, accept (God's will). Dada's cake cutting ceremony was the grand finale.

Dada had arrived in the US during the spring, when the snow was beginning to thaw; now it was fall, and nature had painted its vibrant gold and russet shades on every tree, plant, shrub and leaf. Dada was visiting the Kessler Institute of Rehabilitation, for his rehab therapy. The time was drawing close when he would depart for home.

As long as he was in New Jersey, Dada made it a point to attend the satsang every weekend. Thousands of devotees watched the webcast live on the Mission's website.

Devotees in Pune were agog with excitement when Dada arrived without prior announcement on 14 October 2010. For a few days, due to a muscle pull resulting from overstrain, he was put to complete bed rest; but gradually, he resumed his physiotherapy and got back on his feet. As soon as he was permitted to move out of his room, he came down to the satsang, sometimes walking, sometimes on a wheelchair, to give his upadesh. When Dada entered the satsang hall, it revereberated with the spontaneous claps of one and all. All those sitting outside would rush in to get a good view of their beloved.

'DEAR GOD, BLESS DADA AND MAKE HIM BETTER!'

It was the year 2014. Celebrations for Dada J. P. Vaswani's 96th birthday commenced from 22 July, which was his birthday as per the Hindu calendar. With Dada's love for young ones and the needy, it was appropriate that the party was in the form of a *bal mela*, wherein 700 children were invited from the Pune Municipal School. They were treated to a delicious meal, and were also gifted a bag of goodies and the Marathi version of a book by Sadhu Vaswani.

On 26 July, everyone at the Mission received a tremendous jolt as beloved Dada took ill. He was rushed to the hospital and admitted into the ICCU.

Immediately prayers and chants began, but the most intense of all was the *arambh* or inauguration of the non-stop 108-hour chant of the *Maha Mrityunjaya Mantra*, along with the continuous havan from 29 July. It was a herculean task, but it helped to channelize and reinforce the healing of Dada. Prayerful thoughts were being sent for Dada. The entreaties to the Divine were in a continuous flow, till Dada was miraculously back in our midst at the culmination of this jaap.

Throughout these days when beloved Dada was in the hospital, service programmes went on as planned. Volunteers from the Mission visited an orphanage which houses over 300 street children in their care. A sumptuous meal was provided to them, along with sheets to cover each child. Several group games were gifted to the institution for the enjoyment of the children.

At the evening satsang, the theme was 'Keep the Fire of Prayers Glowing'. The bhajans and kirtan reflected that devotion. The introduction to the theme was followed by its affirmation, dealing with mantras and prayers, positive vibrations and healing prayers for Dada. Silent prayers evolving in the heart were sent out.

The Moment of Calm, designated for 2 August, had this year received tremendous support and enthusiasm from people far and wide, from different walks and positions of life. Special prayers were said for Dada's health and long life; wishes were sung for Dada's birthday.

The uplifting bhajans and kirtan set the mood for the euphoric arrival of beloved Dada at the satsang hall, directly from the hospital. He began his talk by thanking his doctors, who had taken care of him and even accompanied him to the satsang. Referring to his talk on the topic 'Empower Yourself', which he had been unable to give due to his sojourn to the hospital, Dada said that within each one there are infinite energies of the eternal. We are unaware of them, and instead identify ourselves with the body.

We think of ourselves as the body–mind complex, Dada continued. The body is only a garment we wear and the mind is an instrument to work. Ninety-nine per cent of us are not aware of the tremendous power within. Sri Krishna said to Arjuna, 'I am seated in the hearts of all.' These powers need to be unleashed.

To unlock them, difficult spiritual sadhanas are not required, Dada said. The one easy sadhana is to sit in a silent-corner, preferably at the same time and place, where no noise can disturb us. Enter within and ask: What am I? One day, with the grace of God and the guru, the realization will dawn that one is not the physical body. You are *sat-chit-ananda* – the immortal soul in a state of pure bliss.

Dada said he could not continue further with practical suggestions, as he had promised the doctors that he would not talk for more than five minutes.

But before ending, he firmly asserted the immortality of his atman which superseded mere 100 or 1,000 years, for it was there before creation and would continue even beyond dissolution.

The emotionally overcharged atmosphere also proved to be right for the inauguration of the first volume of the *Anjali Sangraha*. An ongoing project, it will be a compilation of every song composed, written, recited or sung by Dada. These songs are truly out of this world, heavenly; they are the outpourings of a yearning and longing soul, for the Divine. The 1,001 pages of the first volume, given away free to the devotees, reflected his every thought, word and action which have always been directed towards the altar of the suffering, deprived and needy.

It was a birthday to remember as several faces were streaked with tears of gratitude to have beloved Dada, despite all the hurdles he had to overcome, in their midst on this auspicious day.

DUTY FIRST

Dada had a fall a few days into the month of March 2016, which required him to rest his knee for over seven weeks to recover fully, as advised by his doctors. The scheduled yatra planned to the US around this time had to be deferred. Despite the pain and discomfort, Dada unswervingly kept his daily appointment with the satsang. From his bed, he continued to deliver several beautiful upadeshes to the sangat in Pune through live videos in the satsang hall and all over the world through webcast.

From his room, Dada gave his Ram Navami message to the sangat. He said, however impure and unclean hearts, words, speech and action may be, the *Pavitra Naam* of Sri Rama has the power to cleanse and purify them all. So sing the Name continuously, Dada urged the devotees. Sing the Name by day and by night, sing the Name silently or loudly. Just keep singing the Name.

From his room, Dada continued to give his usual Sunday morning and Thursday evening upadeshes. He also addressed the sangat on holy days. Dada's talks covered the narrations on Shakuntala, Swami Ramtirth, Baba Farid, Guru Angad, Sister Shanti and Queen Mallika, blessed by the Buddha.

Dada walked down to the satsang hall on 2 May evoking a feeling of gratitude towards the almighty in all hearts.

ELEVEN

Khuda Hafiz

'The heart's longing is fulfilled at last:
And I shall soon enter the vast!
All my sorrows draw to an end
As I am blended as one with the Friend!
Adieu! I go!'
    – Dada J. P. Vaswani, 'Adieu! I go!'

CENTENARY IN SIGHT!

Among the many celebrations was the 24th Sadhu Vaswani Sadhana Camp held in Mumbai, seeing participants from forty-four cities and towns in India and abroad, who came with a deep spiritual thirst which they knew could only be slaked by the practical wisdom and overflowing, unconditional love which Dada willingly poured out on one and all. If the Sadhana Camp was a beautiful necklace, the invaluable gems that made up the necklace were Dada's soul-elevating talks, guided meditation and yoga, bhajans and kirtan, and the spiritually enriching cultural programmes staged by participants. The priceless pendant of this necklace was Dada himself who energized the sessions with his spirited presence. The entire hall echoed with his laughter in the lively and enlightening question and answer sessions.

Dada began his inaugural talk by saying that 'ishq ajeeban vaste' (love for the divine) is so deep that it is equivalent to an iceberg. Only the tip is visible, the rest is hidden. Fortunate is he in whose life there is only love – not just worldly love, but divine love. Such true love is ready to forgive and forget everything. Dada said the purpose of this camp is to become God-intoxicated.

Through the three days of the camp, Dada led us on the journey:

1. The first stage is when we realize that we are caught up in the slumber of the senses. Then suddenly the awareness dawns on us that we need to awaken. We wish to be freed from the snare of the world.
2. The aspirant now sets out on a quest of someone who will guide him in fulfilling his purpose on this earth. He moves out in search of a guru. A guru is the one who gives limitless *atmic* wealth to his disciple and makes him *Atmavaan*. The atmic joy that the guru shares with the disciple far exceeds the worldly happiness which can be brought about by the pleasures of the senses. He leads the disciple to liberation and freedom.
3. In the next stage, the aspirant becomes a sadhaka, jignasu or disciple. The guru trains the disciple to walk the path of truth. The two channels that need to be opened up for this purpose are *viveka* (discrimination) and *vairagya* (detachment).
4. The aspirant moves on to the next stage of becoming a member of the family of the guru – he becomes a *shishu*.
5. Last, the shishu is ready to become a guru himself. Not all of us reach the final stage. It is given only to a blessed few.

The questions from the participants revealed their total absorption of Dada's wise and profound insights:

Q: How do I know where I have reached on my spiritual journey?
A: You don't need to focus on your progress. You must fix your mind on the goal, for the journey is long and arduous.

Q: Dear Dada, please tell me what I should do to be accepted at your lotus feet.

A: The one thing that is accepted at everyone's feet is their footwear! The problem is that we do not wish to be footwear to others! To become footwear only means to become humble as grass, humble as dust. The humble are always accepted.

Q: If we have to choose between being right and being kind, which should we choose?

A: Which is better, to see with the left eye or right eye? My answer is, see with both your eyes! Being right and being kind, go together.

Q: Dada, what is the one ideal that you would wish all of us to practise in daily life?

A: Giving and sharing what God has given you.

The first evening's cultural event comprised of events and incidents from the life of Sant Kabir. Though his beginnings were humble, he soared to great spiritual heights. Dada felt that theatre and music made the narration more realistic, stirring and exalting.

The second evening saw a competition of musical hymns which received valuable assistance from Dada, whose enlightening and explanatory words threw much light on the meaning of the chants, amidst a lot of thrill and laughter.

The third night had a musical presentation on the life of Rumi and his spiritual journey with his master, Shams Tabrez, a relationship on which Dada provided further elucidation.

The grand finale of the camp was a small dance and a skit performed by the youngsters, who almost brought the roof down by their loud proclamations of their love for Dada.

After the hectic schedule in Mumbai, Dada was happy to return home to Pune on 28 December. The Pune sangat were eagerly looking forward to the New Year's Eve satsang with Dada, when Dada was afflicted by severe abdominal pain on 29 December. He was put on a saline drip till the 30 December. But being Dada, he came down for a few minutes to ring in the New Year, so that his beloved sangat was not disappointed. The short film showing the highlights of the Mission events in 2017 left everyone in awe: how could Dada do so much, pour out such love in the service of humanity. Where did all the energy and élan come from? What has the world done to deserve such love?

A guided meditation on love, set the perfect ambience to welcome the personification of love, beloved Dada. In the muted lights of the hall, everyone waved coloured lights in joyous greeting.

Brighter than the brightest lights, Dada's luminous and loving smile lit up the congregation. In his forceful message Dada said: 'Let us bid adieu to the departing year with gratitude, and ring in the New Year with hope and prayer. Thankfulness can transform life; it can turn misfortune into a state of receptivity, sorrow into joy, complaints into gratitude. Thanksgiving fills our hearts with love, and love blesses everything it touches.' Dada ended with a prayer in which the congregation joined him:

O Lord, my Master, my Beloved,
I don't seek to know how,
I don't seek to know when,
I don't seek to know where,
I don't seek to know why,
I only seek you, you, you.

Dada continued:

Create within me a new mind and a new heart that I may be a blessing to many and make us one with the Lord.

The congregation departed from the campus assured that they had made a perfect beginning to the year 2018. Dada was with them again for the New Year evening satsang, and their anxiety and worry about Dada's health having lifted, everyone was eager to absorb his words of wisdom.

Dada said that years ago when he was asked to describe the essence of Sadhu Vaswani's teachings, he had spelt it out as follows: do not live for self, but for others.

When Sadhu Vaswani was asked for a motto for Mira School, he had said '*Kuch na kuch kar jayenge*.' We must leave this world a better place, Dada reiterated, for life is too precious to be spent in the pursuit of pleasure.

The two ideals that Dada placed before us were:

1) Simran, which is constant remembrance of the Lord. This should not just be mechanical, but from the innermost recesses of the heart.
2) Seva or service of the poor and suffering ones.

A true jignasu or seeker should be devoted to these two ideals.

After this short and succinct talk, Dada shared a beautiful poem which he had composed. Then with showers of blessings on everyone for the coming year, Dada went out of the hall, leaving behind him a trail of riches of wisdom and benedictions.

Appropriately enough, *Kuch Na Kuch Kar Jayenge* was the theme the Bridge Builders chose to highlight in the Youth Programme on 14 January 2018, with which the Mahayagna observances began. The week featured many programmes and seva activities that gave expression to the devotion and reverence in which Sadhu Vaswani was held by the sangat.

In his upadesh Dada emphasized the one thought: Sadhu Vaswani still lives and continues to guide and protect us. He said we should aspire to be like *jeevan muktas* who despite living in this world have their consciousness ceaselessly dwelling in that other realm, the homeland of the spirit.

Although Dada participated with full involvement in the Mahayagna, when the problem persisted, his doctors made a decision to take him to Hyderabad for a surgical procedure. He was always taking upon himself our karmas and lightening the load of his devotees.

Dada flew out from Pune on 3 February, late in the evening. Though his face shone with luminance, to some it seemed his eyes held a deep secret within them, which we could not fathom. He was scheduled to have an ERCP (Endoscopic Retrograde Cholangio Pancreatography), with the doctors ensuring that the procedure went off with the least strain on Dada.

He was admitted to the hospital at 6 a.m. on the sixth. By the grace of the almighty, the procedure that was performed on Dada went off smoothly. Despite all the care, every bodily intrusion and every invasion into the fragile form of beloved Dada, did take its toll. But like gold, which on being heated, increases in lustre, Dada too, emanated indescribable brilliance, the aura of his glow visible to all those around him.

On him shimmers the grace of the Lord,
Who in the ecstasy of true love is absorbed.
Within his heart glows the Light Divine
Like burnished gold, his soul doth shine.
The fervour of love keeps soaring,
Permeating all, this love keeps burning.
Such a being is pure and primal individual
In this Perfect One is radiant the Light eternal.

On the second night after the procedure, though physically feeble and unable to utter even a word, the waves of energy that poured forth from Dada were almost palpable. It made us aware of his enormous spiritual presence and strength, and we began to understand the extent he would undergo for our sake.

In Hyderabad, Dada spent most of his time in communion. He said little. But whenever he spoke, his emphasis was on going within.

In spite of his frail health, Dada held a satsang on 11 February, where a large number of devotees gathered. 'Stay connected' was the topic of discussion. As long as we stay connected to the source, he emphasized, energy, intelligence and wisdom will flow into us. If we are separated from the source or if we weaken the connection, we enfeeble ourselves and gradually wither away. How often do we not fill our mind with thoughts which weaken our energy? Therefore, spend some time in silence every day, Dada urged the sangat.

There was but one prayer in the heart of the devotees, as Dada prepared to leave Hyderabad on 13 February. May we keep expressing our gratitude to God for the gift of this priceless treasure, our beloved Dada, whose every breath, whose very existence, is a blessing on Mother Earth and her inhabitants.

While in Hyderabad, he was told by his hosts that mangoes had appeared early in the season. Dada ordered boxes upon boxes of mangoes to be sent to Pune, where he was due to return on the day of Shivratri. Arriving at the airport, he drove to the Mission, and as always, after bowing his head in prayer at his master's sacred samadhi, he went straight into the satsang hall, where devotees were engaged in Shiv Mahima bhajans and kirtan. At the end of the satsang, Dada asked mangoes to be distributed to everybody in the sangat. Mangoes on Shivratri day? With a loving, giving, sharing saint like Dada, miracles and surprise bonanzas were a matter of course! 'Let the message of my life be: give and spread sweetness all around you!' Dada said, as he gave away the mangoes.

In honour of Dada's centenary, the Mission, in association with Jana Seva Foundation, organized a special evening for senior citizens on 25 February 2018. Around 3,000 plus members from senior clubs, old age homes and other organisations were present at the event and each and every elder was made to feel really special. In his address to the senior citizens, Dada offered the following practical suggestions:

1. Don't pity yourself.
2. Always remember, every day brings twenty-four hours or 1440 minutes; my day depends on how I am going to spend these 1440 minutes.
3. Learn to say we can help ourselves, we should be self-dependent.
4. Whatever we do, we should do for love of the Lord. All that we say and do should be our offering at the lotus feet of the Lord. There are a hundred ways of doing any work, but only one is the best. I should do everything in the best way I can.
5. Every day brings new opportunities. Hence every day we should learn something new. The day we have not learnt something new, is a lost day, indeed.
6. We should never forget, that our health is our precious wealth. Hence, we should not eat anything that spoils our health. And to be healthy, we should exercise every day. The queen of all exercises is walking. Every day we should walk for some time. This will strengthen our muscles.
7. We should work patiently. Love should be the law of our life. The day we have not helped someone, a bird or an animal, is a wasted day.
8. Cultivate a relationship with God. Say to God, 'You are my mother, my father, my friend or my Beloved.' When some difficulty arises, we rush to the police and doctor but we do not go to God. Develop a relationship with God. If you do this, you will see many miracles in life and feel God close to you.

On 12 March, a Women's Meet was organized by the Sadhu Vaswani Mission and FICCI FLO, Pune Chapter. The Mission has been in the forefront of women's empowerment ever since the Sakhi Satsang was founded over eighty-five years ago; and it was but natural for Dada to connect with them warmly. His affectionate greetings to his sisters were scintillating; and the Q and A session which followed, found the ladies responding to his crisp and concise responses with applause and cheers. The auditorium was packed to capacity, as many of the FLO members had decided to bring family members along to have Dada's darshan and take his blessings. The session ended with a beautiful guided meditation after which Dada met each and every one of the participants with much love and affection, leaving everyone feeling blessed and elated.

29 March was *Mahavir Jayanti*. Dada paid a heartfelt tribute to the saint who made ahimsa his way of life. At 6 p.m. he left for Lonavla, as the doctors had advised a change of scene; there would be three days of much-needed rest and retreat, before he returned to Pune on 1 April.

4 April brought anguish and anxiety to the devotees, and more pain and suffering for Dada, who came down with shivering and fever. He had to be administered antibiotic fluids on IV. His condition caused grave concern to his doctors, who attended to him with devotion. Dada's pain and affliction continued for fifteen days! Despite the intrusive treatment, not a word of complaint escaped Dada's lips. His eyes glowed with love and gratitude, even as he embraced pain with faith and fortitude.

As the situation did not seem to improve, the doctors pleaded with Dada to visit Hyderabad where another procedure would be carried out. Dada did not seem to be keen on this move. In subtle terms he expressed the idea that we should be ready to accept the will of God. Now, in retrospect, it seems that Dada could see the futility of the procedure. He did not want to dishearten us. But gently and repeatedly he tried to dissuade us. But our unwavering hope refused to give up. To keep us happy he agreed to once again go through bodily suffering.

On 22 April, Dada and a few of us left for Hyderabad, where a stent had to be inserted in his bile duct. A team of doctors travelled with us.

On the night prior to the procedure, Dada had stayed awake almost the entire night with the nectar of the Maha Mantra flowing ceaselessly from his lips:

Hare Rama Hare Rama, Rama Rama Hare Hare
Hare Krishna Hare Krishna, Krishna Krishna Hare Hare.

The entire room seemed to pulsate with the sacred mantra. Every pore of Dada shimmered like a star. Every breath let out a fragrance.

On the morning of 24 April, Dada left for the Asian Institute of Gastroenterology, Hyderabad, where the procedure was to be performed. At the hospital, Dada was warmly greeted by one and all. He was taken to a private room for pre-operation preparations. But Dada's loving smile, his glance of grace comforted the healers who themselves needed to be comforted. The doctor as well confessed to Dada that though they perform precise procedures based on scientific expertise, their faith in the presence of a higher power was deep and unshakeable. He implored Dada to guide them and through his intervention assist them in performing the procedure. Dada, of course, already knew the unfolding of the mystery but continued to give in to our plea. He completely resigned himself not just into the hands of doctors, but also to that divine hand which he knew was at work. He had been patiently and persistently preparing us to accept the will of God. Perhaps, he realized that we were unwilling to accept the inevitable.

'It is not the doctor who treats,' Dada said to the distinguished surgeon. 'He can only entreat. It is God who treats. Blessed be his name.'

A sublime smile played on Dada's lips even as the procedure was in progress. The doctors came and met Dada and conveyed to him that the procedure had gone off smoothly and successfully. Later Dada casually said: 'Success is illusionary! The moment you feel you have achieved it, it slips from your hands. Therefore, let not attachment overwhelm you.'

Dada was once again put through the period of recuperation and revitalizing. Despite the travails his body goes through, bodily suffering was never an issue with him, nor did he ever allow himself to be pulled down by pain. He remained ever joyful, serene and calm, ceaselessly praying for everyone.

> Saints ask for suffering,
> Its true value cognising.
> With the Divine, linked are they so closely,
> Breezing through the ups and downs easily.

During the seven-day stay in Hyderabad, Dada's appetite began to decline. He would refuse to eat anything. On 27 April, a Maulvi, who had happened to hear that Dada was in town, requested the doctors for a quick darshan of Dada, but they gently informed him that this was not possible as Dada could not be disturbed. The Maulvi pleaded to be taken just outside the closed door of his room. They willingly obliged. As the Maulvi began ascending the stairs and approaching his room, uncontrollable tears began pouring down his face. He said that he felt a pull and was being drawn by the force of Dada's spiritual magnetism. He remarked that Dada is not merely a representative of Allah, he is Allah. Dada's every nerve and pore is filled with God; he is a living moving sanctuary of God, the Maulvi insisted, even as incessant tears continued to flow.

ONE THOUSAND MEETS OF *AAO JYOT JAGAYEIN*

In the meanwhile, Sadhu Vaswani centres all over the world observed Dada's centenary year with *Aao Jyot Jagayein* satsangs. The Aao Jyot Jagaein campaign had been launched in 2017 to kindle the light of love which Dada's life has emphasized above all else. It was also aimed at creating greater awareness, not just about the landmark event that was approaching, namely, Dada's 100th birthday, but also to spread his message of universal love. Quite simply, the campaign took the message of Dada's love to people everywhere. In India the campaign reached out to Aurangabad, Lucknow, Ahmednagar, Daund, Nagpur, Indore and other cities. The international centres replicated the effort, holding special sessions to spread the fragrance of the approaching centenary. From Atlanta to Ahmedabad, from Bangalore to Beed, from Accra to Akola, from Dubai to Delhi, virtually thousands upon thousands participated in commemorating hundred years of Dada's selfless, love-filled life.

The month of May saw devotees all over the world preparing for the centenary which was now barely two months away. Hundreds of devoted volunteers met at the Mission headquarters to finalize plans and allocate responsibilities for the auspicious event. Dada saw the sparkle in their eyes, the spring in their steps, the verve in their imaginations, the elation in their spirits and the love in their hearts as they went about translating all our aspirations into reality.

With compassion and understanding he watched but stayed detached. He did not defer his followers lest they feel disheartened. But surely he gave signals, which probably they failed to understand.

But oh, the weakness and strain that Dada went through in those days was heart rending! Minor as they were, the procedures had taken their toll on Dada's vulnerable state of health. He seemed to have lost his appetite completely. What worried all of us most was that the abdominal pain persisted, constraining him to rest in bed. But he never, ever complained, only observing with a smile, 'Pain and illness are unavoidable in this physical body, and we must willingly accept them.'

Now, many devotees experienced indescribable miracles in these days. A mother-to-be who had conceived after a long time was told by the doctors that her foetus may have to be aborted. The mother cried out to Dada in utter despair. Strangely Dada appeared in her dreams for three consecutive nights, shielding the child in his hands. On her follow up with the doctors, she was amazed to learn that the child was safe and normal. Another devotee who was a chain smoker saw Dada standing in front of him. As he bowed down to seek his blessings, Dada held his hand and said to him: My child, you will no longer feel the pull to smoke another cigarette, ever again. The man was incredulous at first but was surprised that he never felt the temptation to smoke again. Dada was reaching out to people in a form that transcended the physical. But Dada's physical body was still in agonizing pain.

THE LAST PUBLIC FUNCTION

30 May was yet another red-letter day in the annals of the Sadhu Vaswani Mission. Marking the ongoing centenary celebrations of Dada, the President of India, Shri Ram Nath Kovind, formally inaugurated the Sadhu Vaswani International School, Pradhikaran, at the headquarters of the Sadhu Vaswani Mission in Pune. Welcoming the president, Dada said, 'Our president is a man with a rich creative mind, a compassionate heart who loves the little ones. He knows it is the little ones of today who will build a new, a better, and a more awakened India of tomorrow. I feel deeply grateful to him that he has honoured this occasion by his presence.'

'We need a new type of education,' Dada said to the mammoth gathering. 'A new education which will touch the life of the student. It is life that is needed. Science is indeed marching on, and our students' brain power is ever increasing, but the problems of India and the nations will not be solved unless we have illumined hearts. We need to train the hearts of our students; they need to be taught that life is larger than livelihood.'

The great visionary and saint that he is, Dada spoke of the divine destiny education is meant to fulfil and reiterated his plea to bring

God back into our educational institutions. 'Teach our children to turn back to God. Let them learn to love God,' he enjoined the educational stalwarts present, 'let them learn to love their fellow beings. In love is the secret of peace which men and nations alike are seeking.'

His speech ended with a prophetic warning: 'Collapse of education is the collapse of a nation.' A thundering applause followed the address. The president arose to lead the standing ovation.

Little did we realize then, that this would be the last discourse in English delivered by Dada at a public function!

DADA'S LAST SATSANG AT THE MIRA HALL

There is something magical about the Mira Hall, the main satsang venue at the Mission headquarter in Pune. Very often, the sangat has seen Dada enter the hall after or even during recuperation and convalescence from his sick bed. On occasions, he has come to the satsang after alighting from an ambulance and paying his obeisance at the sacred samadhi. When he had flown in from Hyderabad after his procedure in February, his first stop was the samadhi and then the satsang. On countless occasions, he had 'dropped in' when he was not expected, just to join the congregation for the *vachan* or the master's recorded discourse. Many devotees would draw close to him and engage him in loving conversation for 'just a few minutes'. Invariably the few minutes would stretch and he would stay to talk to people and bless them with his love and grace.

Many of his silent admirers would notice with concern that their beloved Dada was looking frail and rather weak; their fear and anxiety would prompt them to imagine that they were placing undue strain on his delicate health. But the moment Dada smiled at the gathering and began talking to them, their fear would vanish like insubstantial vapour! What spiritual energy, what intense love, what powerful positive vibrations emanated from those lovely, luminous, radiant, illumined eyes! Of course, the beloved of their hearts was all good and well! Dada was with them in the satsang and all was surely well with the world!

And so it was on that unforgettable Thursday, Dada's day in the satsang, on 14 June. His first appearance did cause a pang, but his million-dollar smile and his loving look and his soulful absorption in the bhajans set right all misgivings. No one, not even in their wildest and most fearful nightmares, could have thought that this would be the last satsang Dada was physically attending here in this material world with them.

Dada was in high spirits, as he related the story of when God created the universe; God had then held a conference of the gods and the angels. He sought their 'feedback' on his monumental creation. Rather timidly, an angel ventured the opinion that God had indeed made the universe exquisitely beautiful, but he had to humbly submit his response, that there was no joy, no exuberance in it. The whole universe seemed dull and arid and it was difficult to imagine how those who came to inhabit the earth would live in bliss and delight. And so, Dada continued, God created *raag vidya*, the science of music! In the early days, he continued, people would communicate with each other by singing.

Dada concluded, this is the one teaching that we need to take with us today: Let us sing the song of love. Love is the only religion. Bind your life in love. Those who have bound their lives in love have touched the highest point. And the first step to bind our lives in love, is to speak sweetly to all.

With those loving words dipped in the magic of his ever-loving heart and spoken in the matchless dulcet, sweet tones which he alone could enrapture us with, Dada left his beloved sangat, with one last final farewell, which nobody realized at that time. They were filled with the ecstasy of having seen their beloved and having listened to his ruh-rihan one more time.

That night, Dada felt uneasy. In the morning, he developed severe abdominal pain with nausea and vomiting. The doctors immediately inserted a Ryles tube to ease the pain which did not seem to abate. In spite of constant agonizing pain and acute discomfort, he continued to engage with us lovingly and cheerfully.

'*Muktidham* is calling me,' he said all of a sudden, startling us.

The doctors attending on him administered antibiotics through IV. When there was no respite in the pain on the following days, we requested Dada to be admitted to the hospital. As we were preparing to take him to the hospital he was preparing his followers to accept whatever lay ahead. Our vision was limited – sure that Dada would recover soon and return from the hospital and resume his routine. Even as he was being wheeled on the stretcher, every heart was heavy with anxiety, every eye was brimming with tears. But the light of hope continued to glow brightly. Dada gave everyone a warm and endearing look and closed his eyes and bowed in reverence in the direction of Sadhu Vaswani's sacred samadhi. He surely knew something which no one around him could grasp. He tried to communicate this to them but they were unwilling, unprepared.

At the hospital, when the tests were over, Dada inquired from the doctors if he could be discharged. The doctors requested him to stay on for a day or two as they wanted to monitor his condition. 'We will review the situation tomorrow,' they assured him. 'What tomorrow brings, who can tell?' Dada responded. He was seeing into a future which he had willed for himself but was hidden from our eyes. Not only we, who were in his vicinity but everyone felt the tremendous uplifting abundance of love that flowed out to all from Dada.

The Mission seemed deserted and desolate; but the master's work always goes on in this temple of service and healing.

18 June had been marked as the date for inauguration of the special centenary gift to beloved Dada, the start of a brand new school for the underprivileged children at Manjri village, near Pune.

Someone unaware of ground realities in India might be pardoned for asking: where is the need for another school in another village?

Institutions of excellence are aplenty in our land; but they are all for people who can pay the right price; for education too, is an enterprise, a money-making venture for businessmen today.

Dada's dream had been to set up such a school for the underprivileged children, who could not afford the price of the best education available to the wealthy and the elite of society. His aspiration had been to start an institution which could offer them the best education and help them imbibe the highest values and ideals along with the required academic inputs that could shape them into successful, well integrated and good human beings!

It was in pursuit of this vision that the Sadhu Vaswani Mission chose to start a Free Education Project in the village of Manjri near Pune. It was to be their offering to their beloved mentor and master, Dada, on his 100th birthday.

The Sadhu Vaswani Gurukul would offer free education to the children of Manjri, from nursery up to class 10. It would also ensure that they acquired skill development by offering vocational courses in electrical, carpentry and plumbing for boys and tailoring and beautician courses for girls. This would be backed by placement services too. In addition, young mothers of the village would be counselled and educated about important values and practices that would help them create a better future for themselves and their children. The children would receive the best quality education in English and the mother tongue. They would receive free books and free uniforms and also be provided with free nutritious breakfasts and mid-day meals.

GOD, BLESS AND PROTECT OUR BELOVED DADA

Dada's balcony door remained closed; and his absence from the Mission weighed heavily on all of us. But there was one thing they could all do; join in the daily chanting of mantras and readings from the scriptures that was already on in full swing at the Mission. God is kind and loving, they knew. He would soon restore their beloved Dada where he belonged, to their midst, to the sanctified Mission campus, and all would be well.

This was the start of what was to be a whole month of what seemed to be a never-ending emotional roller-coaster ride for the devotees, doctors and volunteers in Pune, not forgetting millions of Dada's devotees and admirers the world over.

For those who were attending to Dada at the ICU, these were times tormented with anxiety. They had to be in constant contact with the doctors and take decisions based on their advice. They also had to keep a steady flow of communication with the worldwide sangat and friends and admirers, keeping everyone posted on the state of Dada's health.

19 June brought more anguish. Dada's blood-pressure fell alarmingly low. The doctors pronounced his condition to be critical. Yet, he sat up in bed and spoke to everyone. He was not permitted to eat and drink anything; but his pure and beauteous spirit, his inner silence and peace were mirrored in his glowing countenance. To those of us who sat on the floor beside his bed, wishing to stay as close to him as possible, he said tenderly, 'The floor must be cold, get a sheet to sit on.' How blessed we felt, what bliss it was to be with him.

On the 20th, his condition stabilized and his parameters improved, carrying pulsating waves of relief to everyone. Dada sat up in bed for a while. Babaji Gurinder Singh Dhillon, head of the Radha Soami Satsang Beas, having heard of Dada's health, flew in to see Dada. The two spiritual leaders who loved and revered each other spent some time together. When Babaji took leave of Dada, he held his hand and placed it on his head, as if to seek his blessings. Moved by this beautiful gesture, Babaji repeated the act, reverently placing Dada's hand on his head. 'I am leaving now, Dada, as I don't want to strain you further,' he said to Dada. 'But I will come back to see you very soon, in your own home!'

There were highs and lows, peaks and troughs in the days that followed. Occasionally Dada felt strong enough to sit up for longer periods. Over a week had passed, since he was hospitalized. On 22 June, one of us pleaded with him, 'Dada, we beg you to heal yourself for our sake, so that we can go back home with you!' Dada heard us out; the smile never left his lips even for a minute. With infinite grace and compassion for us he said, 'I am pledged to the Lord, and I cannot withdraw it. I have no will of my own now ... it is his will, only his will that prevails.'

On 23 June, Aamir Khan came to see Dada. To the world outside, he was a celebrity, a superstar and his arrival created a bustle. But to Aamir, Dada was an unfailing friend, a guide, a mentor to whom he always turned in love and faith. He could not contain his tears. He was at once overjoyed to see Dada, but his heart ached to see his beloved in so much pain. He held Dada's hands tightly – soft and tender and kissed his forehead, Dada's love enveloping him all the while. There was not a dry eye in the room, as the two held on to each other unwilling to let go.

The following days found us caught in the pendulum swinging between hope and despair, optimism and low spirits. With the cold hand of fear gripping our hearts, we recalled Dada saying to us, reiterating the message which kept haunting us now: 'The time is fast approaching when this body will no longer be in your midst ... but never forget, I am imperishable, indestructible, immortal, eternal.'

In fact, he had written a beautiful song on this very note:

Thou art an ocean of compassion
Thou art the Light of my life
Shower on me, O Master, thy infinite grace

The repository of wisdom art thou
Thou art the light of my eyes
Seated on the peacock, bless me with your vision

From afar cometh the boat
My time is up now, it will not take me long
Into the great beyond will I merge
Into eternity will I dissolve

My physical form, you will behold no more
Into the matchless light, I now enter
Into the great beyond will I merge
Into eternity will I dissolve

My formless energy will pervade everywhere
Whosoever will remember me, with him I will be there
Into the great beyond will I merge,
Into eternity will I dissolve

Renouncing all worldly pleasures, do thou thyself prepare
O Anjali, seek friendship with the One and Only Fair
Into the great beyond will I merge
Into eternity will I dissolve.

The first week of July were crucial days. We held on to a slender thread of hope, we kept on praying to Dada to shower his grace and compassion on us, by just being there for us. Had he not promised this to us in so many words:

Bound and fettered by our karmas are we,
But saints, liberated and free.
At their will they come on this earth plane or depart
In time eternal, this life to them is but a part.

On 4 July, he was put on an intubated ventilator (ET). This process was necessitated because the doctors felt that he needed all his energy conserved to fight the infection. Intubation is painful and difficult and the physical body of saints is highly sensitive to pain. Dada must have been in agony – yet not a look, not a gesture of resistance came from him.

In anguish, we seemed to hear Dada's words to us, 'I am not that which you take me to be! I am not this body which you think is suffering. I am that which is beyond pain and suffering. I am that which suffering cannot touch.'

On 9 July, Dada's condition took yet another turn for the worse. He had to be given a blood transfusion. When he turned critical, some of us felt that he should be moved to the sanctified ambience of the temple of his guru, the Sadhu Vaswani Mission. In fact, a mini ICU was set up in the Mission, ready to receive him. But the doctors were reluctant to let him leave, as they felt that this might worsen his condition. Indeed, Dada showed a little improvement the following day.

For the few of us who attended on him day and night, to watch him suffer was unbearable, but still we clung on to hope and prayer. But, this too, did not last long. Whenever we lost hope, his compassionate eyes continued to shed the light of love on us, his immaculate divinity dazzled us.

> We would all fold our hands in prayer to the Lord to keep
> showering His blessings on Dada:
> O, our Beloved Almighty Lord,
> This is our plea and entreaty,
> You hold in Your hands the entire universe,
> Keep Dada, Your beloved child, under Your protective canopy,
> May the caress of Your gentle hands heal his every pore, his
> every cell
> Fill his every breath with health, vigour and strength.

Dada's condition worsened further. His eyes were ablaze with beatific light. That light seemed to rise, like high tide, engulfing his entire frame. It was so potent, yet so peaceful! On the night of that day, having heard the doctors' opinion, it was decided that Dada should be brought back home.

Great care was taken to ensure that the ride in the ambulance was comfortable and would ensure Dada's well-being and safety. Amidst the chanting of the Maha Mantra, Dada was wheeled into the ambulance.

At 12:30 a.m. in the early hours of the sacred *Guru-var*, beloved Dada entered into the holy grounds of the Mission. The fires of the Maha Mantra Yagna Havan burned brighter at the sacred samadhi. He was now comfortable in the ICU setup at the residence. He was peaceful as the vibes of the holy ambience imbued new energy into him. We felt that our prayers would bring about his speedy recovery, in these familiar grounds that held him reverent.

By now the Mission was flooded with devotees. Those who received this midnight message struggled to keep their hope alive. Everyone kept awake, chanting, praying the whole night. Maybe, just maybe, coming home to his Mission would make that crucial difference. Maybe, this would bring about the miracle of speedy recovery that they had been praying for.

Would our hopes, the dreams of our hearts be broken, never to be put back together? Would our prayers go unanswered? Would our lives be shattered and our souls left bereft?

But there were devotees who had other kinds of premonitions. One of them saw Dada with wings like a pure white angel flying away from earth.

Another dreamt repeatedly of the number '12', unable to understand what the significance could be.

Yet another saw Dada on a dais, with a beautiful blue and white decor – when she reached Pune after Dada's samadhi, she was startled to see the self-same decor in his samadhi.

In the hushed darkness of the starless night, the world seemed to be crumbling. Dark and comfortless, the future that bore down on us was grim. And in our hearts rose the piteous cry, 'Dada! Dada! How may we hold on to you?'

The night was mute. It had no answers to offer us. And our hearts continued to cry for hope and healing. 'Comforter, where, where is thy comforting? You, Dada who never ever wanted to see a tear in our eyes, what answer can you give to our grieving hearts now?'

At around 8:30 a.m. Dada's pulse began to drop. Knowing the inevitable, it was decided that the devotees be permitted to have his darshan. Long queues formed outside; everyone bravely struggled to contain their tears, but their struggle was futile. The entire congregation was dissolving into tears. But they filed silently past the room where Dada lay. In pure pristine state the very bed seemed to be a heavenly pedestal around which the angels of God were galmouring. A mystical nebula enveloped the room and a celestial fragrance wafted all around. The chant of the Maha Mantra grew intense, and a divine light emanated from Dada.

Dada's breathing became laboured. Our hearts once again cried out:

'O for someone who can show us the way! We looked around everywhere – there was no answer! The molten sky showed no movement, the breeze stood still. Not a single leaf stirred. Our hearts were empty. Our life was dark.'

A pall of heaviness seemed to have settled on everything.

And in the room the machines were whirring and beeping and the chanting of the Maha Mantra kept rising.

It was decided to withdraw all artificial support. The ambience of the room was unfathomably transcendental.

Suddenly Dada opened his eyes, that shone like meteors – as though he was beholding a glorious scene.

His face had a glow that was so soft, so calm, yet so eloquent.

He looked around giving one and all his final benediction and he closed his eyes, never to open them again.

> Soaring beyond the golden clouds
> High above the silvery summits
> Dada brushing past the sun and moon,
> Entered into the vastness of the Unknown
> Entered into immortality!

The farewell song he had composed and left in an envelope in his drawer was sung as his sacred mortal remains were laid in state in the very satsang hall that had thrilled to his words barely a month ago.

Khuda Hafiz!
> The call came to me today all at once.
> Do not tarry, ready Thyself!
> Bidding adieu to all, come with me at the rise of dawn!
> Traversing rivers and mountains, return to your Home!
> Where the sun, moon and stars shine not,
> only the Name Divine abides.
> Where the saints, Beauteous and Radiant, in longing, offer
> *Aarti* to the Eternal!
> Where shines the Light undying– no earthly light, this!
> That resplendent Light, my dear one, beckons you,
> Come let us together go, at once!
> To the Land of Mercy, where there is no trace of sorrow.
> From whence you came, do thou return to that Land, my friend!
> Where they commune in silence, and Love – Love alone doth shine!
> Your dear ones, look for you, keep them not waiting anymore!
> In silence they beckon you, do thou hearken to their call!
> In silence gaze at them, shed unbidden tears
> With deep yearning cry out to them,

With eyes closed, behold the wondrous vision!
Clinging to *Nuri's* Lotus Feet, cross over the stormy ocean of life,
Liberated, once again do thou descend to this earth, *Anjali*!

Dada, death cannot touch you, nor ever separate you from us!
Immortal, Endless, Deathless Thou art
Your home now is in every heart!

TWELVE

Dada Enters the Eternal

'He is never born, nor does he at any time, die. Nor, having once come to be, does he cease to be. He is unborn, perpetual, eternal, ancient. He is not slain when the body is slain.'

– Gita, 2:20

12 JULY 2018, THURSDAY

Tranquil; serene and peaceful; calm and radiant even in his final repose.

That was Dada, the beloved of every heart, as his divine physical form lay in state, in his satsang hall, the selfsame hall where he had captured the hearts of multitudes who had thronged to see him, hear him and gather his blessings day after day, year after year; it was difficult, nay, impossible to imagine he was not there in person now.

But who could say he was not there? His presence felt like a benevolent cloud over the satsang; the large, life-like portrait that had been put up in the nook close to the master's statue, Dada's special corner where his chair and little side table still stood, filled the sangat with love and warmth for him. He was there, with us, watching us, watching over us.

Unending rows of devotees, children, admirers, friends – no, just rows after rows of people whom he truly regarded as his brothers and sisters, came up, tears welling in their eyes, sorrow weighing heavily on their hearts, with bowed heads and folded hands to catch one glimpse of that much-loved saint, whom they had revered and worshipped, to pay their heartfelt respects to the one whose memories could never be wiped out, who would ever live on in their hearts.

Dada often spoke to us of the spiritual heart, distinct from the physical heart, that was located, he said, in the centre of our being. Deep within this spiritual heart, in the innermost recess of the cave of this heart, God dwells, he would tell us. When we heard Dada speak of this so feelingly, with such conviction, for most of us, this only underlined the firm belief that it was Dada who lived in the deepest core of our hearts and souls; he was the light that ever shines in the cave of the heart; his voice, his soulful words, was the music of the *anhad naad* we heard within us, for truly, divinity echoed in his words. Even now, as he lay in the sleep of eternity, his voice seemed to resonate in our hearts as everyone filed past his blessed form.

It seemed as if the line would never end; devotees from across India and all over the world, admirers and followers – men, women and children; rich and poor; the known and the unknown; celebrities and commoners; they came to see the beloved of their hearts in his physical form one last time. He would forever live in their thoughts and prayers; they would always turn to him, think of him and seek his help and guidance in all that they did; but they had lost him in this physical dimension in which they still dwelt; and that was indeed an irreparable loss, which left them lost, bereaved and all alone.

For many, the reality did not sink in. How could he have left? How could he *not* be here in the hallowed grounds of the Mission that was at once his place of worship and home?

The soft, soothing bhajans and kirtan offered solace and much needed comfort to the lost sangat. When the singers let out little sobs or choked over the words, we felt their empathy and knew we were not alone in our grief. In the soothing ambience, Dada's love, tender care and concern seemed to reach out and touch us. In that melting mood, we recalled the words of Sadhu Vaswani:

> Blessed are they that have conquered death. They sleep no more but are awake throughout the ages!
> So live that thou mayst be the death of death.

Had not his perfect disciple done just that? He had indeed become the death of death. How true rang the words of one who captured this truth:

> The Songbird sings,
> We hear no more;
> But the heart knows ...
> To its music, it resonates evermore
> The floweret blossoms,
> We see no more;
> But the heart knows ...
> Its fragrance permeates forevermore.
> You too live to tell the tale of his humility, O Death!
> Entwined in his loving hands you walked away with his physical,
> But remember, in our hearts is enshrined his form mystical.
> Revelling are you too in his music celestial,
> But remember, in our ears echoes his symphony perennial.
> Shining too are you in his bright, guileless smile,
> Yet, remember, it continues to encourage us at every mile.
> All to you is his form, is his very breath,
> Yet, remember, he throbs and pulsates within us, O Death!

All sorrow in this life is due to man's denial of his own divinity, Sadhu Vaswani had taught Dada. 'Declare thy divinity in thy life and conquer death!' the master had stated emphatically. Dada had been the very embodiment of divinity in human form. The divine in him would live on forever.

Dada had also said: 'Man does not die: he only puts off the physical body. If you like, you may say that his physical body has died. Man does not die: man cannot die!'

THE FINAL RITES

The incessant lines of people which had started on the morning of 12 July went on without a break, throughout the night too, until 13 July, 2 p.m. when the darshan time concluded.

The Government of Maharashtra felt it to be their honour and privilege to bestow state honours to Dada. One who had tirelessly contributed to the welfare of the people through his selfless service, his loving kindness, his soulful compassion, his all-encompassing love, his beautiful teachings, his wonderful books and discourses. He had set up schools and colleges, started hospitals, activated welfare and seva programmes for the needy and indigent, extended his mission of humanitarian assistance to remote villagers, and included his feathered friends and four-legged kindred by initiating the internationally renowned meatless day campaign; he had been an ambassador of world peace and the unity of all faiths; he had taught us to rediscover our divinity through his unique Moment of Calm movement.

The state felt it pertinent to commemorate the 'saint of their times', who had chosen to live in Pune and dedicate his works of mercy to all creation; and to spread the message of God and his master.

The national flag was ceremoniously draped over Dada's form and he was lifted gently and carried with tender affection and reverence to the sacred samadhi. For, never, in the years following his master's passing away, had he ever left the Mission campus without praying reverently at the sacred samadhi of Sadhu Vaswani. This *antim yatra*, the final journey, would be no exception to the rule.

A float set out from the Mission campus for a 4 km Antim Darshan Yatra through those very streets on which Dada had devotedly pulled the chariot holding the master's portrait on the annual Rath Yatra. People spontaneously joined the procession. Elders and women stood on terraces and balconies, with folded hands, straining for that one final glimpse. It seemed nature had spread a carpet of flowers for her favourite child.

At about 6 p.m. the *rath* reached the Mission campus. Once again, Dada was taken to the sacred samadhi, where the Gayatri Mantra and the Abhyaroha Mantra (*Asatoma Satgamaya*) so dear to Dada were chanted.

At the samadhi, a six-gun salute was accorded to him, after the president's wreath was placed on him; and the president's tribute was read out, followed by the message of the Chief Minister of Maharashtra.

Sadhu Vaswani's dulcet voice reciting the Gita's twelfth chapter ushered in the atmosphere of a satsang rather than a funeral ceremony. As for Dada's upadesh, it spoke to the grieving devotees straight: What is death? The physical body drops, the bird flies, the cage breaks. Man never dies. He is undying. Do not grieve over the passing away of your dear ones.

Adjacent to the master's final resting place, a special platform was made ready for the *antim samskaras*. Dada's sacred form was placed on a huge pile of sandalwood logs and sticks and *agarbattis*. This was followed by prayers from their respective scriptures by Pune's Bishop, Thomas Dabre, Buddhist leader, Bhante Rajratanji and Sikh priest, Giani Mangal Singh from Dighi Gurdwara. They were unanimous in expressing their appreciation for Dada's universal approach to spirituality and the unity of faiths which he both taught and practiced in deeds of daily living.

The next day the samadhi was covered with a white net. All day, all night, devotees sat before the hallowed samadhi, chanting, praying and just allowing themselves to feel close to their beloved

Dada. There was not a movement in the live long day or the endless night when the sacred space was ever left unattended. Satsangs were held throughout the day.

On 19 July, early in the morning, the havan-fire was lit. After readings from world scriptures, along with kirtan and bhajans the sacred ashes were collected in specially designed copper urns and placed in a beautiful palanquin. Brothers and sisters of the sangat carried the palanquin in a *parikrama* around the Mission campus, where Dada had first set foot in 1951; where he had run and walked and climbed and bustled in the service of his guru and the sangat; where he had been the pillar of strength and support to the bereaved sangat when the master passed away in 1966. The sacred kutiya where he loved to come for prayer and satsang, where he would lovingly bless one and all, seemed more alive with his spiritual presence.

Every evening for the following twelve days, devotees gathered in the satsang hall to observe the solemn obsequies; every day, a special satsang was held, with the bhajans and kirtans that Dada loved; each day a different, new inspirational video upadesh was played, where Dada seemed so alive, spoke with such life and vitality, that the sangat were moved to tears. Even while their hearts grieved, people found it impossible to weep or shed tears; for they could feel his loving, living presence; it seemed to them Dada was there in the satsang with them and that he would also be there as long as they remembered him in love.

The large, life-like portrait of Dada with his hand raised was so beautiful that people felt as if he was looking at them with love in his luminous eyes and assuring them: I haven't gone anywhere. I am here and will be here always.

Seva, satsang and havan were held during all the twelve days. The ambience of the Mission campus during all these days could only be described as heavenly. Not for a moment could anyone, even momentarily, actually feel that their beloved Dada was not with them, for such was the shakti of his spiritual presence, and so great the love and devotion in which they held him. If truth be told, people felt his presence even more strongly than ever before.

The twelve-day ceremonies and prayers were by no means regarded as a farewell to the beloved master. For saints never die. Saints are ever-living entities. Their pure and enlightened souls ever abide with devotees whose hearts are filled with love for them. They are pure consciousness, they take the human form for a lifetime to lead people Godward. When their earthly mission is completed, they are merged in the ever-pervading eternity of divine consciousness. Dada too, dropped his physical form to become part of this higher consciousness. Now, he had become omnipotent, omniscient, and omnipresent, ever guarding and guiding his people. The sangat who had held Dada closest to their hearts, only felt that somehow, their bonds with Dada had strengthened, and that he was enshrined in their hearts forever.

GURU PURNIMA

Can there be Purnima without the full moon? Can we have a Guru Purnima without the guru amidst us?

> Guru bin kaun bataave baat
> Bada vikit yam ghaat…
> Bhrantiki pahadi nadiyan bheechmo ahankarki lat
> Mada matsarkl dharabarasat, maya pavan ghanadhat
> Kama krodha do parvat tade, lobh chor sangat
> Kehat kabir suno bhai saddhoo, kyon karna ye dhat?

But for the guru, who can show us the way?
The way is arduous,
Doubt crosses the mountainous route like a flooded river; the ego forms huge boulders in the river;

Pride and vanity come down like a thundershower from dark
clouds above; delusion tosses us about like a storm;
Passion and anger are like two overhanging cliffs on either side;
ambition, like a thief, stalks us
Kabir says: oh friend! how can we traverse this path?

Can there be a Guru Purnima without the guru? Can we live
life as we did without the beloved in our midst? Was this not the
day which would have ushered in the centenary celebration-filled
Anjali week?

But the moment devotees stood before the sacred samadhi, their
doubts and anguish seemed to lift:

Guru Meri Pooja, Guru Gobinda
Guru Mera Paarbramha, Guru Bhagwanta

Guru is my prayer, Guru is my teacher
Guru is all-powerful, Guru is truly the One.

As the sangat sang the beautiful *Anjali Geet* in chorus, the
positive vibrations alleviated all sorrow.

The satsang concluded with a silent meditation, as the sangat
bowed down in utmost reverence to their master and their beloved
Dada and moved to accept the prasad served.

The evening brought with it the much-needed comfort and
consolation of hearing the upadesh of the masters. The truth hit
everyone hard; from this day onward, his word would have to suffice;
his presence was lost to us forever, here on earth.

YEH NATA RUHANI: DADA'S CENTENARY CELEBRATIONS

Sang hamare, yeh nata tumhari, ruhani ruhani ruhani.

The lilting strains of this moving refrain echoed across the length and breadth of the Mission campus, as the devotees prepared to celebrate their beloved Dada's centenary. True to the words of the specially composed song, their relationship with their guru and master had indeed been a unique, special, life-transforming, death-transcending bond of love and reverence. Thousands of them had poured their hearts and souls into preparing for this grand event. Now, things had changed; he was not with them in his physical presence, but his ever-living spirit and his indescribable spiritual energy and healing vibrations could be felt everywhere in the Mission campus.

31 July, Tuesday, was designated for 'Honouring Hundred Years of a Dedicated Life'. 1 August, Wednesday, was dedicated to 'Honouring Hundred Years of Selfless Service'. 2 August, Thursday, the blessed birthday would be 'Honouring Hundred Years of Unconditional Love'. Many an eye shed a secret tear as the haunting melody echoed and re-echoed in their hearts.

Each of the days would begin with celestial chants and a havan at 7 a.m. before the sacred samadhi; there would be kirtan ras, with uplifting renditions between 11:30 a.m. and 1 p.m. The evening programme would feature guest singers with their melodious songs in the satsang, followed by a special video tribute and upadesh from the masters.

The devotees mingled with each other in love and amity. The centenary celebrations had indeed been a wonderful opportunity for everyone to come together in love and devotion to their one and only beloved. But nothing could fill the void that Dada's absence had left in their lives.

Once, Just Once

With your shimmering glance, let love pierce my heart,
Lighting up a thousand lamps within me, let a responding quiver
    start.
Once, just once ...

In your soothing presence, let me sit, away from the din,
Resting my head on your lap, sprinkled by your love's fountain.
Once, just once ...

Let your flute-like voice enthral me, enchant me,
Calling out my name, sweetly, gently, lovingly.
Once, just once ...

To your calming and gentle touch, make me awaken,
Renewing me, strengthening me to face the day's burden.
Once, just once ...

Shield me in the safe circle of your arms,
Then no storm or siege can cause any harm.
Once, just once ...

Bestow on me your seraphic and disarming smile,
Then I'm weighed down no more, able to walk mile after mile.
Once, just once ...

Nothing is impossible for you, so listen to my plea,
Please, hurry up, fly and come to me.
Once, just once ...

Longing, yearning ... I beseech ...
May the distance keep us apart no more ...
Please, hurry up, make my heart your home.
Once, just once ...

His Master's Mission

'When your dreams include service to others – accomplishing something that contributes to others – it also accelerates the accomplishment of that goal. People want to be part of something that contributes and makes a difference.'

– Jack Canfield

MISSION COMPASSION

Today, devotees and admirers refer to the Sadhu Vaswani Mission as 'the Mission with a Vision' or as 'Mission Compassion' and Dada's utter devotion to his master's ideals has resulted in a quantum leap in the growth of the Mission's services and programmes over the years. Dada has been the moving force and the inspiration behind these multifarious activities, as the hundreds upon hundreds of committed and devoted volunteers who have made their entire working life an offering to the Mission, would avow.

What measures the success or the achievements of an institution? It is not just about milestones and accomplishments and statistics, but about how many lives you have touched, how many souls in distress you have reached out to, how many weary pilgrims you have helped lift their heavy loads, sharing their burden, making them feel there is someone they can turn to ... it's about what you give back to humanity, in return for the life that God gifted to you! Measured in these terms, it would be quite true to say that the Sadhu Vaswani Mission has lived up to the ideals of its founder: Service of the poor is worship of God.

Pune has been privileged to be chosen as the Sadhu Vaswani Mission headquarter since the early 1950s: the city opened its doors and its heart to two of India's most respected spiritual leaders – Gurudev Sadhu Vaswani and Dada J. P. Vaswani, keeping alive the light of those ideals of love, kindness, peace and compassion with which the organization was first founded. These ideals are still cherished by the thousands of dedicated volunteers as they go about their service activities.

'How do you manage to oversee and administer such a vast organization?' an interviewer once asked Dada. 'How did you conceptualize and build and nourish all those hospitals and schools and clinics and oh, so many other institutions and programmes and movements?'

'I do nothing!' Dada replied, with his trademark smile. 'I plan nothing; I implement nothing. All that has been built, all that the Mission has accomplished, has happened by the grace and blessings of the master. What he wills, comes to pass, at the right time, at the right place.'

In a way, the Sadhu Vaswani Mission today is a representation of the vision of a living saint who asserts again and again, 'I am nothing! The master is all-in-all.'

SATSANG

Sadhu Vaswani asserted, 'The noblest work is to cultivate the soul.' With this focus, the pivot around which the Mission's activities revolve is the satsang. At least thrice daily, the devout and faithful gather in the sanctified atmosphere of the Sadhu Vaswani satsang hall to utter the Holy Name, to participate in soul-stirring bhajan and kirtan sessions, to recite from the holy scriptures and to renew their faith and piety in the Almighty. The recorded upadeshes of Sadhu Vaswani still hold listeners spellbound. 'Your life on this earth is but a journey, a brief sojourn. Your native home lies beyond this earthly plane; and the passage to the native land is through the satsang,' we are told.

Dada would constantly urge one and all to join the fellowship of the satsang. 'Do not ever forsake this beautiful, purifying, blissful experience, that is so freely available to all of us,' he would tell the devotees. 'It is as easy as walking in and taking your seat. The power of the satsang will take care of the rest ... Indeed, the divine presence of a realized soul, a guru, is in itself a boon, for it brings peace and harmony to your soul, just through the spiritual vibrations that his presence generates. Satsang is the flowing waters of the spirit. It is the melody of the Name Divine. It cleanses both the heart and mind.'

A sister once came to see Dada in a very perturbed state of mind. She said that she had been greatly agitated, of late, by a personal crisis that had rocked her life. She needed to talk to Dada and was anxious for advice. Dada suggested that as it was nearly time for the evening satsang, she should attend the same, and then come to talk to him.

She agreed, and went away to join the satsang, which was about to begin. It was a Tuesday, which in the Sadhu Vaswani Satsang, is given over to a period of meditation – that is, after a brief kirtan and aarti. When the satsang was over, there was a brief session of prayer and silence at Sadhu Vaswani's sacred samadhi. Following this refreshing and uplifting session, Dada sent for this sister, for she had indeed appeared very disturbed.

She came running up to meet him and said, 'Yes, Dada?'

Dada had to gently remind her that she had wanted to meet him urgently, over a matter that had been troubling her.

'Oh, yes, I remember,' she said, with a smile. 'But Dada, I really feel I don't need to trouble you and take away your valuable time now. I have found the answers to my questions, the solution to my problem.'

She explained that the moment she walked into the satsang, she had felt a sense of peace and calm descend upon her. As she heard the kirtan, she felt tears flowing from her eyes, unbidden. The day's *vachan* from the Nuri Granth seemed as if it were deliberately addressed to her. She participated in the aarti, which she found to be a healing, purifying experience. In the meditation session which followed, she was actually able to hear her inner voice speak to her, and the terrible weight of anxiety and worry that had been pressing down on her, lowering her morale and her spirit, seemed to lift like a cloud. At the end of the session, she felt that she was a new person, ready to take on life. She had not only received inner guidance to approach her own problem, but was also filled with a sense of well-being, courage and confidence. In fact, till Dada sent for her, she had almost forgotten that she had gone to him earlier that evening, in a distraught condition, seeking answers to questions that overwhelmed her. Such was the effect of satsang on her.

Indeed, most of the sangat can vouch for the fact that satsang is an abundance of positive energy.

THE SACRED SAMADHI

Every month, people from all over India and the world, make it a point to spend a few days or even a few hours at the Mission. The sacred samadhi, enshrining Sadhu Vaswani's holy ashes is located in a serene and beautiful, green nook of the Mission campus, adjacent to the Gita Mandir. Over the years, it has become a place of pilgrimage to thousands of devotees who flock to this sacred shrine of their beloved master.

The life-like statue of Sadhu Vaswani seems to smile upon the devout pilgrims who come to bow at his feet. His kind and loving eyes seem to look into their very souls. As brothers and sisters of the sangat sit at the sacred samadhi in silent meditation, they are blessed with an uplifting sense of peace and joy.

The truth is that thousands upon thousands of devotees and seekers still look upon Sadhu Vaswani as their beloved guru and master: he may have dropped his physical body; he may have departed from this earth-plane; but he lives on, he lives amidst us, in our deeper consciousness. From the personal experiences shared by many seekers, the sacred samadhi of Sadhu Vaswani and the holy kutiya where he lived, still resonate with the most positive and healing vibrations, and even strangers and first-time visitors who come to these sacred spots, say that these vibrations are palpable – and that they feel a profound sense of peace and tranquillity when they sit to meditate there.

The Sacred Samadhi is now endowed with twice the sanctity, since a new structure is coming up at the spot where Dada's mortal remains were consigned to the flames. Adjacent to the Master's samadhi, but a step lower, as Dada would have wished, work on the new structure started in August, soon after the Centenary celebrations. While the builders asked for a period of six months to level the ground, pave the plot and raise the basic structure, the kar seva of devotees ensured that the temporary structure was raised in half the time! While a new marble statue of Dada has been commissioned from master sculptors at Jaipur, the temporary structure with its *akhand jyot* (permanent lit up lamp) houses a magnificent lifelike portrait of Dada Jashan (oil on canvas) with his charming smile and piercing glance which seems to look into the very souls of the devotees. While the Master stands in celestial splendour, Dada, the perfect disciple, seems to engage us in an enchanting conversation!

SERVICE TO NEEDY FAMILIES

'Do as much good as you can, to as many as you can, in as many ways as you can and as often as you can,' Dada would urge his devotees.

Selfless service is thus at the core of the Mission's activities. In bearing witness to this great ideal, innumerable social service programmes are tirelessly carried out at the different centres all over the world.

It was Dada J. P. Vaswani's firm conviction that the teaching of profound spiritual truths can wait until the poor and the hungry are provided with life's most basic necessity – that is, food to keep their body and soul together. Dada Bhandara is the ever-hospitable kitchen where food is cooked and distributed to the poor and needy and to institutions which look after the underprivileged. Feeding of *yatris* and giving away *prasadi* for satsangs is a daily activity.

Dada melas (funfairs) are organized regularly for the underprivileged, such as orphans, coolies, the aged, blind and disabled, as well as public servants such as nurses, social workers, postmen, *sevaks, sevikas* and municipal workers. They are warmly welcomed as the Mission's special guests on these occasions and offered a delicious spread of eatables to choose from at their will. They also receive thoughtfully chosen gift articles to take home with them. A variety of entertainment programmes are arranged especially for their pleasure. The Mission volunteers spare no effort to see that these special guests have a lovely time on these occasions.

In Pune, the Mission's seva department organizes regular service programmes under which hundreds of needy families receive monthly rations, household utensils, as well as help in cash and kind from the Mission. Electricity and gas connections are provided to those underprivileged families who cannot afford them. The Mission also undertakes the construction of toilet blocks, proper drainage facilities, and the repair of leaking roofs, in the homes of the underprivileged.

Vocational training programmes are offered free of cost to underprivileged women. Full and partial need-based scholarships are offered to needy students at the Mission's many educational institutions. Help in cash and kind is offered to needy families whose daughters are to be married.

RELIEF AND REHABILITATION

The Mission's volunteers have always rushed to help victims of natural disasters like earthquakes, floods and famines. Their dedication and determination were highly lauded by state governments during the earthquakes in Latur and Gujarat, during the tsunami in Tamil Nadu and the Kosi floods in Bihar, and during the cyclones in Kerala. They serve silently and humbly, without seeking publicity or intruding into people's lives.

They open temporary emergency hospitals/dispensaries in disaster-struck areas and offer food from temporary kitchens they set up in these regions. They tend to the sick and the wounded with paramedical teams. They offer help in cash and kind to people who are rendered homeless. In many cases, they have been involved in township rebuilding projects such as ninety-two new homes built for the 1993 Latur earthquake victims, 450 new homes built for the 2001 Gujarat earthquake victims, and ninety-four homes for the 2004 tsunami victims.

The Mission has also undertaken village upliftment programmes in the rural areas of Maharashtra and Gujarat to improve the quality of the life of villagers. This includes village adoption schemes, education for children, free medical camps and imparting training to enable them to be financially independent. Other activities under this service include digging of wells in draught-hit districts, provision of drinking water, tree planting, maintenance of electricity supply, soil conservation, irrigation and self-employment programmes.

NEW EDUCATION CAN MAKE THE WORLD NEW

Both Sadhu Vaswani and Dada believed in education as a transforming force, where humanism is blended with the spiritual ideal. As Sadhu Vaswani expressed it so powerfully, 'The secular, in its right expression, is humanistic: and the secular must not be cut off from the root of all – that is, the Spirit.' While our ancient system of education was aimed at bringing out the God in man, Dada would often rue that our current system of education insists on keeping him out of our learning. That is why education today, he felt, has become soul-less.

The Mira Movement in Education founded by Sadhu Vaswani believes that the One Light shines in all scriptures of all races and religions. Named after Mira, whom Sadhu Vaswani saw as a free spirit, and a symbol of true bhakti – dedication, absolute and total, she was an advocate of that true freedom for women, which grows out of love of God and service of the poor.

The Mira School which he founded was regarded as an oasis in our educational desert even in those early days. Even today, visitors to the Mission's colleges and schools are invariably amazed and profoundly impressed by the atmosphere and spiritual positivity of the daily Sanctuary gatherings. Sadhu Vaswani did not merely specify the Sanctuary as a 'compulsory' period; he also gave it a theme: viz. 'The Art of Living' – and this, it must be made clear, was as early as in 1933.

Today, the Mira institutions include no less than three Sadhu Vaswani International schools run by the Mission centres in Delhi, Mumbai and Hyderabad, as well as schools in Mumbai, Ahemdabad, Baroda, Rajkot and Bangalore; and the Mira College in Pune founded by Sadhu Vaswani himself. Among the newest additions to the fold are the Sadhu Vaswani College of Nursing, inaugurated in the year 2006; and the Sadhu Vaswani Institute of Management Studies, inaugurated in July 2010, at the Mira Campus at Koregaon Park, Pune; and an exclusive institution for teachers, the Sadhu Vaswani Institute of Teachers' Training, inaugurated in 2012. A brand-new Sadhu Vaswani International School has also been inaugurated in Pradhikaran, Pune. A new addition to the family was the Little Lamps Nursery, inaugurated on 22 September 2017 in London, the first Sadhu Vaswani school outside India. The Sadhu Vaswani Gurukul, Manjri, offers a completely free high-quality education with all facilities to the underprivileged children of the area.

When people asked Dada what was special about Mira education, he would outline the unique features of this education, using Sadhu Vaswani's own words:

+ Education is a matter of the spirit, and not just acquisition of paper degrees.
+ The end of all knowledge is service of the poor and the lowly, the sick and the afflicted, the oppressed and the handicapped.
+ While students are taught and trained to show good results in their examinations, the emphasis must always be on character building, service, heroic living and spiritual unfolding.
+ True education cannot stop with the development of the brain alone; therefore, the Mira Education, as envisioned by its founder, aims at a triple training – of the head, the hand and the heart.

Sadhu Vaswani's ideals for Mira institutions were indeed lofty. He wanted each one of them to be an ideal institution and for its teachers and students to reflect those ideals in deeds of daily living. Thus, he gave Mira institutions a four-fold ideal: Simplicity, Service, Purity and Prayer.

Taking this vision forward, Dada too, was a firm believer in education as a transformational force: 'Put the child right and the world will come out right,' he emphasized. Quite firm in the belief that a 'Godless' curriculum can only be a wasted effort, he insisted that we must educate our children, first and foremost, to know God and to love him. He stated forcefully, 'If we make God a reality to our youth, we will surely find that they grow in those true qualities of character without which life has no meaning or significance.'

HEALING WITH LOVE AND COMPASSION

Helen Keller pointed out that though this world is full of suffering, it is also full of the overcoming of suffering through love and compassion. Dada, a great healer of the spirit, holds the well-being of all people very close to his heart.

Once, when Dada was in Mumbai, he happened to witness an incident that left a deep impression on his gentle heart: an old man lay dying on a busy road. Thousands of vehicles whisked past him. Countless pedestrians crossed the road where he lay unconscious. But no one took any notice of him.

The moment Dada's eyes fell on the man, he asked the driver to pull over. He got off and went to his side. The old man was indeed in a critical condition. With the help of the friends who were with him, Dada had the old man carried to the car.

Then began the harrowing search to find a humane hospital, clinic or nursing home that would admit the man and give him the medical care that he needed so badly. In vain did they drive from one hospital to another, callously being turned away by impatient administrators and unsympathetic nursing staff, mechanically refusing any treatment simply because the patient did not have a name or address which they could put on record.

At long last, a little-known hospital in the suburbs accepted him. He received treatment for three days and then breathed his last.

Deeply saddened by the insensitive and callous attitude of the hospitals, Dada made a resolution that with God's grace and the blessings of his master, he would undertake to build a hospital where even the poorest of poor would not be turned away; where a patient would not be reduced to a mere case number but be treated with due love and respect.

Around this time, a philanthropic patron of the Mission came to offer a donation to the Mission with the request that a hospital project may be carried out in the memory of her dear, departed husband. At that time, the hospital that was no more than a dream in Dada's heart, began to shape itself into reality.

On 9 January 1989, the dream was realized, as the Inlaks & Budhrani Hospital was inaugurated by the hands of the Nobel Laureate Mother Teresa.

Today, the multi-discipline hospital is the flagship institution and part of the prestigious Sadhu Vaswani Mission's Medical Complex. The Morbai Naraindas Cancer Institute and a Healer's Home, inaugurated by His Holiness the Dalai Lama, were added first on 24 November 1995; this was followed by the super-specialty hospitals, Kirpalani & Kundnani Eye Institute inaugurated on 2 August, 2003 by L. K. Advani, then Deputy Prime Minister of India; the Fabiani & Budhrani Heart Institute, commissioned on 4 June 2006; and the Sadhu Vaswani College of Nursing commissioned on 1 September 2006. The ideal that Dada has placed before these temples of healing speaks volumes for his love and compassion, 'Every patient is a picture of God. To serve him is to worship God.'

The hospitals function as genuine philanthropic, not-for-profit institutions of medical care.

For Dada, medical care is more about healing, help and compassion, over and above diagnostics, prescriptions, surgery and treatment. Thus, he took a keen interest in the Mission's hospitals, to ensure that the healing touch was always present.

During the early days, Dada was a frequent visitor to the hospital, often slipping quietly into the wards, without prior announcement or fanfare. As in the good old days, he would go around visiting patients in the wards, offering them fruits and biscuits, and the love of his ever-compassionate heart. How their faces lit up when they saw Dada!

Once, when Dada had left a ward and was on his way to the next, a young girl came down the corridor, and was pleasantly surprised to see Dada. She had left her ward to take a walk and a breath of fresh air, and her joy knew no bounds when she recognized Dada, whose discourses she had often seen on TV with her family.

'Dada, Dada,' she kept repeating, holding his hands and shedding tears of joy. 'I am so happy to see you! I am so happy to see you!'

Dada graciously acknowledged her love-filled greeting and offered her some biscuits and fruits. As she tried to touch his feet, Dada noticed that she herself was walking barefoot. Loving and selfless as ever, Dada offered his own footwear to her so that she would not catch a chill from walking on the cold floor. The young girl's eyes widened in amazement as Dada bent down and placed his soft sandals at her feet. He made her wear the sandals, even as the ward nurse came to take her back to her bed.

Her eyes brimming with gratitude and a look of wonder still in her eyes, the girl returned to the ward. She placed Dada's sandals reverently beside the bed and kept on gazing at them. 'I have seen an angel,' she whispered to the nurse, who tucked her in bed.

LIMBS FOR THE LIMBLESS

Once Dada was asked, 'What is the best exercise for the heart?'

His reply was, 'Bend down with compassion and lift up someone who needs help.'

Over ten years ago, to commemorate Dada's 90th birthday celebrations, the Sadhu Vaswani Mission's Medical Complex conceptualized the seva programme that became really close to our hearts: Enable the Disabled. Our inspiration came from Dada, and he gave his blessing and support to this wonderful initiative to put people back on their feet; restore the use of lost or amputated limbs; to help the physically challenged to walk again, work again, and live life to their best potential. The idea was not just to restore limbs, but to give them self-confidence, to add meaning to their lives, to restore dignity to them, to enable them to contribute meaningfully to their families and society at large – in short, to bestow on them a new lease of life.

We are told there are hundreds of thousands of people in India, who have lost a limb due to various reasons like accidents, infection, diabetes or amputation; and are deprived of their ability to earn a livelihood and unable to support themselves or their loved ones. The dedicated team of orthopaedics and administrators of the Sadhu Vaswani Medical Complex, and the best prosthetists in Pune, set up the Enable the Disabled Initiative. It would be no exaggeration to say that this 'gift of mobility' has given many people, men, women and children, a reason to live life anew.

There are about 10,000 underprivileged people alone in various parts of Maharashtra who lose a limb for some reason or another, be it an accident, infection, diabetes, or a tumor. The Mission's goal is to eradicate this handicap in the state by reaching the number of 10,000 artificial limbs. Thousands of generous donors all over the world are contributing to make this scheme a grand success!

CANCER IS CURABLE

Dada had heard from friends and devotees about the arduous efforts undertaken by cancer patients and their families from Pune, who had to travel to Bombay for treatment of the dreaded disease. His impulse was to set up a special cancer treatment facility in Pune, which could offer healing and care to these patients. His dream came true when the Morbai Naraindas Budhrani Cancer Institute was inaugurated on 24 November 1995, becoming the first comprehensive cancer treatment facility in Maharashtra outside Mumbai.

'Cancer ... Let's beat it!' is the upbeat, optimistic slogan with which this hospital dedicates itself to a relentless campaign against cancer. Here, diagnosis is aided by the best equipment and radiation therapy is delivered through world class systems such as linear accelerator, micro sectron HDR, simulator and treatment planning computer. A dedicated and expert team of medical and surgical oncology specialists is available to treat patients with care and compassion – the hallmark of Sadhu Vaswani hospitals.

The Morbai Naraindas Budhrani Cancer Institute (MNBCI) has been recognized as a hospital under the Times 'Icons' category. The senior authorities of MNBCI were recently felicitated at a function held by the Times Group at Hyatt Regency, Pune.

SIGHT FOR THE SIGHTLESS

Dada's heart always went out in anguish to the many who are afflicted with blindness, especially the poor, illiterate villagers, unaware that ailments like cataract can be cured by a simple surgery and continue to live in darkness, often abandoned in old age by their children. The Mission's K. K. Eye Institute offers such people a new life. Today, the K. K. Eye Institute is a centre of excellence in eye-care, with its highly acclaimed Sight for the Sightless initiative, offering the best quality of treatment to the rich and poor alike. It also provides expert ophthalmic care with quality and compassion. It is dedicated to its mission to combat eye disease and reduce avoidable blindness through a comprehensive approach to eye care. It is committed to the goal of eradicating preventable blindness in the areas around Pune, by focusing on comprehensive eye care services, education, training and community services with the best of technology and skills.

Indeed, by any standards, the institute is a one-of-its-kind eye-care hospital and has done commendable work among various underprivileged and vulnerable groups like peasant farmers, stonecutters, tribal people living in remote hill areas, as well as slum dwellers in the cities. Truly, this hospital has lit up the lives of tens of thousands of people by the beautiful gift of sight.

CARDIAC CARE FOR THE COMMON MAN

On Dada's 41st birthday, in his message of blessing, the master had said, 'The heart of Jashan pulsates with the pain of the poor and the lowly, the downtrodden and the destitute. In his heart is a beautiful blend of the love of God and love of the suffering children of God … In his heart shines the light of compassion. Not many of you know how selflessly he serves the poor, beholding in them images of the Lord … It is only when your heart is full of compassion that you feel the pain of another …'

True to his master's perception, Dada has always taken tremendous efforts to reach out to the underprivileged and the needy, and it has been his earnest aspiration to bring affordable and compassionate medical care to the ailing ones. When devotees decided to celebrate 18–24 February (the week of his quadruple by-pass surgery) as Thanksgiving Week, it was Dada's insistence that made them take up the highly appreciated service activity of offering free angioplasty and free bypass surgeries for needy patients.

Little wonder then, that the Fabiani & Budhrani Heart Institute has not only blossomed into a leading cardiac care specialty hospital, but also translated Dada's vision into reality by offering free and concessional procedures including angiography, cardiac catheterization, angioplasty, permanent pacemaker implantation, balloon angioplasty and the other cardiovascular services – all these to alleviate of suffering of humanity.

The community outreach team of the institute, comprising a cardiologist, resident doctors, nursing and paramedical staff take their camps to the outlying districts, providing hundreds of patients with a range of free screenings, including consultations with a cardiologist, ECG, blood pressure and blood sugar level testing. Patients requiring further cardiac treatment are guided to the hospital for free or concessional treatment.

BRINGING MEDICAL CARE TO YOUR DOORSTEP

The Sadhu Vaswani Ashram Medical Centre, Khandala, offers medical outreach to the poorest of the poor. Started in 1994 as a free dispensary for poor Adivasis (tribal people), it is now a full-fledged medical centre, treating as many as 50,000 patients a year. The centre has a drug store which dispenses free medicines to all the patients.

Two mobile vans with doctors visit small villages in and around Lonavla and Khandala to treat poor patients in small villages and hilly areas where tribal people live. Apart from diagnosis and treatment, free medicines are provided to the patients. The mobile clinics visit villages on fixed days of the week, ensuring follow-up and continued care to the patients. Over one lakh people have benefited from this service.

The centre attracts medical students from all over the world to study its rural health programme.

JIV DAYA: COMPASSION TOWARDS ANIMALS

Emphasizing Sadhu Vaswani's belief that all creation is one family, where birds and animals are man's younger brothers and sisters, the Mission fulfils his ideal of reverence to the voiceless and defenceless creatures by feeding birds and animals, regularly.

A mobile veterinary clinic, offering compassionate medical care to domestic animals and farm cattle in their own habitat, visits outlying areas in Pune District. Two doctors travel on the mobile clinic providing antibiotic, anti-inflammatory, anti-histaminic and anti-ectoparasitic injections, as well as homeopathic medications wherever possible.

SAK AND THE INTERNATIONAL MEATLESS DAY CAMPAIGN

Sadhu Vaswani was a staunch advocate of animal rights and held very close to his heart the principle of reverence for all life. Dada's tireless efforts to spread the message of his master have borne fruit in the form of the SAK (Stop All Killing) Association and the commemoration of Sadhu Vaswani's birthday, 25 November, as an International Meatless Day and Animal Rights Day.

Many states in India, including Maharashtra, Gujarat, Karnataka and Andhra Pradesh, have banned the slaughter of animals on 25 November. Even countries as distant as Brazil have responded enthusiastically to this campaign of compassion. Every year millions of pledges are received from people (directly and through the mobile app and social media) who vow to go meatless on 25 November.

'Is not life God's greatest gift to each and every one of his creatures? How can we take away that which we cannot give?' asks Dada. Sensitive thinking people all over the world have paid heed to his message of love and compassion.

The impact that Dada has on people must be seen to be believed. His moving appeals to 'live and let live' and emphasis on compassion to all living things have proved to be so irresistible that confirmed non-vegetarians have sworn to stay away from meat for the rest of their lives.

Dada's advocacy of vegetarianism as a lifestyle rather than a mere dietary choice, has always been a passionate concern with him. In his extensive travels around the world, he has constantly sought to awaken people to the importance of vegetarianism. As a result, his followers recognize that the best offering they can make to him – more important than money or seva – is a pledge to turn vegetarian. For many of them this poses a real challenge and giving up meat becomes for them a major turning point in life, one of self-discipline and self-restraint. It implies living life with conviction and daring to be different from others around them.

HERO DAYS

'In all religions the Light is thine,' sang Gurudev Sadhu Vaswani. In his weekly discourses, Dada J. P. Vaswani would narrate thrilling events and anecdotes from the lives of the great ones who have blessed humanity, both in the East and West. Days sacred to Krishna and Christ, Buddha and Muhammed, Moses and Guru Nanak, Kabir and St Francis, Zoroaster and Bahaullah are observed by the sangat with special prayer meetings and service programmes. These days are known as 'Hero' Day as Dada would say, 'It is not in physical courage and military valour alone that heroism is to be found.' After all, as Mark Twain pointed out, physical courage is seen to be aplenty in the world, while moral and spiritual courage is very rare.

On these Hero days there are special programmes for helping social institutions such as orphanages, old age homes, schools for the physically challenged as well as free day care centres and creches for the children of construction workers run by various organizations for the underprivileged sections of society. This includes meeting the basic needs of these institutions, besides distributing food and other necessary items to them.

Upholding the ideal of universal love and the brotherhood of all men, the annual Muharram procession passes the campus of the Sadhu Vaswani Mission every year. Devotees and volunteers led by Dada, lovingly serve their Muslim brethren with sherbet and boiled grams.

Once, when Dada was in tremendous pain and advised complete rest, the participants of the procession who had looked forward to receiving his blessings, not finding him there as usual, enquired where he was. When they were told that Dada had been advised rest owing to an injured back, they brought the *Alam* (their sacred banner) to Dada in his room. Dada took the sacred Alam in his hands and said, 'Imam Hussein is one of the heroes of humanity. He was brave as a lion and inspired love and devotion in the hearts of his people. He sacrificed his life in a fight against tyranny and injustice. His life has been a source of inspiration to untold millions through the centuries.'

This was akin to the mountain coming to Muhammad. The Muslim brothers were touched and departed with good wishes for Dada's speedy recovery and said that they were sure, in the following years Dada would personally come and once again greet the Muharram procession.

There was another instance, when the *warkaris* (pilgrims) from Alandi on their annual walking pilgrimage to Pandharpur, brought a huge procession to the Sadhu Vaswani Mission. They first sang 'Vithala' and 'Tukaram' bhajans at the sacred samadhi of Sadhu Vaswani; and then, hearing that Dada was in pain, the group moved up to his residence to sing kirtan in his presence. The associations had come with a special reason: to confer upon Dada, their 'Sant Ratna Puraskar'.

Accepting the award, Dada said that his Guru Sadhu Vaswani bade him not to be just a bhakta – but a bhakta of the bhaktas, a servant of the devotees of the Lord. He said, 'You are all true bhaktas and I bow down to each one of you. You all come from different parts. The call of warkaris should be: We all are one. May the warkari movement grow and inspire more and more on the path of devotion.'

Dada was also presented a statue of Lord Panduranga of Pandharpur.

At the end, in a moving scene, the warkaris requested Dada to hold their *veena* and their Tulsi Vrindavan, which he did in utter humility. It was indeed a sight fit for the Gods to behold!

THE GURUKUL IS LAUNCHED

In the words of Sadhu Vaswani, the foundation of true education is reverence, *shraddha* – reverence for all: for those that are above us, those that are with us, and those that are beneath us. And it was his dream that a gurukul be set up by the Mission, where this quality of reverence is instilled in the hearts of the students. This precious dream came true when Dada inaugurated the Sadhu Vaswani Gurukul as part of Sadhu Vaswani's 39th Mahayagna celebrations, in 2005. As Dada said in his inaugural address, for many years, he had wanted to set up such a gurukul where the youngsters would get real education rooted in Indian ideals, values and cultural heritage.

Today, several centres in India and abroad have set up their own gurukul. Summer camps and vacation workshops are conducted for children and young adults.

THE MOMENT OF CALM

'Love, love, love thine enemies,' said Sadhu Vaswani. 'And though they hate thee as a thorn, thou wilt blossom as a rose.' Following his master's teaching in letter and spirit, Dada has always held up the ideal of forgiveness as a supreme virtue.

It was in keeping with this ideal that on 3 June 2012, while Dada was on a yatra to the US, a public function was held at the Marriott Hotel in Chicago, to launch a new worldwide initiative which Dada referred to as 'The Moment of Calm'. The organizers of the meet announced that starting that year, August 2nd would be celebrated as a 'Day of Forgiveness', which would culminate at 2 p.m. IST, in the Moment of Calm. The purpose of forgiveness, which leads to inner calm, is essential to cleanse our souls. Signing up for participation in this movement commenced from that evening.

Launching the movement, Dada said: 'The treasure of this inner calm that forgiveness brings to us should be experienced by all of us at least once every day. But if we are unable to do so, then let us enjoy and experience it at least once a year!'

Dada pointed out that our minds are usually turbulent, disturbed and agitated, whereas our natural state is that of calmness. We need to go within to reinstate it. We can only do so by letting go of all resentment, grudges, disturbances, pettiness, selfishness, vengeance and other such negative attributes.

In order to provide a taste of this calm, Dada guided the audience in a 20-minute meditation session. After the revitalizing meditation, followed a volley of questions and answers. It was an extremely enlightening, stimulating and satisfying evening for all those who attended.

OUR TRYST WITH TECHNOLOGY: WEBCASTING

There are many devotees worldwide who want to hear the precious recorded discourses of Sadhu Vaswani and to participate in special satsangs at the Mission with their beloved Dada throughout the year. From 2002, the Mission started webcasting numerous special events and functions through the year, starting with the inauguration of the renovated Mission premises and Rev. Dada's birthday celebrations from 27 July to 2 August, which were successfully webcast live from Pune. This involved live streaming of video and audio content on the web in real time. Now, virtually all the important programmes are webcast live on the website or on Facebook.

There is also a new-look website, www.sadhuvaswani.org, through which devotees can log on to get regular updates on Mission activities, to learn about events planned in the near future and to listen to rare recordings of upadeshes given by Sadhu Vaswani and Dada J. P. Vaswani – made available to the public for the first time.

A new app, Simply Love, has been launched which includes Dada's thought for the day, stories for every occasion, and a unique question and answer section 'Dada Answers', where Dada answers questions put to him. Devotees and admirers also stay updated with events and happenings at the Mission through social media platforms.

DARSHAN: A DREAM COME TRUE

Bollywood star Aamir Khan, a great admirer of Dada, inaugurated Dada Darshan during Dada's 93rd birthday celebrations in 2011. Darshan is a one-of-its-kind unique marvel, exhibiting the life and teachings of the master, Sadhu Vaswani. It is actually a 100-minute wonderful walk-through show, which takes you into a different era in which the master lived and moved and spoke to admiring audiences. Dada has urged the Mission administrators to keep the entry free to all visitors, so that all humanity may see and benefit from the Master's teachings.

THE EXPANSION OF GITA MANDIR

The newly constructed Gita Mandir, adjoining the sacred samadhi imbued all hearts with joy. This wasn't just a structure. It symbolized the fulfilment of the Master's dream of never-ending humanitarian activities of the Mission. The Gita Mandir is now a beautiful five-storey structure, housing a mini satsang hall, an auditorium, a library and offices of the Sadhu Vaswani Mission.

TRANQUIL TUESDAYS

For many years at the Sadhu Vaswani Mission, Tuesday evening satsang has been dedicated to kirtan and meditation. But Tuesday, 25 August 2014, saw the start of something new: guided meditations with Dada.

The Tranquil Tuesday meditation sessions are different. The ambience is aglow with warm purple lights, soft floor chairs, and Dada's soothing voice in the guided meditation, which make the evening truly memorable.

Tranquil Tuesdays have attracted a wide following since then, and are described by regulars as a spiritual journey that occurs every Tuesday from 6:45 p.m. to 7:45 p.m. These peace-filled sessions now follow a regular pattern, deeply appreciated by the participants: ecstatic kirtan by renowned singers, followed by a guided meditation in English by Dada. Each Tuesday, a renowned singer fills the satsang hall with melodious chants. Providing a calming ambience that transcends the daily routine, Tranquil Tuesdays have become a favourite among many Puneites.

SADHANA CAMPS

Sadhana camps are a unique feature of Dada's special programmes for the devotees. The camps have become highly sought-after as spiritual retreats, whether they are held in India or abroad. The three-day camps, which may be described as an exercise in spiritual fitness, have proved to be truly uplifting, transforming experiences for participants, often transporting them to a beautiful world of the spirit. Dada gives each camp a special theme to focus on, and his discourses and the daily meditations are based on this theme. The camps include guided meditations, yoga, *akhand kirtan*, service activities, games, cultural programmes, question-answer sessions, campfire and discourses by Dada. The camp ends with a kirtan which sends divine vibrations that can purify one's inner being.

Most important of all, the Sadhana Camp would offer participants the privilege of being in spiritual nearness to their beloved Dada.

Silence, Dada says, is the language of the soul. Therefore, all participants, during the duration of the camp, communicate in the language of the soul, and avoid all unnecessary talk. They are expected to wear simple, modest, preferably white clothes, to ensure that their clothes do not distract their attention from their sadhana.

Respecting the fact that their time at the camp is truly precious, they avoid worldly activities like reading the newspaper, listening to the radio or watching TV, talking on the telephone, and shopping, while they are in this secluded heaven! Above all, they enjoy three and a half days of freedom from the cell phone.

Outside the sessions in the hall named Nuri Sabhagriha, leisure hours are spent wisely and well, practising silence, meditation or in study of spiritual literature. Outsiders and visitors are not allowed.

The first Sadhana Camp was held in Chennai in the year 1981 and since then, over a hundred such camps have been held all over the world, under the auspices of many centres, to provide the spiritual recharge and re-energization that all true disciples need from time to time! To the very end of his life, Dada showed tireless commitment to attend these camps personally and rekindle the spiritual flame of every aspiring soul who came to participate.

REACHING OUT TO THE WORLD:
SADHU VASWANI CENTRES

A visit to the Mission headquarters in Pune is the dream and aspiration of thousands of devotees. But there are several of them who are not fortunate enough to travel frequently. And there are many whose commitments to their homes, work or business prevent them from coming to Pune, although they earnestly desire to participate in and contribute their mite to the good work the Mission is carrying on. In the interests of these people, the solution was to extend the work of the Mission to the towns and cities in which they happen to live. Philanthropists contributed to the effort, and the result has been that several branches and centres of the Sadhu Vaswani Mission have sprung up all over India and abroad.

These centres help preserve and propagate the ideals of the Mission and connect the new generation of youth living in foreign lands with their Sindhi and Indian roots. The centres reach out to their respective local communities by organizing service programmes such as free medical care, feeding the homeless, visits to charitable institutions and animal welfare organizations. The Mission works hand in hand with Buddhist, Christian, Hindu, Jewish, Muslim, Sikh and other religious groups to promote a secular spirit of understanding among all cultures and communities.

Within India, Sadhu Vaswani Mission centres are located at Adipur, Ahmedabad, Bangalore, Baroda, Bhopal, Bikaner, Chennai, Coimbatore, Indore, Kolhapur, Kolkata, Mumbai, Nagpur, Nasik, New Delhi, New Mumbai, Pimpri, Rajkot, Secunderabad, Solapur, Sumerpur and Ulhasnagar.

Africa has Mission centres at Accra in Ghana; Casablanca in Morocco; and Lagos in Nigeria. Johannesburg in South Africa also has its own centre.

Asian centres include the ones at Guangzhou in China, Hong Kong, Jakarta in Indonesia, Osaka in Japan, Penang in Malaysia, Manila in the Philippines, Singapore and Dubai.

Europe has centres at Las Palmas, Ceuta, and Malaga in Spain, and London in Great Britain.

North and South America have centres at Atlanta, Boston, Chicago, Hawaii, Los Angeles, Miami, New Jersey, Orlando, San Francisco, Shreveport, St Louis, St Thomas, and Washington D. C. in the US; Barbados in the West Indies; Ottawa, Toronto, and Vancouver in Canada; and Iquique in Chile, Curaçao, Panama City, Colon, San Juan, St Maarten and Trinidad.

The devotees and volunteers who spearhead the activities at the centres are people with a great sense of dedication and commitment to the master's ideals. The centres draw their inspiration and raison d'etre from the Mission headquarters in Pune, considering themselves as smaller tributaries that flow into the ocean. For them, Dada is God, guru, mentor and master, all rolled into one. As one of them puts it so eloquently, 'Dada is the source of our sustenance, the magnet that draws us all together, keeps us motivated and inspired, and is our guiding light!' They imbibe his teachings through daily/ weekly satsangs and try to translate his vision into their activities. Devotees stay connected through satsang, seva as well as through Facebook and social media.

THE BRIDGE BUILDERS

In the early nineties, a sense of bonding and a new wave of aspiration arose among the young adults, teenagers and volunteers in their early twenties; these were 'mission children' who had grown under the benevolent shade of the Mission seeing and hearing Dada ever so often, in the satsang, during Mission events and seva activities, and ever eager to offer their energy and active help to the Mission elders and stalwarts like Baba Gangaram, Shri Atu Relwani, Shri H. T. Sadhwani and others. At times it included laborious tasks like shifting chairs and benches for public functions; at times it was helping with social service initiatives like visiting hospitals and orphanages; whatever the occasion, these eager youngsters were always there to assist to the seniors.

Working together, the thought crossed their minds almost in unison, that they should channelize their energies and give a new direction to their efforts by forming a youth group geared towards service to the community, and getting closer to Dada through exclusive gatherings and meetings of the youth, for the youth and by the youth. The core team met Dada and shared their ideas with him.

Dada heard them out patiently, and with his characteristic flair, encouraged the youth to organize themselves into a formal group known as the Bridge Builders under the auspices of the

Mission. Thus began the popular youth satsang, with its unique no holds barred question-answer sessions, where the youngsters could ask Dada anything they wanted, on any topic that troubled them, intrigued them or got them thinking. The questions were spontaneous, and Dada's answers were always on target: sure, swift, beautifully articulated and always satisfying. Side by side, their service activities grew by leaps and bounds; enthusiastic youngsters visited orphanages, old-age homes, slums, hospitals and lepers' colonies, carrying gifts and food cooked in the Bhandara and offered lovingly by the Mission.

Young people from abroad visiting the Pune headquarter of the Mission were warmly welcomed to these meetings; they were so deeply inspired and impressed with the youth group that on going back to their countries of residence, they started their own Bridge Builders groups. Dada blessed them abundantly, and by the first decade of the new millennium, the Bridge Builders was a worldwide movement.

Dada gave them the motto: Hope, Help and Heal. He also penned a beautiful anthem for them, which is sung with reverberating joy and energy across the world. In Pune, their community service programme, Footprints, embraces environment protection, animal welfare, talent hunts for the youth as well as proactive service events which bring them closer to the underprivileged and marginalized groups with whom they spend time, spreading love and joy, and their own special brand of help and healing! They conduct monthly youth programmes including plays, musical evenings and innovative shows which never fail to enthrall the young and old alike. They also organize the monthly YES, or Youth Ekadashi Satsang at the kutiya making the night vibrate to their pure energy, and melodious singing.

The movement has given them the valuable gift of loving and giving, and sharing what they can with the world. Ask any Bridge Builder, and they will tell you that their life has been transformed by Dada's influence and grace.

GITA PUBLISHING HOUSE

One of the Mission's busiest departments is the publication department. Over 300 titles of books and booklets written by Sadhu Vaswani and Dada J. P. Vaswani in English and Sindhi, as well as their translations in Hindi, Marathi, and world languages, have been published by the Gita Publishing House (GPH) and Mira Publications. For over half a century, GPH has worked hard to make the writings of the masters accessible to countless readers all over the globe.

The books are valued and appreciated by thousands of people as the soul-stirring writings of Sadhu Vaswani appeal to the spirit, while those of Dada J. P. Vaswani are especially relevant to the modern man. Rational, simple, practical and laced with wit and humour, the books reach out to all readers who seek the wisdom of saints and sages. Magazines and newsletters brought out by GPH include the popular *East and West Series*, a Hindi magazine, *Dil Ka Dwar Khol* and a children's magazine, *Mira* (for children up to the age of twelve).

The Mission also publishes *Shyam* (a Sindhi fortnightly newsletter), *Sant Mala* (Sindhi monthly) and *Sant Sahitya* (a free monthly newsletter in Sindhi). A colourful Meatless Day Newsletter is also brought out every month from October to January, to promote the campaign for vegetarianism.

GPH also actively takes part in national and international book fairs held in Delhi, Kolkata, Frankfurt, New York, London, Abu Dhabi and Beijing.

ANJALI STUDIOS

The Mission's audio-visual department aims to harness the developments in technology to preserve, reproduce and propagate the teachings of the master, ensuring that the power of his message is not lost to future generations.

The revolution in the world of communication has enabled digitization of the audio recordings of Gurudev Sadhu Vaswani and make his beautiful discourses freely available to satsangs held all over the world. The latest endeavour in this direction is to produce accompanying visuals with subtitles in English, for the benefit of people who attend the Mission's public functions.

There is a compact but highly professional audio studio which helps preserve recordings in the latest format. Hundreds upon hundreds of discourses and upadeshes have been digitized and archived, and CDs/DVDs of meditations and talks are released and sold at minimal rates.

The in-house video division makes it a point to record all the happenings at the Mission headquarter, including Dada's talks and discourses. Anjali Studios has successfully coordinated the telecast of Dada's discourses on various TV channels.

Anjali Studios also runs a souvenir stall which offers artefacts with images of the masters to aspiring souls from all over the globe, who treasure every little memento that they can carry home with them, from the hallowed Mission campus.

PILGRIM PRODUCTIONS

Pilgrim Productions is an in-house visual communications cell. Pilgrim Productions records and archives rare photographs as well as audio-video material on the masters. With the help of industry experts and contributing artists, the department has successfully produced movies and documentaries on the masters and Mission activities. These films are premiered at special programmes in the satsang and also circulated to the Sadhu Vaswani centres all over the world.

Select Bibliography

Chapman, Rick, 'The Perfect Master', *The Cross and The Lotus Journal*, vol. 19, no. 2, 2018, pp. 20.

Connolly, John, *The Book of Lost Things*, (New York: Atria Books, 2006).

Hammarskjold, Dag, *Markings*, (United States: Vintage Books, 2006)

Roosevelt, Franklin D. and John Grafton (ed.), *Great Speeches*, (United States: Dover Publications, 1999)

Vaswani, J. P., *Sadhu Vaswani: His Life and Teachings*, (New Delhi: Sterling, 2002)

Henry Wadsworth Longfellow Quotes. BrainyQuote.com, BrainyMedia Inc, 2019. https://www.brainyquote.com/quotes/henry_wadsworth_longfello_385716, accessed June 13, 2019.

Jack Canfield Quotes. BrainyQuote.com, BrainyMedia Inc, 2019. https://www.brainyquote.com/quotes/jack_canfield_637647, accessed June 13, 2019

On Devotion: Amma Says. AmritaPuri.org, Mata Amritanandamayi Math, 2019. https://www.amritapuri.org/6681/on-devotion.aum, accessed June 13, 2019.

Thomas Carlyle Quotes. BrainyQuote.com, BrainyMedia Inc, 2019. https://www.brainyquote.com/quotes/thomas_carlyle_143133, accessed June 13, 2019.

'The Higher Pantheism' by Alfred, Lord Tennyson, PoetryFpundation.org, 2019. https://www.poetryfoundation.org/poems/45323/the-higher-pantheism, accessed June 13, 2019.

A rare photograph of little Jashan from his school days, seated on the extreme left.

Young Jashan, calm and unruffled as the waters of the lake.

Jashan in the loving lap of his master.

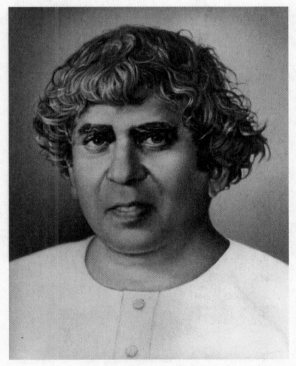

Sadhu Vaswani: Dada's master and mentor

Dada feeding the needy with love and compassion.

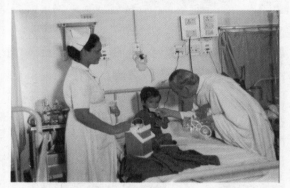

Dada bringing a smile on the face of a sick child.

Dada sharing his vision with Mother Teresa.

A light moment between His Holiness The Dalai Lama and Dada.

Dada in a warmhearted conversation with Prime Minister Narendra Modi.

Dada being awarded a D Litt by the then President of India, Pranab Mukherjee.

Dada enthralling an international audience with his wisdom and humour.

A citation being conferred on Dada.

Dada: The epitome of tranquillity

Dada's ever-open arms welcoming one and all.